ON HIS MAJESTY'S SERVICE

JULIAN FRANCIS GODOLPHIN

ON HIS MAJESTY'S SERVICE

HOW THE KING PRESERVES THE BRITISH CONSTITUTION

Biteback Publishing

First published in Great Britain in 2025 by
Biteback Publishing Ltd, London
Copyright © Julian Francis Godolphin 2025

ISBN 978-1-83736-014-7

10 9 8 7 6 5 4 3 2 1

A CIP catalogue record for this book is available from the British Library.

Set in Adobe Caslon Pro and Montecatini Pro

Printed and bound in Great Britain by
CPI Group (UK) Ltd, Croydon CR0 4YY

FSC
www.fsc.org
MIX
Paper | Supporting
responsible forestry
FSC® C013604

In memoriam John Hopkins, John Maples and Jeremy Heywood.
For teaching me to pay attention to the man behind the curtain.

'To understand how we're governed, and hence the power of the Prime Minister, you have to understand the power of the Crown. It's like the Trinity: God the Father is the Queen – she's just there and nobody knows very much about her; God the son is the Prime Minister – who exercises all the patronage and has all the real power; and God the Holy Ghost is the Crown – the Royal Prerogative – and the Crown is the state-within-a-state, surrounded by barbed wire and covered in secrecy.'

TONY BENN

CONTENTS

PART IV: THE PREROGATIVES OF DISSOLUTION AND ASSENT

AUTHOR'S NOTE

Throughout this work, the terms 'king' and 'queen' are used interchangeably unless the context suggests otherwise. When lowercase they refer to the monarch in more general terms, whilst King or Queen denotes a particular regnant monarch. 'Sovereign' and 'monarch' are used in a similar manner without distinction. Likewise, the term 'crown' is used to refer to the institution, whether in its capacity as an individual or collective, of which the monarch is the personal, human manifestation. Similarly, terms of gender will be used in an interchangeable way, as will the singular and plural as appropriate. The aim is to describe an entity free from grammatical distinction.

PROLOGUE

'All my life people have been telling me, "You can't do that." And I've always proven them wrong.'

If you had to sum up Boris Johnson's world view in a single phrase, this would surely be it. A bold statement uttered in a time of stress to Geoffrey Cox, who was Attorney General at the time, it contained a world of meaning for those who were privy to the public life of this most polarising of Prime Ministers. To Johnson it simply explained the phenomenal success he had enjoyed in his life, which had brought him to the threshold of greatness. Yet for those who surrounded him, it was the echo of his doom. For the tragedy that lay at the heart of the Johnson story was that the closer to the summit he progressed, the less freedom of action he would enjoy – discovering far too late that Downing Street would be a prison from which he would long to escape.

I first had the pleasure of meeting this most fascinating of characters in the spring of 2004, when I was engaged in the quixotic quest to impeach Tony Blair over his actions in the Iraq War. Such endeavours naturally ensured that I met most of the 'characters' present in the House of Commons, not least amongst them the

Honourable Member for Henley. But it was not until that November that I received my first insight into his character, an insight which has stayed with me to this day. Addressing the Horatian Society of Lincoln's Inn two days after his dismissal from the shadow Cabinet, Johnson entertained us all with his wit and knowledge of the poetry of Horace, casting into a cold shade those academic speakers who sought to follow him. What was most significant, however, was that during his performance Johnson openly identified himself with Mercury – the messenger of the gods and the guide of the dead to the underworld – admitting there was a resemblance between himself and the deity.

What struck me most about this at the time was not the hubris in his allusion to being like a god but the fact he had chosen to identify himself with the Roman aspect of Mercury and not the more common Greek identity of Hermes. At first, I thought this was merely because Horace, as a Roman writing in Latin rather than Greek, had identified himself with Mercury, which explained Johnson's later-day emulation. But as I pondered this further, I wondered if there was something more to it than that? Could the answer to Johnson be found in the ancient world rather than the modern?

Two things stand out in Johnson's choice of divine patron that would have parallels with his premiership. The first has to do with the nature of Roman religion around the time of Horace. Unlike their Greek counterparts, the Roman religion was not based on concepts of divine grace but rather on a contractual partnership between man and gods. It was ritualistic in form, with little to no moralistic element. So long as the ceremonies were observed correctly, there was no obligation on a Roman to think or act in any moral way. Second, Mercury was not a primary god but rather a servant of the gods. Far from being a master of communication, he was rather a conveyor of messages from others, most notably Jupiter, the king of the gods. Mercury served a higher power and was not the directing force of the cosmos.

Interesting observations to consider as we seek to understand the forces at play during Johnson's premiership, for he was confronted by the realities of the British constitution in a more direct way than any of his immediate predecessors were. In examining the actions of his time in office, we see the hidden hand of the monarchy in the smooth running of our governmental systems and the way in which the monarch's influence ensures our Prime Ministers do not breach our constitutional settlement. At certain key moments when Johnson attempted to get his own way, he found that he could not achieve his ends. A higher power prevented it, for he was but a servant to a force greater than himself.

Johnson entered office in a more precarious position than any of his predecessors since James Callaghan in 1976. His party held no majority and was dependent on the support of the DUP to pass its legislative agenda. Theresa May's attempts to secure an agreement for the UK's exit from the European Union had not only split the Conservative Party in two but had created the most hostile environment in Westminster since 1912, dissolving the bonds of trust between the Commons and the executive. Johnson had promised to 'Get Brexit Done'; Brexit deal or no Brexit deal, the UK would leave the EU on 31 October. If he failed, his premiership would be over in three months. His team was determined this would not happen and so they looked for ways to achieve the impossible. Every trick in the book was considered and dismissed, save one: prorogation. The ending of the parliamentary session meant the possibility that the government could frustrate its opponents and regain control of the parliamentary timetable, which May had lost.

The plan was simple. In retrospect, too simple.

Prorogation would last five weeks, from 9 September to 14 October. Then, the new Queen's Speech would be presented, giving the government control of the agenda for a further couple of days. If no agreement was reached by the time of the European Council meeting on 17 October, a no-deal Brexit would be inevitable, and Parliament would have only five working days before prorogation to prevent Johnson from pursuing a no-deal Brexit. As prorogation was considered to be a 'non-justiciable' (not capable of being decided by legal principles or by a court of law) process, Johnson and his team were quietly confident that the courts could not interfere, thus preventing any challenge to their policy. The plan appeared to be foolproof. Events would prove all these assumptions to be somewhat wide of the mark.

The reaction to the plan was swift. The implications began to dawn on courtiers, civil servants and politicians, many of whom first heard the news whilst enjoying their summer holidays. Of central importance were Mark Sedwill, the Cabinet Secretary, Sir Edward Young, the Queen's private secretary, and Peter Hill, the principal private secretary to the Prime Minister, who were all concerned that the monarch may have been politicised amid a national crisis. Palace officials were furious that No. 10 had attempted to bounce them with a decision made whilst the Queen was in Scotland. There had been no warning or briefing provided by Downing Street, leading to concerns that the Queen would not be fully informed as to the actions she was being asked to approve. Not since the nadir of Margaret Thatcher's premiership had relations been so strained. Exercising the monarch's right to be informed, the palace sought its own legal advice, which suggested that although the issue was potentially non-justiciable, the request placed the Queen in a very difficult position by forcing her to act on legally dubious advice from the Prime Minister. Reluctantly, the palace provided the Queen's consent but let No. 10 and the Cabinet Office know they were far from happy. We can only imagine how events would have turned out had the palace's legal advice stated the process was illegal. Royal intervention had been avoided by the narrowest of margins, and the Prince of Wales and Duke of Cambridge let it be known that the monarch's reaction would be very different in future reigns.

The Privy Council approved prorogation on 28 August, causing a tidal wave of anger in Westminster ahead of Parliament's return on 3 September. In response, a coalition of the disaffected from across the House came together, under the leadership of Dominic Grieve, Oliver Letwin and Hilary Benn, to introduce a bill to frustrate the government's actions. This was a move that enjoyed the very public support of the Speaker, John Bercow, who assisted the rebels in their cause. Known as the Benn Act, the legislation stated that if the House of Commons had not consented to either a Withdrawal Agreement or no deal by 19 October, the Prime Minister would be compelled to seek an extension of the withdrawal date to 31 January. Progress of the legislation was swift, with majorities in both Houses being formed as outraged Conservatives joined forces with the opposition to get the measure on the statute books before prorogation.

The reaction in Downing Street was vitriolic. Johnson took his revenge on the colleagues that had voted in support of the bill by revoking the whip from twenty-one Conservative MPs and destroying his fragile majority in the process. By removing no deal from the table, Johnson felt that Parliament was compelling him to accept a deal that was not in the national interest. This could not be allowed. Johnson looked for ways in which to frustrate Parliament's actions. He gave serious consideration to blocking royal assent to the bill and asked Cox to explore whether he could advise the Queen not to give royal assent and to provide him with a legal opinion that could buttress his actions. Not since the reign of Queen Anne had a Prime Minister contemplated such action, but nor had they faced such a complete loss of control of the Commons. The government could no longer get its way, as the Commons insisted on frustrating the policy of the executive. An example needed to be made that the administration would not simply abrogate its functions to a chamber that lacked the mechanisms for directing the machinery of the state.

Johnson was keen on the idea, which had support within the wider legal community, but Cox was less enthused with the proposal for two primary reasons. The first was that it would drag the Queen into a controversy that could threaten the political neutrality of the monarchy itself. The second was that such a radical act could only antagonise Parliament, further leading to a complete collapse of our political system. How the Commons would react to such a naked use of royal power was simply unknown. Given the electoral maths, it was almost certain that the government would lose a confidence vote, further weakening the UK's negotiating position with the EU. These concerns were reflected in the response of the palace. The Queen's advisers doubted that the Prime Minister could compel the Queen to refuse assent, given the lack of support enjoyed by the administration in the Commons. The word leaked out that the Queen would refuse such a request, ending the debate within Downing Street with a heavy finality. Johnson had been told it could not be done, and he had to accept it. The Benn Act received royal assent on 9 September.

Johnson's frustrations mounted further following the passage of the Benn Act. He faced the reality that he had lost control of the Commons and could not break the impasse, as the Fixed-Term Parliaments Act prevented him from calling an election. This legislation had been introduced by the coalition government to regulate the UK's election cycle to a set five-year period. The only way an early election could take place now was for either the government to suffer a defeat on a confidence motion or else for two-thirds of the Commons to vote to call an election. For Johnson to achieve either result he needed the support of the opposition, as he lacked the votes needed to secure passage of the required motion. For their part, the Labour Party and the other opposition parties had no interest in assisting the Prime Minister given their fears over a no-deal Brexit. An election was off the table for now and Johnson once again found he could not get his own way. An ironic position to be in, given the fact his predecessors could have relied on the monarch's ability to dissolve Parliament in similar circumstances.

Attention now turned to the courts as the government's attempts to prorogue Parliament were challenged across the UK, leading to the Supreme Court agreeing to hear the case. On 24 September, the court savaged the government's position by not only stating that the issue was indeed justiciable but that the Prime Minister had acted unlawfully in advising the Queen to prorogue Parliament for such a considerable period of time in the midst of a national crisis. Whilst many in the Cabinet and legal profession saw the judgment as flawed and politically motivated, ignoring as it did historical precedent and political motivation, they still concluded it was justified by the Prime Minister's behaviour. Our constitution relies heavily on conventions that outline accepted behaviours by our politicians, but the Johnson administration was breaching those conventions to such a degree that the court had no option but to intervene in an area of activity that was historically out of bounds to judicial oversight.

The result was that Parliament was found to still be sitting and that the Prime Minister was exposed as someone who sought to act illegally. Johnson was left with no option but to call the Queen and offer an unreserved apology for his actions in the lead-up to the prorogation.

Johnson's stock was falling fast with the palace and word leaked out that Charles and William were furious with how the Queen had been treated and were less than impressed with the Prime Minister's actions. The withdrawal of this wider royal support would make its impact felt shortly afterwards. The deadline of 19 October approached, when the Benn Act would compel Johnson to seek an extension to the Brexit deadline, and civil servants feared the Prime Minister would trigger a constitutional crisis as he had let it be known he did not consider himself bound by the Act and would simply ignore it. Cox and Richard Keen, the Scottish Advocate General, were deployed to tell Johnson he had no option but to send a letter requesting an extension. He simply had to do it. Outraged by the thought, Johnson raged at his staff and the meeting broke up, leading to further concerns as to the PM's ability to govern the country.

Dominic Cummings called a meeting for the morning of 4 October to discuss ways in which Johnson could circumvent the Benn Act with limited involvement by officials. To frustrate this, officials pressed for the inclusion of James Eadie, leading counsel to the government, and Helen MacNamara, the deputy Cabinet Secretary, who in Mark Sedwill's absence was the most senior civil servant. The meeting proved heated from the start. Johnson made it clear he would not send the letter to the EU. Faced with such a blatant statement of intent from Johnson, MacNamara had no choice but to inform him the civil service could not support him and would down tools if he proceeded in such a fashion.

Speaking bluntly, she told the turbulent premier and his principal aide, 'The police don't work for you in that situation, Dom, they work for me. They work for us. It's not your building. These aren't your people. The police work for the Queen. We all work for the Queen.' As silence fell in the wake of such a bold statement Eddie Lister, Johnson's chief strategic adviser, asked the crucial question: 'Can the Queen sack the Prime Minister?' To this, MacNamara heatedly responded, 'Do you really want us to have to advise the monarch that she is going to have to ask you to stand down?'

As a visibly shaken Johnson deflated in the wake of such a challenge, the meeting broke up. This most bombastic of premiers, the man who did not take no for an answer, found to his surprise that he served at Her Majesty's pleasure. Jupiter had spoken and Mercury had little option but to listen. There was a moral curve to the universe after all. The letter was duly sent.

With a deadline extension agreed, the pressure on the Prime Minister began to ease, as he found that he now had the space to build the support for a general election, made possible by the passage of the Early Parliamentary General Election Act 2019. Johnson emerged triumphant at the polls and his opponents suffered a resounding defeat, ensuring that he could at last deliver Brexit as promised.

But no sooner had one crisis abated than another hove into view. Covid-19 broke upon our shores and the nation went into lockdown. On 27 March 2020, Johnson tested positive and went into isolation, informing the nation that his symptoms were mild. However, within nine days it was touch and go as to whether he would live or die. This confronted the government with the problem of how to handle a political succession during a pandemic. As Johnson was taken to hospital on 6 April, he let Sedwill know that he wanted Dominic Raab to deputise for him during his convalescence and the arrangements were duly made. By Sunday, it was clear that Johnson was getting worse and that he now faced a 50-50 chance of survival, an outcome that was conveyed to his distressed partner.

On Monday, the Cabinet faced the very real possibility that the Prime Minister may die within hours and that the administration would lose not just its head but its lodestar, depriving the government of its driving force. As the country lacked a formal line of succession to the premiership in these circumstances, conversations were held at the highest levels to determine a way forward. The Queen was informed that she may need to act swiftly and a conference call with the Cabinet was arranged. Clearly in shock, the Cabinet deferred to Sedwill, who drew up a plan of action. Two options presented themselves. If the Prime Minister was ventilated, a stand-in leader would need to be approved. They would lead the government until such time as the Prime Minister recovered and resumed his duties. A letter to the Queen was drafted to this effect. If, however, Johnson fell into a coma or died, the Cabinet would have to formally vote on a candidate to be appointed Prime Minister ahead of a formal leadership contest in the Conservative Party. In this instance, the candidate should be someone who did not intend to seek the leadership themselves and would only hold office until a successor was elected. As an incapacitated Johnson could not resign due to being in a coma, the Queen would formally dismiss him from office ahead of appointing a new premier. It was duly agreed that Raab would assume office in these events, and he prepared himself for the unthinkable. An address to camera was filmed informing the nation of the sad news and the incoming political succession whilst the Queen prepared to fulfil her duty. The event never came, however, as Johnson rallied that night and began his slow progress to recovery.

Amazingly, in the first three months of the Johnson premiership the power of the Queen had been wielded on several occasions to control the actions of this most wayward of Prime Ministers. Then, just a few months later, she was preparing to wield her power of dismissal in order to manage the prime ministerial succession.

In the following pages, we will come to explore the historical enormity of these actions and their place within British constitutional history – for this is the story of the royal prerogative.

PART I

THE PREROGATiVE OF SOVEREIGNTY

1

THE KING'S MAJESTY

During the afternoon of 8 September 2022, the long reign of Queen Elizabeth II came to a gentle close as the woman who had been our monarch and the fixed point of our national life for seventy years breathed her last. Rushing to her bedside was the man who was transformed in that singular moment of apotheosis into our new king, assuming in an instant the burdens to which he had prepared for his whole life.[1] As he absorbed the momentous news of his mother's death, King Charles III became the forty-third sovereign of our country and head of the Commonwealth of Nations.*

He had succeeded to the greatest and most permanent office in the land, for he was now the head of state, the guardian of the law and the font of all honour not only within this country but in fourteen other Commonwealth realms around the world, a burden he assumed at the grand old age of seventy-three – a time of life when many of us have laid down the obligations of work in anticipation of a well-deserved retirement. And yet as the ancient and half-forgotten cry of 'The Queen is dead, long live the King' echoed

---

* Marked from the point of 1066 and the uniting of England under one king.

from Land's End to John O'Groats, we found ourselves confronted by a reality long contemplated but little prepared for. How would our lives change now that the Queen had left us? How would the new king's reign differ from that of his mother? To what extent was his inheritance one of mere ceremony and duty? Did the King wield any real power in modern Britain or did he merely represent an institution whose time had passed?[2]

In truth, the King has entered into one of the most complex of all roles, for he is as much a symbol as he is a man, a living embodiment of the bond of national unity that holds this United Kingdom together. In every political system around the world there is some visible symbol upon which the people can centre their patriotism and so define their national character. If we look across the Atlantic to our American cousins, we can see this principle clearly expressed in the value they place upon their flag, whilst our French neighbours focus their attention upon their republican tradition as the very symbol of France. We, on the other hand, reserve this form of emotional appeal for our monarch, who is deemed and required to portray all our virtues whilst shunning all of our vices – a view which Winston Churchill felt moved to express on numerous occasions. The crown, he once remarked, was 'the symbol which gathers together and expresses those deep emotions and stirrings of the human heart', adding that it 'has become the mysterious link – indeed, I may say the magic link – which unites our loosely bound but strongly interwoven Commonwealth of nations, states and races'.[3] In this way, the sovereign lends what has often been described by commentators as 'glamour' not just to our political system but to our society as well.

The monarchy links us to our heritage in a sublime way and in so doing gives our daily struggles a sense of perspective and gives our efforts hope for the future. This is because the King stands as a link with our past, during which untold calamities and crises have been overcome. That feeling of an abiding connection with times gone by gives us great inner strength in times of trouble and explains the enduring appeal of our monarchy today. We feel that we are joined not just to our history by the presence of our King but to our future as well, through his family and, more importantly, his heirs and successors. In his radio broadcast prior to the coronation of George VI, Churchill summoned up this historic association to describe the ceremony that was to take place. He told his listeners, 'From ancient times all classes have shared in it [the coronation] with rejoicing,' before expounding that 'the British constitutional monarchy embodies the traditions of a thousand years. The King will be crowned tomorrow not only under a ritual which has come down from the Plantagenets and Tudors but which revives forms and customs of Anglo-Saxon times.'[4] The sovereign thus stands at the nexus of both past and future and so provides a sense of certainty in a transient and mortal world.

If the King is to succeed in the role that fate has ordained for him, he must be seen to embody these values and represent us all collectively. He must strive to be above and outside of all partisan activity, whilst recognising the wellsprings from which these conflicts arise. He must be, as far as is humanly possible, impartial to the competing views of the different sections of our community whilst being compassionate enough to understand them. Above all, he must be the keystone of our political system, giving his full backing and assistance to the government of the day regardless of its political persuasion and ensuring in the process that our constitutional principles are upheld. To this end, the monarch must avoid all attempts to sway him to any particular political expedience of the moment by those who feel that his own outlook may be closer to theirs than their opponents'. The King must continually stand above these day-to-day battles if he is to represent the nation as a whole.

We get a flavour of this from the very earliest days of Queen Elizabeth's life. When the young princess accompanied her parents on a tour of South Africa in 1947, she was very much the remote and unknown heir to the throne. This was a situation that dramatically changed when she spoke to the wider empire and Commonwealth for the first time on her twenty-first birthday. In a speech that was old-fashioned and stilted by today's standards, Princess Elizabeth sought to make a connection with her generation. 'Although there is none of my father's subjects, from the oldest to the youngest, whom I do not wish to greet,' she began, 'I am thinking especially today of all the young men and women who were born about the same time as myself.' In so doing, she summoned up the camaraderie of the war that had just ended and the opportunities peace presented to the empire and Commonwealth. But then she made a surprising detour. What came next was very much a personal manifesto that encapsulated the importance of our constitutional monarchy and her place within it. It was an attempt to spiritually link her to the younger generations and so reforge this mystic bond that sustains the monarchy. So iconic has this speech become and such was its effect on the people of the time and to this day that it is worth quoting in full. She told her listeners:

There is a motto which has been borne by many of my ancestors, a noble motto: 'I serve.' Those words were an inspiration to many bygone heirs to the throne when they made their knightly dedication as they came to manhood. I cannot quite do as they did, but through the inventions of science, I can do what was not possible for any of them. I can make my solemn act of dedication with a whole empire listening. I should like to make that dedication now. It is very simple.

I declare before you all that my whole life, whether it be long or short, shall be devoted to your service and to the service of our great imperial family to which we all belong. But I shall not have strength to carry out this resolution alone unless you join in it with me, as I now invite you to do. I know that your support will be unfailingly given. God help me to make good my vow and God bless all of you who are willing to share in it.[5]

With these words, a young Elizabeth summed up the nature of the role that she would inherit in just a few short years. She was to become a living embodiment of the nation and her role was to serve the people in that capacity, a position she solemnly dedicated herself to. Such was the power of this statement that it formed the keystone of the mourning that greeted the news of her passing, encapsulating as it did her life and reign.

This epitomises the symbolic nature of the office, for it is in many ways the sovereign's task to mask and temper change and in so doing, remove the fear and anxiety that innovation can engender in the wider community. This was a role the late Queen played to perfection. In this way, the monarch ensures domestic harmony whilst creating a space for organic change to occur. The ceremonies and traditions that centre around them reassure us by their reference to our historic past whilst diminishing the emotional response that may greet any political changes that find their way onto the statute book. By this alchemy, Britain has been able to be both a stable and progressive society, enjoying unparalleled domestic harmony over the centuries.

But this is a civic benefit that is achieved at a price, for we expect our king to be both a symbol and a human being. We want personality without peccadilloes, glamour without vanity, modesty without shyness, a sense of duty without dullness, a sense of humour that does not mock us, a life devoted to service and yet one that is recognisably similar to our own. In short, we want what no human being could ever be; we want them to be perfect. It is this disconnect that has become most apparent in the digital age as our royal family becomes ever more visible. Their problems are now exposed for the world to see, and we are aware as never before that behind all the pomp and circumstance lies real people with real problems. With the Queen's passing, it now falls to a man born in the ashes of the Second World War to define how this role can be recast for the world in which we now live.[6]

So this is the public and representational role of the King's life as our sovereign. Yet what of his constitutional role? In short, does he wield any real authority or has our parliamentary democracy so shorn the office of its powers that it is now nothing more than a gilded sinecure?

We may live in a monarchy in the strict sense of the word, but it is one tempered by the fact that it is a constitutional monarchy, which makes all the difference. Far from being a country ruled by one absolute and singular ruler, we in Britain have for centuries lived in a state in which our sovereign reigns according to the established principles enshrined in our constitutional tradition. This distinction between absolute and constitutional monarchy has a long and illustrious pedigree in British history, stretching far back into the Middle Ages. In the fifteenth century, for instance, the English political theorist Sir John Fortescue famously defined the two states of monarchy in his book *On the Laws and the Governance of England.* He posited that there were two types of kingdoms in the world. The first was ruled by kings that made laws and imposed taxes solely on their own initiative and the second was governed by kings that respected laws and only engaged in activities that had received the assent of their people. Of the two, Sir John argued, it was undoubtedly the second which was the most successful and secure.[7]

This was a contention that was far from universal in the sixteenth and seventeenth centuries, as English and Scottish monarchs sought to adopt the concepts of absolute monarchy so fashionable in Louis XIV's France. But the common sense of the British people could not believe that any human being, even a king, could be infallible. It was on this issue that the English Civil War was fought, and although Charles I's son would eventually inherit the throne, no future sovereign would be able to claim that their actions were based upon a divine right to rule. From this moment on, it was agreed that the king must govern with the consent and support of Parliament. As a result, the concept soon developed that the king's command must always bear a minister's signature since the monarch was answerable to Parliament for their actions. If things went wrong, it was the minister that was held liable for the error not the king, who simply replaced the disgraced minister with another. In the process, this ensured that ministerial advice was always available to the sovereign to help govern their actions. Cabinet government was formed as a result of this innovation, establishing that ministers were the ones who increasingly made most of the political decisions, which they defended in the House of Commons. At the same time, the monarch slowly retired from active political life.

The Bill of Rights and the Act of Settlement that flowed from the Glorious Revolution of 1688 confirmed and strengthened the principle that government was undertaken by the sovereign and their constitutional advisers (i.e. their ministers) alone and not by the sovereign and any personal advisers whom they may happen to choose at any given time. By their actions in 1688, Scottish and English politicians had reached a truly radical understanding of the political structure in both kingdoms. They had accepted the principle that monarchs derived their legitimacy not from God but from Parliament and, through that institution, the people.[8]

Which brings us neatly to Walter Bagehot, the journalist and banker who occupies a central position in any discussion of the British constitution. In the midst of the turbulent year of 1865 – when Britain was griped with battles over the Second Reform Bill, Europe was confronting the first of Bismarck's three wars of German unification and the US was emerging from civil war – he penned his seminal work *The English Constitution* and secured his place in our political history.[9] So influential is this work that scholars and commentators can hardly mention the words 'monarchy' or 'Cabinet' without some reference to his book. Its lively written style combined with Bagehot's historical knowledge ensures this work continues to be read to this day. If we are, therefore, to dispel the glamour that surrounds our monarchy as an institution we must start with Bagehot.

This is because Bagehot has been central to the royal family's education since 1894, when a young Duke of York attended lessons with J. R. Tanner, fellow of St John's College, Cambridge, and an expert on maritime history and constitutional matters.[10] He was instructed on the kingly side of statecraft through the lens provided by this work. In this way, Bagehot's famous trio of rights for a constitutional monarch became embedded in the mind of the man who would become George V. In his 'Notes on Bagehot's *English Constitution*' he observes these rights thus (emphasis in original):

During the *continuance* of ministries the Crown possesses, *first* the right to be consulted, *second* the right to encourage and *third* the right to warn. And these rights may lead to a very important influence on the course of politics, especially as under a system of party government, that monarch alone possesses a '*continuous political experience.*'[11]

In doing so, George completed a circuit that had been created by Bagehot thirty years before. For Bagehot had simply invented these three rights by stating them as a matter of fact, summoning them from thin air as rules of the constitution.[12] And by accepting them as such, George V firmly established them in the lexicon of our political system, ensuring that all future monarchs were accorded these rights without question – a tradition that has been passed from one monarch to another until this present time.

In her biography of George VI, Sarah Bradford informs us that the young Prince Albert derived lasting knowledge on the monarchy from his time at Cambridge via the 'brilliant exposition on the subject by way of Walter Bagehot'. She asserts that this learning influenced his approach to his role as king when called upon to serve following the abdication of his brother in 1936.[13] Viewers of the TV series *The Crown* will also be aware that Queen Elizabeth was similarly fed on a diet of Bagehot when she received her instruction in kingship from Sir Henry Marten, provost of Eton, in 1938.[14] Kenneth Harris has noted that Charles III has covered the same ground his mother, grandfather and great-grandfather trod before him.[15] In this way, the Bagehotian trio of rights has become a fixed point in our constitutional settlement, affecting not only how our monarchs view their role but how they can and should use their influence at any given moment. This has been reflected in the pronouncements of the Queen's closest advisers in recent times. For instance, Sir William Heseltine, the Queen's private secretary, stated explicitly in 1986 that the Queen had 'the right – indeed the duty – to counsel, encourage and warn her Government'.[16]

Alongside these rights, Bagehot is also responsible for the way in which we view our constitutional settlement. This is because he divided our political system into two parts – the dignified and the efficient. In so doing, he ascribed all the ceremonial, symbolic and 'dignified' functions to the monarchy whilst assigning the mundane administrative functions or the 'efficient' to the political government of the moment. In this way, he highlighted that in all but a few key areas the monarch acts on the 'advice' of their ministers and as such has no real autonomy in their actions.[17]

That said, I think it is important that we pause here for a moment to discuss what exactly we mean by the term 'advice', as it plays such a key part in the British constitutional system. When the term 'advice' is used it is important to understand that there is both formal 'Advice' and informal 'advice', with each having a different legal character.[18] In a constitutional monarchy, it is a crucial requirement that the sovereign remains politically impartial and this is achieved through the principle that almost all public acts of the monarch are taken on the 'Advice' of their ministers. 'Advice' of this kind can only be given by a minister and is of such a binding nature that the sovereign has no choice but to accept it. To reject it would lead to the resignation of the government, forcing the monarch to find new ministers who would hold office as the sovereign's personal choice. Such actions would potentially place the monarch in direct opposition to a majority in the House of Commons and to one or more political parties, indicating in the process a political partisanship that no constitutional monarch could long survive. The doctrine that the sovereign only acts on the 'Advice' of their ministers thus protects the monarch from political involvement because it recognises the reality that all official acts are essentially the decisions of the government of the day, who are held responsible for them by the people. Put simply, the monarch is not the instigator of the government's actions and thus is not to blame for their outcomes.[19]

Informal 'advice,' on the other hand, is not binding and can be given by monarch, minister and other political actors or citizens. The right to advise, for instance, is informal as the monarch can advise a Prime Minister not to do a thing but the Prime Minister is under no obligation to follow that advice.[20] Although the monarch can never formally 'Advise' the government, there are several occasions when ministers cannot formally 'Advise' the sovereign, a point I shall return to in a moment.

Bagehot believed that the monarch had no part to play in the efficient part of the constitution as all effective actions were undertaken by ministers. In doing so, he misled his readers by implying that the monarchy was simply above and separate from the political competition that defined the efficient part of the state. This in turn created the image that we hold today of the monarchy as existing on a separate plain to our politicians, that the essence of constitutional kingcraft is that the sovereign reigns but does not rule. In general, this conventional wisdom is indeed correct. The monarchy is not *party* political in nature, but this does not mean it is not political. The crown has a central and crucial role to play in our political system due to something called the royal prerogative. Put simply, these are the sovereign's political powers, which are seldom discussed in wider society and are instead confined within legal debates and academic study.[21]

Following the line taken by Peter Hennessy, Anthony Seldon,

Vernon Bogdanor and others, I believe we need to discuss these powers, their importance and their use openly if we are to truly understand how our constitutional system works. Lord Blake perhaps said it best in his Gresham College Lecture in 1984 when he argued that 'I do believe the vestigial powers of the British monarch do matter' but that 'they should be exercised ... with the greatest tact and discretion'.[22] This view was taken up by Peter Riddell in 1994 when he argued that it was perfectly acceptable for people to discuss the monarchy and its role in modern Britain without being thought of as disloyal to the system in some way. Instead, he felt, 'In the Crown's own long-term interests, the fog over its political role needs to be lifted.'[23] A sentiment I fully agree with, but where to begin?

A good place to start might be the King's role within our constitutional monarchy. This role is largely a symbolic one, but this symbolism is, however, given substance by the existence of his prerogative or reserve powers. These are those discretionary powers that reside in our head of state, enabling them to uphold and maintain the fundamental constitutional settlements of the system of government of which they are head.* These powers are vital to the wellbeing of our political system, as they ensure the effective operation of the government and provide the last line of defence against government action that breaches fundamental constitutional principle. The monarch is not merely the symbolic guardian of the British constitution but is the one person who holds the powers of last resort for its own protection.[24]

Seen in this light, our King is a rather more active participant in the constitution than is usually felt to be the case, for he is the

---

* Alongside the United Kingdom, Charles III is the head of state of fourteen other countries, which each have their own similar but separate constitutional systems.

protector, guardian and defender of the constitution. This is a role that is highlighted in the King's Coronation Oath, where he swore to 'govern the Peoples of the United Kingdom of Great Britain and Northern Ireland, your other Realms and the Territories to any of them belonging or pertaining, according to their respective laws and customs'.[25]

This oath, which was originally laid down in the Act of Settlement 1701 and is used by all subsequent monarchs to this day, is not just some minor piece of symbolism but is in fact a central part of the sovereign's assumption of office. When the oath was originally included in the Act of Settlement, it was not viewed by its authors or Parliament as some minor issue separate from the overall revolutionary settlement but was a deliberate creation that broke with the historic precedent. The oath, more than any other act, symbolised the revolutionary nature of what had taken place in 1688 and was seen as the condition on which each individual monarch held the crown. Any breach of this condition by the monarch could be used as grounds for their forfeiture of the throne by Parliament.

We can see this more clearly when we look at the wording of the original oath the sovereign took prior to 1688, which affirmed that the laws of the land were merely the gift of the king to their subjects: 'Sire, do you grant to be held and maintained the just laws and liberties of this realm, and will you, so far as in you lies, defend and strengthen them to the honour of God?'[26] In so doing, it indicated to the people that the king was both above them and could not be bound by them. As the king's authority flowed from God, no mortal power was equal to theirs or capable of removing them from office. The new oath did away with this concept entirely. From now on, the monarch was accountable to the law in much the same way as their subjects were. Moreover, they were the law's guardian and primary enforcer. As such, their position in office rested on their just execution and defence of the rule of law.[27] A fact that was reinforced by Acts 12 and 13 of William III's reign, which affirmed:

> the laws of England are the birthright of the people thereof; and all the kings and queens who shall ascend the throne of this realm ought to administer the government of the same according to said laws; and all their officers and ministers ought to serve them respectively according to the same.[28]

In this way, the rule of law was enshrined and accommodated within the ancient legal maxim *rex non potest peccare* – the king can do no wrong – as a continuing part of British constitutional practice. By so doing, the crown, Parliament and the courts had mutually recognised the fact that the executive had no innate prerogative power to suspend or to alter either statutes or the common law. All executive decisions must therefore be made in accordance with the principles, procedures and requirements set out by the law as contained within either statute or common law.[29] As the monarch is considered by the law to be incapable of wrongdoing, the courts assume that if the government is found to be in breach of the law, the advice given to the monarch must have been at fault. This is because they presume the crown's intentions are to always act con-stitutionally. Ministers can be found to be at fault, but the monarch is assumed to be blameless.

This is a process we can see at work in the recent Supreme Court judgment in *R. (Miller) v. the Prime Minister*. When called upon to decide the lawfulness of the Queen's prorogation of Parliament in 2019, the court found the advice the Prime Minister gave the Queen to be in error, thus invalidating the act. The court made clear that it was the flawed advice provided to the Queen by her advisers that led to an illegal act being committed, not the Queen's order that was illegal, ensuring she received no blame for the action.[30]

The logic upon which this convention is built is that the head of state is always obliged to act in a manner that is in accordance with the law as it then stands and traces its pedigree back to Magna Carta in 1215. The implication of this assumption is that by extension the monarch is not obliged to act upon any ministerial advice, regardless of how much support the government has in Parliament or the country, that requires them to knowingly breach the law or constitution. This principle was outlined by Professor Pitt Cobbett in relation to Australia and the Governor-General, but his observation is just as relevant for the UK itself.* He says:

> The Governor-General is at once entitled and bound to refuse to act on the advice of his Ministers, in a case where this would involve a breach of the law. The Constitution, as we have seen, constitutes the Governor-General the chief executant and guardian of the law and its due observance is a duty he owes ... to the community over which he presides, whose permanent wishes must be presumed to be embodied in the laws deliberately made by Parliament and whose permanent interests are identified in their strict observance.[31]

Seen in this way, we can be reassured that the sovereign's reserve or prerogative powers should be exercised in a manner that is consistent with and supports fundamental constitutional principles, such

---

* In Australia and the other Commonwealth realms, the Governor-General or Governor exercises the sovereign's prerogative powers in the name of the monarch as a viceroy. In law, the powers remain the King's and they can technically override or bolster their Governor or Governor-General.

as representative government. These principles include the rule of law and the separation of powers.[32] As a result, the monarch forms a nexus for the three primary principles of our democracy and ensures both the spirit and function of the British constitutional system.

The way in which the British constitution has developed means it does not embody just one but many constitutional theories, all of which can have relevance at any given time. Monarchic rule, parliamentary struggle, revolution, democracy, custom and law are all combined to form the cohesive whole that we know today. Although communal oversight and a diffusion of power have existed in the English and Scottish political systems for centuries, democracy itself is a late arrival to the constitutional party. Much of the system that exists today was developed before democracy was an accepted let alone desirable outcome. A fact Anthony King highlights well when he recognises:

> The United Kingdom was a monarchy before it became a constitutional monarchy. It was a constitutional monarchy before it became a system of government built around ministers of the Crown. It was a system of government built around ministers of the Crown before it became a parliamentary system. And it was a parliamentary system before it became a parliamentary democracy. Democracy ... was a novel feature grafted on to a pre-existing constitutional structure.[33]

This is why Tony Benn said that it was important to understand the powers of the crown if we are to truly understand how we are governed.[34]

Democracy in the UK is thus a form of 'liberal democracy'. This fact defines its substance as a system of representative and responsible government in which voters elect the members of a representative institution, namely the House of Commons. The government of the day is then largely (but not exclusively) chosen from amongst its members and is, in turn, accountable to the Commons and through it, to the electorate itself. The Reform Act of 1832 began a process where representative democracy was progressively accommodated within the existing political structure, and the nature of the electorate and its composition have continually changed over the decades to arrive at our current point in time.[35] All of which means that our current system of a liberal, representative and indirect democracy is neither flawless nor immutable but continually changing to meet the needs of the country.

We must, therefore, neither overstate nor dismiss the current and historical importance of democratic institutions within the UK. Parliament is the supreme legislative body within the country, having established that there is no source of law more authoritative than an Act of Parliament in the Civil War of the 1640s and the Glorious Revolution of 1688.[36] This principle, however, is founded upon the unique authority Parliament derives from its representative nature and thus its link to the people. Had the House of Commons not contained within it an element of democratic principle in the seventeenth and eighteenth centuries, it is unlikely it would have been able to bend the crown and its ministers to its will. Yet we must always keep in mind that although Parliament may be supreme in legislative matters, it is not the supreme executive authority within our country. That honour rests in the hands of the monarch, as head of the executive, and through them their ministers and the Cabinet as embodied in the concept of the crown, a notion that was developed over the centuries to distinguish between the personal and the political acts of the monarch as the realities of Cabinet government became more established.

This split in the functions of the crown, or executive authority, led to the evolution in the UK of a binary executive comprising a head of state (the monarch) and a head of government (the Prime Minister) who between them fulfil the executive functions of the constitution.[37] What this means in effect is that the monarch is considered to act in two distinct and separate ways that encompass both their personal constitutional role and their public governmental role. In the first, the monarch has a wide degree of autonomy and can perform their functions as they see fit, whilst in the second their acts are those of government ministers, over which they have no control.

The overwhelming majority of executive acts fall into the second category and are exercised by the Prime Minister and the other ministers of state without the involvement of the monarch of the day. The personal functions of the head of state, however, are different in nature and can be broken down into three specific areas. The first is the formal and residual constitutional functions that require the monarch to become directly and personally involved in the political process. The second is the ceremonial activities that the monarch regularly undertakes, such as public engagements, commemorations or rituals. The third, and perhaps the most important, is that the monarch represents and symbolises not just the state but the nation too. In this capacity, they form and provide the physical embodiment of the unity that makes us a national community.[38]

The powers of executive action, legislative initiation and judicial oversight were collectively fused together in 1688 to form the theoretical concept called the 'King-in-Parliament', to which was ascribed the concept of parliamentary sovereignty that lies at the heart of our constitution.[39] This concept ensures that an Act of Parliament is the highest form of law recognised by the courts and has the ability to perform any action that Parliament has devised. We can see this theory at work in the preamble to all Acts of Parliament, which states, 'Be it enacted by the King's Most Excellent Majesty, by and with the advice and consent of the Lords Spiritual and Temporal, and Commons, in this present Parliament assembled, and with the authority of the same, as follows...' Only a bill passed by the House of Commons and the House of Lords that has received the assent of the monarch will be viewed by the courts as having this supreme character to which all entities in the kingdom must bow. As no form of power is greater than an Act of Parliament, the King-in-Parliament is seen by the courts as the supreme law of the land.[40] It is because of this concept that Vernon Bogdanor could say, 'The Constitution can be summed up in just eight words: What the Queen in Parliament enacts is law.'[41]

As a concept, parliamentary sovereignty has, over the centuries, proved itself extremely capable of being able to balance effective government with liberty and freedom because it is based on a harmonious principle which requires the three branches of government to cooperate with each other to administer the country. The goal has not been to create a system in which separate branches of government are each free to exercise their authority subject to being checked and balanced by the actions of the other two, as is the case in the US. Instead, the British system encourages cooperation between the monarch, Parliament and the courts, allowing for the development of several different points of view and opinions, which must be balanced in policy creation. For the government to act, it must do so through debate, consultation and individual participation, which creates a degree of consensus before a decision is implemented. Legal decision-making must be based on the broad consent of multiple interests of society and once the decision is arrived at, all three branches collaborate to ensure its implementation.

Should this harmony be disrupted or abandoned by one branch, it falls to the other two to intervene and reinstate the harmonic procedures. In this way, the monarch, Parliament and the courts each have a role in ensuring the proper functioning of the system.[42] It is through an acceptance of this concept that our system allows for a fusion of the executive and legislative powers. This fusion between the legislature and the courts and the courts and the executive was recognised until the creation of the Supreme Court in 2005. Before this, the highest court in the kingdom was located within the House of Lords and the Lord Chancellor was both a government minister and the highest-ranking judge.

Ensuring the system works effectively and that the 'efficient' and 'dignified' parts of the executive can function harmoniously together means that both the monarch and their ministers accept a framework and series of presumptions on how the system should work. These are:

1. The sovereign must act on the advice of ministers in the exercise of most but not all executive functions.
2. Ministers must accept all the political consequences for their decisions.
3. The monarch must be politically impartial.
4. Ministers must not act in a way that draws the monarch directly into the political process.
5. The sovereign must accept the advice and support of their ministers, thus ensuring the sovereign cannot have an independent policy.

This framework reconciles the monarchy with the reality of parliamentary democracy, whereby the will of the people, as expressed by the House of Commons, prevails.[43]

This book is therefore focused on the use of those powers that are vested in the monarch personally and which can be used to ensure the effective operation of the political process. As mentioned earlier, the King performs several personal functions as our head of state and this work seeks to explain the powers required to meet the first of these functions – in other words, to highlight and explain through historical examples exactly what we mean by the formal and residual constitutional functions that may require the monarch to become directly and personally involved in the political process. I will highlight not only the role our monarch plays in our political process but also the options open to the King in how he can exercise those powers, should he be called upon to do so during his reign. In this way, I hope to contribute to the public understanding of how our constitution truly operates.

I will explore the existence of those powers, collectively known as the royal prerogative, which the King retains independently of the legislative authority of Parliament. In so doing, I will discuss historic examples of their use and the limits under which they operate, all in the hopes that we can discuss our political system in a sensible way based on an understanding of the constitution.

In these pages I intend to hold up a mirror to our constitution to show you how royal power is wielded, eschewing in the process the comforting myths that underpin much of the political debate around executive authority. My watch words will be the same as they were for William Blackstone: 'A competent knowledge of the law should form the basis of everyone's political education.'[44] It is only when we are honest with ourselves about how our country is governed that we can truly seek to shape our political destiny.

Thanks to the operation of the Act of Settlement of 1701, Charles, as heir apparent, succeeded immediately and automatically to the throne upon the death of his mother. He was thus empowered to act in his constitutional role from that moment onwards, though how he will perform this function is yet to be revealed. When this happened, we were collectively privy to an act that has in the past been witnessed by only a few of our national leaders and statesmen, thanks to the decision to televise the Accession Privy Council – a decision that may hold some clues as to the King's future actions. This ceremonial body was convened for the first time in seventy years in the confines of St James's Palace, there to do what no living person in the country had done before: proclaim a new monarch.

Surrounded by the members of his Privy Council, the King confirmed his desire to be known as Charles III, ending decades of speculation as to this somewhat minor point. Of more interest to us was, however, the declaration he made to those present. In emulation of his ancestors before him and with a voice shaking with emotion at the loss of his mother, the King said the following words.

My Lords, Ladies, and Gentlemen.

It is my most sorrowful duty to announce to you the death of my beloved Mother, The Queen … I am deeply aware of this great inheritance and of the duties and heavy responsibilities of Sovereignty which have now passed to me. In taking up these responsibilities, I shall strive to follow the inspiring example I have been set in upholding constitutional government and to seek the peace, harmony and prosperity of the peoples of these Islands and of the Commonwealth Realms and Territories throughout the world.

In this purpose, I know that I shall be upheld by the affection and loyalty of the peoples whose Sovereign I have been called upon to be, and that in the discharge of these duties I will be guided by the counsel of their elected parliaments. In all this, I am profoundly encouraged by the constant support of my beloved wife.[45]

In these few words, his first official statement as our new monarch, the King encapsulated the nature of his role and his new responsibilities. He expressed his duty to act as the protector of the constitution, an act that is combined with that of his duty to be our national symbol, who seeks the peace and harmony of their people. In such rituals are the truths of our political system to be found, for often they are not the hollow meaningless acts that some ascribe them to be but living and significant moments.

The oath given, King Charles will now seek to define his office in a new way for a new age, but much will depend on how he meets the needs to balance the 'dignified' and 'efficient' parts of his role. This is because, as our sovereign, he is the oil in the wheels of the state, constantly working to ease us into a harmonious whole instead of splintering us into antagonistic parts. It is the sovereign's job to constantly smooth out the differences of opinion that arise in civic discourse, both on public occasions and in the privacy of an audience.

This job will continue for the rest of the King's life and will come to dominate the life of his son and grandson thereafter. True, he will experience the world in a unique way, will live in comfort and even luxury and will be regarded with immense interest and perhaps even affection. But there will be no occasions in which the cares and worries of the world can be cast aside for a moment's rest, no weekends without the pressures of work and no remission from responsibility until the moment of his own death. Who amongst us would willingly apply for such a role?

2

THE KING'S PLEASURE

The royal prerogatives have their origins within the mists of time, stretching back to the dark years following the fall of the Roman Empire in the west. A poetic notion to be sure, but one that does not provide us with much light or understanding in our current times. What it does show is that the prerogative flows from the ancient powers of our kings of old and thus it is antique in nature, preventing its effective categorisation. It is not the artificial creation of some distant law-giver, but rather it has grown and developed alongside the nature of kingship within these islands, from the Saxon war bands of the sixth century to our modern constitutional monarchy of today. It was, and to some extent remains, inherently grounded in the foundations of our fundamental constitutional beliefs, principles and practices. It is separate from the mundane consideration of more modern concepts like democracy, predating, as it does, Parliament by several centuries.[1]

These powers, privileges and immunities that are attributed to the king were not created by the common law but were merely recognised by it as a legal reality in later centuries. This is because their origin lay within the very nature, functions and attributes of kingship itself and are as much a product of custom as the common law is. The royal prerogatives originated as the personal powers of the monarch, which grew and developed as kings transformed themselves from commanders of roving war bands into leaders of large geographic entities.[2] Some gave the monarch certain rights, such as to any treasure troves that may be discovered; some gave immunities, such as the crown's immunity to being sued; and some imposed duties, such as the ancient obligation to protect their subjects from harm.[3]

Albert Dicey has provided what has generally been regarded as the standard definition for what the prerogative powers are, stating:

> The prerogative appears to be historically and as a matter of fact nothing else than the residue of discretionary and arbitrary authority which at any given time is legally left in the hands of the Crown ... Every act which the executive government can lawfully do without the authority of an Act of Parliament is done in virtue of the prerogative.[4]

As these powers flow from the remnants of the powers and privileges that were enjoyed by our medieval kings and queens, they are fixed in law, capable neither of enlargement nor diminution. They are determined to exist or not by the courts through the actions of common law. This means that the crown cannot claim a new prerogative power where one did not exist before, for it was 'three hundred and fifty years and a civil war too late to do so' according to Lord Justice Diplock in 1965.[5]

The prerogatives are thus relics from our distant past, but this in no way implies that they are not important or meaningful tools of governance today. The conduct of foreign affairs, for instance, is carried out under the scope of the prerogative, as is the organisation, control and disposition of the armed forces. Parliaments are summoned and sit as lawful assemblies under the warrants issued by the crown and all bills must receive royal assent before they can become laws. Likewise, the crown is not considered to be bound by any statute unless it is explicitly stated as being so bound by Parliament, and the appointment and regulation of the civil service is a matter solely for the prerogative.[6]

These powers are to some extent living history and we should therefore start our discussion about them in our distant past. In so doing, we need to recognise the seminal fact that royal absolutism never found root in the soil of these islands. Medieval kings of England and Scotland were indeed powerful, enjoying unique social and military privileges as the principal feudal landlords, but they were not all-powerful. There were accepted limits placed on their authority by the political traditions of their kingdoms. Their rights and duties were spelled out in coronation oaths and from 1215 onwards, English kings were constrained by their promises under Magna Carta.

We have Henry II to thank for the establishment within England of the institutions of settled government. His reforms to the operation of the executive and judicial functions of the kingdom helped establish a recorded law code for the first time.[7] Legal memory therefore only extends as far back as the coronation of Richard I, even though the common law's roots are recognised as stretching further back in time.[8] Thanks to his energy and imagination, Henry ensured that by the end of the twelfth century, England was arguably the most sophisticated and effective monarchy in Europe, in large part thanks to this unbroken legal tradition.[9]

This is a fact that is reinforced when we realise that the first great treatise on English law appeared early in the thirteenth century. In this work, Henry de Bracton affirmed the central tenent that 'the king must not be under man but under God and under the law, because law makes the king'.[10] Such a statement could not have been made but for the Henrician reforms of the previous century. It also helped that it was a principle that could be imposed on the king by the relative wealth and power of the earls and barons – men who could enforce their rights by the sword if needs be. This fact was proven on the fields of Runnymede in 1215, when the earls and barons compelled King John to accept limits on his power through the Magna Carta, signed by the king at the end of the First Barons' War.[11] Far from being a revolutionary document, Magna Carta recognised and codified a wider body of legal traditions in one place and so reflected the political consensus of its time. Political innovation thus compelled our kings to accept 'the necessity of taking the nation into partnership' in the governance of the realm.[12] All of which meant that by the fourteenth century, English kings had acknowledged the prudence of recognising a convention that taxes should be levied with consent and laws promulgated with the approval of the prelates and barons.

Two events in our medieval history stand out to highlight the development of this doctrine that kings ruled by force of law and forfeited their rights if they broke it. The first was the removal of Richard II from the throne in 1399. The charge laid against him was not incompetence or unworthiness, but rather that he had broken the law by claiming that the lives, liberties and property of his subjects were his to dispose of. This assumption so outraged the barons and gentry that it sparked the rising of Henry of Lancaster, which compelled Richard to abdicate. Parliament was summoned to approve the abdication but went further than required by formally deposing Richard. This created a power vacuum they then sought to fill by confirming Henry as the new king.

The second event of note was the assumption of the crown by Henry Tudor in 1485. Here was a man with neither a hereditary nor legal claim to the throne who simply assumed the crown following his victory at the Battle of Bosworth. Keen to ratify his position, Henry duly summoned Parliament, which happily converted his possession into a legal title through statute. In so doing, Parliament became not just the body through which the king governed but the accepted kingmaker of the land. Henry's actions thus confirmed that laws did indeed make kings.[13]

This brings us neatly to the moment in time when the prerogative steps forth into its own and we can begin to recognise it as a separate entity in law. The Tudor revolution transformed the way in which the kingdom was governed, as the monarchy enlarged the sphere of its activities and increased the effectiveness of its control – a situation that was aided by three key social changes that occurred during this period. The first was that the power of the nobility declined markedly over this period as their numbers and wealth had been decimated by the Wars of the Roses. The second was the rise of the merchants, gentry, knights and squires in wealth and importance. Keen to secure their rights and privileges, they were willing allies for the Crown and in exchange for protection and promotion, they supported the expansion of royal power during this period. And the third was the English Reformation, in which Parliament assisted Henry VIII in breaking the power of the Catholic Church, increasing royal revenues and the king's authority in the process.[*] [14]

All of this ensured that the king was transformed into both the

---

[*] A fact highlighted by the career of Thomas Cromwell.

temporal and spiritual head of the country and the very pinnacle of the state. The monarch's new position as both the actual ruler and the representative of the nation led to distinctions being raised as to which powers fell within his prerogative. Some were considered to be 'inseparable' as it was impossible to imagine a king without them, whilst others were felt to be 'absolute' because the king had an uncontrolled discretion as to their use.[15] This debate was engendered by the fact that the king increasingly began to administer the realm through his council and the use of his prerogative powers, an innovation made necessary by the fact that whole new areas of governmental activity had now opened up which had yet to be incorporated into the existing governmental structure. To supplement the existing law and create new laws where none existed increasingly became the business of what was termed the 'King-in-Council', using the royal prerogative.*

Despite this increase in the direct use of royal power, it would be wrong to assume that that the Tudor monarchy had become absolute. The Tudor kings and queens continued to balance this new activity with the more traditional roles undertaken by Parliament and the courts. In this way, the prerogative sat beside and complemented existing practice rather than replacing it outright.[16]

To balance this increased authority, Bracton's principle was again restated during this period by Fortescue in his *Governance of England*, which argued for the merits of constitutional monarchy that we discussed a few pages back.[17] Tudor monarchs and their advisers, as a result, had to accept the supremacy of the law and the centrality of Parliament in the governance of the kingdom.[18] Seen in this light, the Tudor monarchy sought to operate within the rules of the

---

* 'King-in-Council' refers to the monarch exercising executive authority, as opposed to legislative (King-in-Parliament) or judicial (King-in-Court).

constitution as they were then understood and this was accepted by Parliament and the courts as lawful. This was a situation that changed somewhat upon the death of Elizabeth I.[19]

Elizabeth's Stuart heirs and successors chose to operate in a more direct way than Englishmen were accustomed to and so lacked the subtlety of their predecessors. Instead, they sought to proclaim their divine right to rule. A conflict was all but inevitable as they looked to divert more power into the king's hands. The challenge to this royal assertion would first arise within the courts, as common law judges resisted royal claims to be dispensers of the law. Led by Sir Edward Coke, the Chief Justice, former Speaker of the Commons and Attorney General, the courts began to assert the supremacy of common law over the prerogative.[20] They sought to reduce the prerogative from an unlimited discretionary power to one that was simply a part of the common law.[21] This was a proposition that was summed up in the ruling in a landmark legal case: 'The King hath no prerogative, but that which the law of the land allows him.'[22] In so doing, the courts laid the legal framework that allowed parliamentarians to mount a more serious rebellion when Charles I tried to dispense with Parliament entirely. The restoration of the monarchy in 1660 ended the turmoil of the Civil War, but it was achieved by an acceptance that the king governed within the limits of the constitution and that his power was defined and limited by law. Charles II adjusted to this new reality, but his brother James unwisely sought to unravel this settlement, leading to a further rebellion.[23]

These momentous proceedings were set in motion by the flight of James II and the arrival of William and Mary in London following an armed landing in Torbay on 5 November 1688. The power vacuum created by these events instigated the election of the

English Convention Parliament following a summons from William. The Parliament met for the first time in January 1689 to resolve the crisis.[24] In recognition of James's absence and his acceptance of Catholicism, they took the momentous step of declaring the throne vacant and offering the crown to William and Mary who were to be appointed joint monarchs of England – and, by extension, Ireland as a dependent realm – following their acceptance of the Declaration of Rights and the rule of law. This extraordinary result emerged from a series of compromises that saw theories of social contract and divine right mingle in a way that sought to obscure the revolutionary nature of the Convention Parliament's actions and explain them in terms of existing constitutional practice.[25]

This innovation was itself made possible by a political compromise that saw English politicians vote for constructive abdication and by extension the removal of a bad king whilst evading the central question of whether subjects could lawfully perform such an act in the first place. A series of laws were therefore passed in the subsequent years that aimed to remedy this failing by further limiting royal authority. So important were these Acts that they came to be collectively known as the revolutionary settlement.[26]

Events in Scotland were to follow a similar process after the summoning of the Convention of the Scottish Estates by William on 16 March 1689 with the consent and support of the Scottish Privy Council. Although the Scottish Convention, like its English counterpart, could not be classified as a true Parliament as it had not been summoned by the king, it did have the unique power to discuss a specific issue as a sister institution to Parliament – in this case, who should occupy the Scottish throne. Historically, the convention had been summoned by the king for the purpose of raising taxes, but given the circumstances it was felt to be the best constitutional vehicle in which to discuss the future of the Scottish crown.[27] The Scots were to have a far more difficult and innovative debate on this question than their English counterparts, as they could not simply claim, as the English had done, that James had abandoned the throne. This was because James had not been present in Scotland during the crisis – or for the vast bulk of his reign for that matter – and so could not be said to have fled Scotland.

The Scots had long had to deal with the reality of an absent king since James VI had left to assume the throne of England in 1603 and so they found themselves unsure as to how they should proceed. Whereas English politicians argued that James had abandoned his throne and country by converting to Catholicism and fleeing to France, Scottish politicians argued instead that he had forfeited the throne by his misuse of power. In so doing, they accepted the fundamental point that had been so studiously avoided in England that subjects did indeed have the power to depose a king.[28] James, and by extension executive authority itself, was placed on trial by the convention to determine if power had indeed been misused, establishing in the process a standard by which the judicial use of authority could be measured and lawfully established. James was ultimately found to be in breach of this standard and was thereby deemed to have forfeited the throne due to a number of transgressions that were then listed by the convention in the Articles of Grievances and the Claim of Right. These documents formed the basis on which William and Mary were formally offered the Scottish crown, which they accepted on 11 May 1689.

With their acceptance of the throne, the convention became a Parliament and transformed the Articles of Grievances and the Claim of Right into Acts, which form part of the constitutional settlement of Scotland and by extension the United Kingdom to this day. The Scottish convention's behaviour fundamentally changed the constitutional practices of the time, as they had shown that monarchs derived their legitimacy not from God but from Parliament and thus the principle of the divine right of kings, so long promoted by the Stuarts, was finally ended.[29] All of this meant that within six months of James's flight from Britain, a profound transformation of the constitution had been achieved. By two very separate routes, both English and Scottish politicians had arrived at the same destination and established the twin principles of the rule of law and parliamentary sovereignty that would go on to form the basis of British constitutional practice to this day.

The origins of our current constitutional settlement are thus to be found in these monumental changes that occurred during the period 1688 to 1720 and the resulting shift of political power from the sovereign to Parliament. The Bill of Rights (1689), the Claim of Right (1689), the Mutiny Act (1689), the Triennial Act (1694), the Treasons Act (1696) and the Act of Settlement (1701) form the core of this revolutionary settlement.[30] These Acts transformed the constitution, shifting the balance of power from the sovereign to Parliament by, amongst other things, enshrining the supremacy of Acts of Parliament over all individuals and institutions within the realm, including the king himself. Alongside this, they ensured free elections to regularly called Parliaments, freedom of speech in parliamentary debates, the right to jury trials and the need for the consent of Parliament to wage war at the behest of another country.

By fundamentally transforming the constitutional landscape, these Acts provided the fertile environment for the evolution of a head of government who was separate from the sovereign.[31] The Bill of Rights and the Act of Settlement, for instance, confirmed and strengthened the principle that government was undertaken by the sovereign and their ministers alone. By their actions, Scottish and English politicians had reached a truly radical understanding of the political structure in both kingdoms, as they had accepted the principle that monarchs derived their legitimacy not from God but from Parliament and, through that institution, the people. Parliament was thus able to determine who was legitimately king and arrange for succession to the throne independently of the church or the concept of primogeniture – a power it exercised to the benefit of Sophia, Electress of Hanover, and her heirs in 1701.

The revolution of 1688 fixed the principles of our modern constitution in place and its essential character has changed very little to this day. Unlike the French Revolution a century later, which ushered in a new system of governance, this British revolution set out to return the political system to the state that it enjoyed before the arrival of James II.[32] It therefore did not set out fundamental new principles of governance but merely codified existing practice in a way that prevented further disagreement. Both the Bill and Claim of Rights were largely declaratory of existing law and ensured that rights which had been proclaimed in a piecemeal fashion in the past were now firmly established in the constitutional structure. The monarch's prerogatives remained, but they were now more than ever before subject to the overriding power of statute and the regulation of the courts.[33] What made this retention of the royal prerogative politically palatable was the growing use of these prerogative powers by ministers who were increasingly held to account for their use within the House of Commons. This process led to the development of a dual-headed executive, in which the day-to-day administrative roles of government were separated from those of kingship.

Under this constitutional settlement, the sovereign is the head of state and nominal head of the government, which is referred to as His or Her Majesty's Government. Their primary role is to select as Prime Minister the person who can command a working majority in the House of Commons and invite them to form a government. The Prime Minister, who is the actual head of government, then selects the Cabinet, choosing its members from amongst their supporters, or party, in the House of Commons. These individuals are then recommended to the sovereign, who formally confirms their appointment to office. The Cabinet determines policy collectively and is jointly held responsible for all acts of said government by Parliament and the people. The sovereign does not consult with ministers privately about policy, nor do they attend Cabinet meetings or seek to determine governmental actions.

As a result, the crown provides the legal basis for all governmental action and occupies the conceptual place held by the head of state in other countries. But just to confuse matters further, the crown is both a concept and a person, which can at times blur the distinction between the public actions of the government and personal actions of the king. Although the powers are personal in nature, they exist today to ensure good governance rather than the personal whim of an individual. The prerogative must, as a result, be seen as inherently linked to its function, as these powers, privileges and immunities are vested in the sovereign for the purpose of governance – in other words, to ensure the government can function.[34] In the words of Sir William Holdsworth, 'The principal motive force of the executive power in the British Constitution has always been the royal prerogative.'[35]

Although the legal relationship between the legislature, executive and judiciary has altered little in its form since 1688, the operation of the executive and legislature has been transformed.[36]

The constitutional structure remains the same, but the way it operates is very different. This transformation had become clear by the time Walter Bagehot began to contemplate the nature of the constitution, a process that happened piecemeal over the centuries and was driven by a series of events from the Hanoverian succession and the Napoleonic Wars to the passage of the Reform Acts, which shaped the way in which the government operated. The most important of these was the increased dependence of the monarch upon Parliament for not only legislation but more importantly taxation, a process that was fuelled by the rising importance of the House of Commons within Parliament and the development of the party-political system within the Commons itself.[37] Individual ministers became increasingly responsible to the Commons and the government's authority flowed from the support of the majority. This was compounded by the lack of attendance at Cabinet meetings by the Georgian monarchs and the consequent emergence of a 'Prime' Minister, who increasingly chaired the Cabinet and led the government. This resulted in a government whose policy was made by the Cabinet and whose members were increasingly drawn from and answerable to the House of Commons.[38]

The division of the executive between a head of state and a head of government cemented our current conception of a constitutional monarchy. Under this system, the sovereign remains the formal head of the executive, but the vast bulk of the legislative and prerogative powers of the crown are exercised not by the monarch personally but by ministers in the king's name.[39] For this process to work, the sovereign must be politically neutral, operating on a level above party politics. This is because almost all public acts of the crown are taken on the advice of his or her ministers who are responsible to Parliament and the electorate for their actions. When ministers advise the monarchy, their advice is generally of such a binding nature that the sovereign has no choice but to accept. If the king should reject the advice offered, they risk the resignation of the government, an act that would compel the monarch to find another government that would hold office as the king's personal choice rather than that of the House of Commons. In so doing, the monarch would signal their opposition to one of the main political parties of the state – a situation they could not long survive.[40]

The irony of all this is that the concept of political neutrality and the need to follow ministerial advice came about to protect Parliament and the people from the arbitrary use of royal power, whereas today the very same process protects the monarch from the negative political consequences of the use of executive authority, which is instead absorbed by elected politicians. This process is buttressed by three conventions. Firstly, the monarch can only be advised by their duly appointed ministers; secondly, the king's public statements reflect the advice of their ministers whilst their private statements ensure government ministers are not compromised; and thirdly, the sovereign must accept the advice and support of their ministers. In this way, the system reconciles monarchy and democracy by ensuring the will of the people prevails.[41]

The monarch's true impact on governmental action does not therefore come from the direct use of power but rather from their exercise of influence on the decision-making process itself through their regular meetings with the Prime Minister, their receipt of all government papers and, as time goes on, their longevity in office.[42] This is a more personal and passive use of power than we are trained to expect from politicians, but it can be just as effective. The monarch should not, therefore, be seen as a mere cypher for the government of the day but as an independent actor on the political stage.[43] This is a fact Disraeli highlighted in 1872 when he told his audience in Manchester:

> I know it will be said that the personal influence of the Sovereign is now merged in the responsibility of the Minister. I think you will find a great fallacy in this view. The principles of the English Constitution do not contemplate the absence of personal influence on the part of the Sovereign; and if they did, the principles of human nature would prevent the fulfilment of such a theory.[44]

The leading biographies of the most recent monarchs clearly show that the sovereign is an active head of state who is engaged with the daily process of governance. This influence is most clearly proven by Bagehot's trinity of rights: the right to be consulted, the right to advise and the right to warn. These rights embody a high degree of influence, for as Bagehot states:

> A king of great sense and sagacity would want no others [no other powers]. He would find that having no others would enable him to use these with singular effect. He would say to his minister: 'The responsibility of these measures is upon you. Whatever you think best must be done. Whatever you think best shall have my full and effectual support ... I do not oppose, it is my duty not to oppose, but observe that I warn.' Supposing the king to be right and to have what kings often have, the gift of effectual expression, he could not help moving his minister. He might not always turn his course, but he would always trouble his mind.[45]

In short, a wise use of influence and advice will obviate the need for the monarch to directly exercise those residual political powers that are vested in them in a personal capacity.

Tensions can, however, arise within the system if the monarch is felt to express a political opinion or if a Prime Minister pursues a domestic policy that generates a considerable amount of civil unrest. This is because the monarch may find themselves torn between their personal and political roles – on the one hand, supporting the government, whilst on the other, ensuring national unity. Such an event happened in 1984 when the government clashed with Arthur Scargill's National Union of Mineworkers. The images that played out on the nation's TV screens of the police clashing with striking mineworkers had the feel of a civil war about them that was not lost on the Queen. Seeking to embarrass the government, the miners' union publicly appealed to the Queen to 'speak up on our behalf' as they sought to pressure her into entering the political fray.[46] Although the Queen continued to publicly support the government throughout the strike, she privately had a great deal of sympathy for the miners and was unimpressed by Margaret Thatcher's policies.[47] The Queen had personally been more comfortable with the post-war consensus politics of earlier governments that had tried to maintain industrial peace. As a result, a royal whispering campaign developed against the government's policies generally and the Prime Minister in particular.[48]

The tabloid press became filled with stories that were both personal and political. They revealed to the nation that Thatcher hated going to Balmoral and was regularly kept waiting by the Queen during her weekly audience at Buckingham Palace.[49] All of which would have been bad enough, but the political disagreements between the two women over foreign and especially Commonwealth matters were also disclosed in the process.[50] Things came to a head in July 1986 when *Today* published a story exposing the quarrel for all to see. This story was allegedly based on information supplied to the paper directly by the palace press office itself, which claimed that the Queen had urged Thatcher to support sanctions against South Africa. If true, such an allegation implied the direct interference of the monarch in the development of British foreign policy, a clearly political matter that was within the purview of the Cabinet alone. *Today* informed its readers, 'She [the Queen] fears Britain's stand on trade sanctions could lead to the breakup of the Commonwealth. The queen gave the prime minister a discreet warning during a private audience at Buckingham Palace.'[51]

Such a sensational revelation was quickly followed up within the more dignified pages of the *Sunday Times*, which reported that the Queen regarded Thatcher's approach to governing as 'uncaring, confrontational and divisive'. It went on to state that the Queen felt that Thatcher was damaging the national consensus and that her clashes with the unions would produce long-term damage to the nation.[52] These revelations laid bare for all to see the rift that had developed between Buckingham Palace and Downing Street and in so doing broke the cardinal rule of confidentiality and political neutrality that lies at the heart of the premier-monarch relationship.

The political fallout was swift, and the Queen found herself in an exposed position that could potentially have damaged her position irretrievably. Upon investigation, Michael Shea, the Queen's press secretary, was identified as the source of the story, giving the exposé the potential to create a full-blown constitutional crisis, as it was felt to be unlikely that such an experienced professional would have acted in such a way without the backing of the Queen. Such was the level of concern within the country about South Africa's racial policies and the government's clash with the miners' union that neither Thatcher nor the Queen emerged unscathed from the scandal. The government's poll ratings slumped and the Queen was strongly suspected of having crossed a constitutional line.[53] Keen to re-establish the status quo and reduce the tension between the palace and No. 10, Shea left the Queen's service within a year and the royal whispering campaign was formally ended.[54] All parties had learnt their lesson. Although the monarch and Prime Minister may disagree about policy privately, it must never become public as conflict can only lead to both institutions being damaged.

The king can therefore only exert their influence within the framework of the constitutional rules around ministerial advice, a point that was highlighted by Lord Esher in a memorandum he presented to George V regarding the Home Rule Bill in September 1913. In considering how he should act, Esher told the King that he must accept:

> Every Constitutional Monarch possesses a dual personality. He may hold and express opinions upon the conduct of his Ministers, and their measures. He may endeavour to influence their actions. He may delay decisions in order to give more time for reflection. He may refuse assent to their advice up to the point where he is obliged to choose between accepting it and losing their service.
>
> If the Sovereign believes advice to him to be wrong, he may refuse to take it, and if his Minister yields, the Sovereign is justified. If the Minister persists, feeling that he has behind him a majority of the people's representatives, a Constitutional Sovereign must give way.[55]

This is advice that was built upon by Sir William Heseltine, the Queen's private secretary, when he looked to defuse the row between

No. 10 and the palace in the summer of 1986. Writing to *The Times*, he laid down three propositions that needed to be met to ensure an effective relationship between monarch and ministers. These were:

1. The Queen has the right, and indeed the duty, to express her opinions on government policy to the Prime Minister.
2. The Queen must act on the advice of her ministers, regardless of her own opinion, in most but not all situations.
3. Communications between the Queen and the Prime Minister must remain confidential.[56]

As you can see, the first premise and the third are linked and operate to prevent the monarch from publicly criticising the government. Royal influence can only ever be used privately, a fact which ensures and maintains the political neutrality of the sovereign.[57]

So, we have examined the general principle, but now here is where things get complicated, for everything we have just discussed only applies during the existence of a ministry and when the government is itself operating within the accepted constitutional principles. They do not apply when a ministry ends through the death, incapacity or resignation of the Prime Minister; when a Prime Minister seeks a dissolution of Parliament; or when the Prime Minister is acting in an unconstitutional manner. On these rare occasions, the king retains the ability to act unilaterally and without the advice of ministers. Why should that be the case, you may well ask? Well, it all has to do with the monarch's role as guardian of the constitution.

As we have discussed, the prerogative powers are those powers reserved to the crown, which ensured the effective operation of the executive. To this end, a degree of discretion is still to be found in their operation, as it is recognised that the sovereign has a duty to maintain the fundamental constitutional principles of the UK. It is only when the prerogative powers are exercised in a constitutional crisis that their existence become notable and their nature and scope a subject for public debate.[58] To aid our understanding of this process, the Public Administration Select Committee identified three categories of prerogative powers in 2004. Their report breaks the prerogative down as:

1. The sovereign's constitutional prerogatives – that is, the discretionary powers that remain within the sovereign's personal use. These include the right to: advise, encourage and warn Ministers; to appoint the Prime Minister and other ministers; and to assent to legislation.
2. The legal prerogatives of the crown – such as the right to sturgeon, whales, certain swans, and the right to impress men into the Royal Navy. More significantly, the legal principle that the Crown can do no wrong and that the Crown is not bound by statute, save by express words or necessary implication.
3. Prerogative executive powers – the powers that historically have resided with the sovereign but which now, by constitutional convention, are exercised by government ministers acting in the sovereign's name. They include the making and ratifying of international treaties, the conduct of diplomacy, the governance of overseas territories and the deployment of the armed forces.[59]

If we examine the non-exhaustive list of prerogative powers in current use, drawn up in 2013 for the House of Commons Political and Constitutional Reform Committee, we can see how these three categories work in practice. The powers include:

1. The appointment and dismissal of the Prime Minister;
2. the summoning, prorogation and dismissal of Parliament;
3. giving or refusing royal assent to bills;
4. legislating by prerogative Order in Council or by letters patent;
5. exercising the prerogative of mercy (e.g. to pardon convicted offenders);
6. making treaties;
7. waging war by any means and making peace (including powers over the control, organisation and disposition of the armed forces);
8. issuing passports and providing consular services;
9. conferring honours, decorations and peerages; and
10. making certain appointments (including royal commissions).[60]

The first three powers are recognised to be the sovereign's personal constitutional prerogatives, exercisable by them as head of state according to their own discretion without, or contrary to, ministerial advice.[61] Some legal experts, such as Rodney Brazier, have preferred to use the term 'reserve powers' rather than 'personal prerogatives', as a way of 'emphasising that these powers are in reserve, to be used in exceptional cases, and are not at all powers which might be used regularly or routinely'.[62]

Although this is an admirable attempt to reconcile royal discretion with our constitutional conventions around ministerial advice, it does not clarify as well as it intends. This is because several of these powers are exercised regularly and are not confined to periods of crisis or only used in exceptional cases. The appointment of a Prime Minister or the granting of a dissolution, for instance, happen at regular intervals and so form part of the regular operation of the constitution. Now it is true to say that, due to accepted conventions as to the use of these powers, no discretion will be exercised by the monarch in normal circumstances. But such a recognition does not change the fact that no external ministerial force can compel action as to their use.[63] To this end, Brazier et al. are right in asserting that these powers only become worthy or of note during a crisis that requires the sovereign to operate outside accepted custom.

Worth noting here is the degree to which the key players in the political drama all ascribe to the belief that the maintenance of a separate field of independent royal action is not only necessary but beneficial to our political system. As we saw during the formation of the coalition government in 2010, the party leaders went out of their way to ensure that the Queen was not compelled to enter the political arena by using her powers to appoint a Prime Minister. All accepted the political need to ensure that a crisis did not develop in which the only possibility for resolution was for the Queen to act.[64] Their actions help highlight the important convention that the monarch must accept the advice and support of their ministers. To ensure the monarchy remains politically neutral and above the fray, politicians have a duty to ensure that the government can continue in a way that does not require royal action. This can require them to bend on political principle to achieve an acceptable outcome, even if it is to their detriment.

The strength of our political system is its suppleness, which ensures our constitutional settlement can bend when confronted by political storms. Centrally important to that suppleness is the existence of a set of powers that can be used by a non-political actor in a manner that helps maintain the constitutional consensus when politics breaks down. As it is accepted that the king cannot be bound by precedent, the uses of these powers remain flexible enough to meet any occasion that may arise.[65] Thus, in 1910, Lord Esher could argue that there ought not to be a general discussion as to the use of the prerogative by the king as 'the principle is entirely dependent upon the circumstances in which the prerogative is used'.[66]

A sound argument and one that has been proven by the actions of legal and political commentators ever since. We only have to look at the debate around the ability of peers to serve as Prime Minister to see that. It is generally accepted that following George V's appointment of Stanley Baldwin as Prime Minister in preference to Lord Curzon in 1923, only MPs can be considered as candidates for the premiership. But a close examination of the records of the time shows this not to be the case, as the King was clear when questioned on this point by Lord Curzon that he was not seeking to create a general doctrine with regards to appointment but rather to make the best choice in the circumstance of the time.[67] Which helps explain how George VI could contemplate just a few years later the appointment of Lord Halifax, believing that his peerage was no bar to his candidacy.[68]

Whilst I would support the proposition that the sovereign's personal prerogatives should be viewed as necessary and used with a wide degree of discretion, I do not support the view that they should be uncircumscribed. This is because the foundation upon which these powers and discretions stand is the monarch's role as the defender of the constitutional order. It therefore follows that any use of personal discretion by the king must accord with the constitutional principles that he is seeking to defend. The king's authority flows from his legality and as such, he cannot break the law for whatever reason. The inherent conflict involved in the belief that the monarch must be both politically neutral but also willing and able to act when required can only be resolved by the sovereign, recognising their duty to preserve our constitution in a manner consistent with accepted practice.

Which brings me neatly to the premise of this book. As we enter a new reign, we are left wondering how the King will differ from his mother in his approach to the use of his prerogative. The long reign of Queen Elizabeth II has conditioned us to a certain form of royal behaviour, but as we have discussed, the monarch is not bound by precedent. It will be for the King to decide how he should act when called upon to deal with the political issues that are bound to arise in the future. The example of his ancestors will be a guide, but he will also need to pay attention to the circumstance of the moment if he is to weather future storms unscathed. In many ways, our late Queen was blessed to have presided over a relatively calm and stable political period in British history. The conflicts of the 1970s and Brexit aside, her reign lacked the drama that George V's suffered and so we have not seen the use of the royal prerogative in such a public way for many years.

The early days of the King's reign have already been eventful, and it may be that we are entering a period of greater uncertainty and political turmoil than was the case in our quieter past. To that end, it seems timely that we should delve into examples of how the prerogatives have been used in the past so that we can condition ourselves to their potential use in the future. I will therefore use the following pages to examine how the prerogatives of appointment, dismissal, dissolution and assent have been used in the last century in both Britain and the other principal Commonwealth realms to see what lessons they can teach us.

PART II

THE PREROGATiVE OF APPOINTMENT

3

THE KING'S FIRST MINISTER

The first prerogative we will examine is the power of appointment, for it is universally accepted that the monarch alone has the power to appoint a Prime Minister. This is because the office is a creature of the executive and there is no constitutional actor that can compel the monarch to appoint someone to the post. As a result, the power cannot be delegated to another and must be exercised in person. This is a reality that was clearly shown in 1974, when Edward Heath called a snap election whilst the Queen was on a tour of the Pacific. When Heath informed her that he intended to resign, the Queen was forced to cut short her tour and fly back to the UK in the middle of the night to accept his resignation in person and appoint Harold Wilson.[1]

In exercising this power, the monarch is understood to be appointing not just a Prime Minister but a government. A Prime Minister so appointed becomes the monarch's principal adviser and they must act in the way they are formally advised to by their premier. When a Prime Minister resigns or dies in office, however, the government's mandate expires with them and so the monarch no longer has responsible ministers, a fact which ensures this power can only be exercised at the sovereign's discretion. Such a situation creates the space that allows the monarch to consult widely to determine which individual would be best placed to serve as their Prime Minister.[2]

Whilst this remains the constitutional position today, just as it did 300 years ago, the sovereign is nevertheless bound by a series of political, legal and procedural considerations in their use of this power. The monarch's discretion has also been further constrained by the tangential evolution of a clear party structure within Parliament, with each party having a process by which leaders are elected. These factors combine to create a situation in which the monarch appoints the leading political figure of the day to the premiership with little direct involvement on their part. Yet situations can and do arise when they may need to exercise a more direct role.

It is because the appointment of a Prime Minister is made without formal advice or submissions from the Cabinet, which has anyway ceased to exist with the loss or resignation of the Prime Minister, that the monarch is free to consult widely on whom to appoint. This right becomes most important and of the greatest value to the constitution when there is doubt about the choice but is far less important when the appointment is obvious, as it is in most cases.[3] This is a point that was highlighted by Ronald Fraser, assistant private secretary to King George VI, in 1949 when he told Sir Norman Brook, the Cabinet Secretary:

> The choice of Prime Minister by the King is not made on the formal advice or submission ... In many cases the choice is clear but the King has an absolute right in all cases to consult anyone he pleases. This right may of course be of the greatest value in cases where there is doubt about the choice; such as in the event of the

death of a Prime Minister in office, the resignation of the Prime Minister for personal reasons, a complicated political situation and so forth. Never the less, as the King should not exercise, or appear to exercise, any political bias, he would normally choose as Prime Minister the leader of the Party having the largest number of seats in the House of Commons.[4]

If we survey the political landscape of twentieth-century Britain, we can see how this process worked in practice. During that period, three events took place that required a degree of royal discretion. First, when there were several party leaders with a claim to national leadership at the same moment, as occurred in 1923. The election of that year had produced a startling result, with the Conservatives losing their overall majority but remaining the largest party with 258 seats. Labour and the Liberals between them had returned 349 seats, giving them a majority of ninety-two. The Liberals' gains were bigger, but Labour remained the second-largest party with 191 seats. The electoral maths allowed for several outcomes to occur at the same moment. The Conservatives could have sought to remain in office as a minority, Labour could have assumed office as a minority or with Liberal support, a non-party government could have been assembled under an acceptable statesman or a Liberal government could have emerged with either Conservative or Labour support. In the end, following consultation with the King, both Conservatives and Liberals agreed to Ramsay MacDonald assuming office as Prime Minister of the first Labour government.[5]

Second, when the nation was confronted by a profound crisis that threatened its existence and prevented the existing political structure from functioning effectively, as occurred in 1931. Faced with the need to make significant budget cuts due to the effects of the Great Depression, the Labour government collapsed. Keen to ensure there was no political crisis in the midst of an economic crisis, the King encouraged the party leaders to agree to a compromise. The result was a national government comprising elements of all three parties, with MacDonald as Prime Minister. During the discussion, the issue of who would be Prime Minister was hotly debated with both Stanley Baldwin and David Lloyd George being considered. It was the King's preference for MacDonald, however, that resolved the matter, allowing for the national government to be formed.[6]

Third, when a Prime Minister was either incapacitated or else died in office, as almost happened in 1953. Following a state dinner held for the Italian Prime Minister, Winston Churchill suffered a stroke that raised the possibility of his dying in office or else being unable to perform his duties. As there was no clear successor due to Anthony Eden being out of the country for surgery, it was agreed that if either eventuality took place, the Queen would appoint Lord Salisbury as an interim Prime Minister until Eden returned.[7] We will go on to discuss all three of these examples in greater detail in the following pages.

Australia similarly provides us with fertile ground in which to explore the operation of the prerogative of appointment, for that country has experienced the deaths of three Prime Ministers in office since 1939. The corresponding political vacuum these events created was only filled due to the exercise of the crown's discretionary power along the lines outlined by Ronald Fraser. The first of these tragedies occurred in 1939 with the death of Joseph Lyons. The succession was confused because Robert Menzies had just resigned as deputy leader of the United Australia Party on policy grounds, thus causing a vacancy in the posts of both leader and deputy leader.

The Governor-General, acting on their own initiative and without advice, appointed as interim Prime Minister Earle Page, the serving Deputy Prime Minister and leader of the junior coalition party, the Country Party – an outcome made possible because there was no clear line of succession until the United Party elected a new leader.[8] The second was in 1945 when Frank Forde was appointed interim Prime Minister following the death of John Curtin. Things were made far simpler for the Governor-General in this instance, as Curtin had appointed Forde as acting Prime Minister due to his deteriorating health, thus allowing time for the Labor Party to elect Ben Chifley as their new leader.[9] The last was in 1967 when, following the disappearance of Harold Holt at sea, the Governor-General appointed John McEwen, the Deputy Prime Minister and leader of the Country Party, interim Prime Minister until the election of John Gorton as the new leader of the Liberal Party.[10]

In cases such as these, the sovereign can be expected to have a wide degree of freedom in the use of their power of appointment, but in so doing, they would seek to work within the existing political structure to build a wide degree of support within the House of Commons.[11] The forces of history itself have shaped the way in which the monarch exercises their appointment powers to the degree that a constitutional monarch would not now seek to impose their own wishes on Parliament as would have been the case before 1688. Instead, they would work with the political parties to ensure their government has the widest political support possible.

To aid the monarch in the exercise of their duty they are governed by what I call the Golden Rule, which sets out the criteria that must be met by an individual before they can be appointed to office. This rule encapsulates the legal requirements that have developed and shaped the office over the centuries and is binding to such a degree that many people feel that it has rendered the monarch's freedom of action void. But what exactly is the Golden Rule? Put simply, it is that the monarch must appoint as Prime Minister the individual who can form a government which will have the confidence of the House of Commons.[12] This simple sentence comprises the magic formula that instantly transforms an ordinary person into a Prime Minister – nothing more and nothing less. All our Prime Ministers have met this test to gain office and all have been forced to resign when they can no longer demonstrate that they can achieve it. Fundamentally, the rule both protects the political neutrality of the monarch and provides a degree of structure as to how they exercise their prerogative of appointment by providing the threshold that politicians must meet to be considered for the office. In this way, it is left to the political process itself to decide who is best able to run the country at any given moment in time.[13]

Although the Golden Rule may appear simple in construction, it is in fact a precise formula that synthesises the various forms of governance that have operated in the UK over the centuries. It recognises that although initially the appointment of any minister was in the personal remit of the sovereign, the increasing need to secure the support of a majority in the House of Commons has effectively constrained the monarch's freedom of choice.[14] The advent of mass franchises and organised political parties in the nineteenth century further modified this system, as candidates for office now needed not only a majority in the House of Commons but control of their political machine and the support of the voters as well.[15]

All successful Prime Ministers are able to demonstrate that they enjoy the confidence of their political party and through it the majority of the House of Commons, which ensures they have the support of the monarch. Seen in this light, the Golden Rule is a highly pragmatic and flexible tool that allows for secure governments to be formed in a myriad of outcomes that helps underpin the UK's political stability.

So, there we have it. If an individual can meet the requirements of the Golden Rule, they will be appointed Prime Minister and remain in office until such time as they can no longer meet these requirements. It will be for the Prime Minister alone, in all but the most extreme and extra-constitutional circumstances, to decide when that situation has arisen, either personally or on behalf of the government.[16] When such a situation does arise, it has been suggested by the Political and Constitutional Reform Committee that a Prime Minister has a duty to remain in office until it is clear as to who should be appointed as their successor, but accepted practice does not reflect this.[17] Constitutionally, the Prime Minister has no obligation to stay in office once they feel they can no longer meet the requirements of their appointment under the Golden Rule, and they are free to resign at any time. They do not and cannot formally advise the monarch on whom their successor should be, as this is a matter for the sovereign alone. It is fair to state, however, that no responsible Prime Minister would place the monarch in a perilous political situation. As such, they should do all they can to ensure that there is a viable political successor whom they can recommend that the sovereign should send for.[18]

The gaining of political power in Britain is thus fairly simple. All an individual has to do to claim the premiership is to be able to satisfy the Golden Rule, and then they are in office for as long as they and they alone can meet the rule's requirements. The appointment is immediate and requires no formality, as the clerk of the Privy Council points out: 'The Prime Minister accepts office by attending The Queen in private audience. The appointment – and [appointment] as First Lord of the Treasury – takes effect from that moment. At audience the new Prime Minister kisses hands. There are no other formalities.'[19]

When a vacancy in the office occurs due to the resignation or death of a premier, the monarch ceases to have a principal adviser and so no formal 'Advice' on who should be appointed can be given. This is because the commission to form a government is granted to an individual in a personal capacity and it cannot be handed over to a designated successor.[20] Hence, if a premier resigns or dies in office, their resignation or death terminates the government, just as their appointment creates one. Ministers would remain in office as caretakers until new ministers are appointed, but they would lack the ability to bind the monarch's actions. It is only when a new individual is appointed Prime Minister that a government once again comes into being. As a result, it is within this space of time between the loss of one Prime Minister and the appointment of another that the monarch has almost total discretion on how to act and whom to appoint.[21]

This constitutional fact, however, clashes with the political need for the monarch to be impartial and depoliticised. To ensure that this neutrality is achieved, the Golden Rule regulates how the monarch exercises their discretion at this most critical of times. The two-part test ensures that any politician appointed can carry on the business of government in such a way as to not politically embarrass the monarch. In most cases, the person who can form a government that has the confidence of the House of Commons is clear, leading to no genuine exercise of personal discretion by the head of state.[22] So, whilst the monarch will formally exercise their reserve or prerogative power every time they appoint a Prime Minister, they will rarely exercise any actual discretion as the Golden

Rule will bind their actions. This creates, in all but crisis situations, a distinction between the monarch's formal appointment and the actual choice of a Prime Minister.[23]

Although this may well be the practice most of the time, there are occasions when a greater degree of freedom for the monarch may well be needed to solve a political crisis. In 1931, for instance, the Labour government, when faced by the economic crisis of the Great Depression, was unable to agree an economic plan to meet the emergency. Faced with a divided Cabinet and a pending budgetary crisis, Ramsay MacDonald contemplated resignation and notified the palace accordingly. At his audience on 23 August, MacDonald outlined the Cabinet's position and the weak standing of the government, given its minority status, to a troubled sovereign. Under these circumstances, the King should, MacDonald told him, prepare himself to accept the possibility of MacDonald's resignation if a US loan could not be secured in the next few hours. In anticipation of this event and to ensure a swift transfer of power, MacDonald recommended that the King consult with the other political leaders to ascertain their thoughts on the situation, so he would be prepared for the transfer of power if the need should arise.[24]

Recognising his duty in such a situation, George V accepted his Prime Minister's advice and subsequently held separate conversations with Sir Herbert Samuel, standing in for David Lloyd George who was confined to bed after an operation, and Stanley Baldwin. Both men confirmed that the Liberals and Conservatives felt that a national government was needed in this current economic crisis and they would be willing to serve under MacDonald in such an administration. Should MacDonald resign, however, Baldwin indicated that he was ready and able to form an administration that would seek Liberal support to ensure a majority in the Commons.[25]

At 9 p.m. the same evening, MacDonald was notified that the New York bankers who had been approached to supply the loan would only provide short-term credit to the government so long as certain conditions were accepted – conditions which would have required the Cabinet to make significant cuts to its planned expenditure. The Cabinet discussed these proposals and by eleven to nine agreed to accept the cuts, but as this majority was too small to ensure the success of the policy in the House of Commons or the unity of the government, MacDonald decided he had no choice but to resign.[26]

The King, however, refused to accept MacDonald's resignation when he presented it later that evening, much to MacDonald's surprise, and instead suggested that MacDonald should meet with Conservative and Liberal representatives the next day to see if a political solution to the crisis could be found. George V told his Prime Minister that 'he was the only man to lead the country through the crisis and hoped he would reconsider the situation'.[27] Faced with this royal display of favour, MacDonald hesitated and asked whether the King would confer with Baldwin, Samuel and himself to discuss the position the next morning, to which he received a positive response.[28] Armed with this assurance, MacDonald returned to Downing Street to inform his colleagues of the result of the meeting and to seek their approval for him to meet with the other leaders the next day, which they duly gave.[29]

Primed by their conversations with the King the day before and urged on by his call to action, the three leaders met in the Indian Room of Buckingham Palace at 10 a.m. on 24 August. Driven by the urgency of events, they swiftly made progress on the key principles of governance, drafting a memorandum calling for the formation of a national government in a little over an hour. With political clarity established and the foundations of a majority government laid, MacDonald once again offered his resignation to the King, who now accepted it. He then promptly presented MacDonald with a commission to form a new administration. MacDonald's resignation ended the existence of the old Labour administration and his acceptance of a new commission brought forth into being a new national government.[30]

It is clear from the records of this period that without the King's initiative, there would not have been a national government in 1931. On three separate occasions within a twenty-four-hour period MacDonald had tried to resign and each time he had been dissuaded from doing so by the intervention of the King. Although it is important to note that at no point during this period did the King lack a Prime Minister to advise him, the King did exercise his power of appointment to not only prevent MacDonald from creating a vacancy but to also gain Liberal and Conservative support for MacDonald heading a coalition government. Had MacDonald formally resigned, the King would have been left with no choice but to send for Baldwin to form a new administration. Yet by preventing a vacancy occurring, George V retained the power of initiative to compel the political parties to a destination he felt best served the national interest – the formation of a strong, cross-party government.

This power, combined with his accepted prerogatives to consult, advise and warn, had allowed the King to prevent a constitutional crisis in the midst of an economic emergency whilst ensuring the governance of the country continued along the accepted constitutional principles of the time.[31] Far from being seen as an unconstitutional intervention by the monarch, George V was praised by the vast bulk of the political class for his actions, which were held up as an example of how a constitutional monarch should behave. Had he failed, the King was certain that 'there would have been a national disaster in a few hours, as a general election was out of the question'.[32]

Similar views were held by all political parties except for the bulk of the Labour Party who, perhaps understandably, felt MacDonald had betrayed the party by his actions. Harold Laski recounts that:

> It is notable that, in the formation of the National Government, no attempt was made by the King to elicit the views of the great bulk of the Labour Party who transferred their allegiance from Mr MacDonald to Mr Arthur Henderson. It appears certain that the impetus to the peculiar form of new administration came wholly from the King, Mr MacDonald was as much the personal choice of George V as Lord Bute was the personal choice of George III. He is the sole modern Prime Minister who has been unencumbered by party support in his period of office ... We need not doubt that the King acted as he did wholly from a conception of patriotic obligation. But since it was known that a Baldwin Premiership was confidently expected at least as late as the night before the break-up of the Labour Government, it is not, I think, unreasonable to term Mr Ramsey MacDonald's emergence as Prime Minister of the National Government a Palace Revolution.[33]

As Laski makes clear, the King's failure to consult the wider Labour Party was the central issue with regards to his actions as far as many in the Labour Party were concerned, but broadly, he accepted that the King had a right to act in the way that he did. And yet this rebuke for his failure to consult the Labour Party fails to appreciate that the King could only have consulted Labour politicians if the Prime Minister had advised him to do so or if the Prime Minister had resigned. In this instance, neither event occurred. MacDonald had recommended that the King consult with Samuel and Baldwin, ensuring that these conversations were constitutionally proper, but no such licence was given for a conversation with the Labour Party, which MacDonald rightly saw as lying within his prerogative as leader of the party. So, although it may appear at first sight that the King directly intervened in the political process, his actions were eminently constitutional. He restricted his actions to consulting with other political leaders and providing informal advice to Mac-Donald on what actions he should take, whilst always accepting and following the formal direction of his Prime Minister.

What the formation of the national government clearly demonstrates is that in certain circumstances, often involving a national crisis of some sort, a genuine choice may potentially arise as to whom the monarch appoints as their Prime Minister. For, as John Saywell highlights:

> Situations do arise ... where the simple and well-known precedents and conventions do not apply: where there is no majority party, or where it is leaderless; where an alliance of groups has forced the retirement of the government but is itself without cohesion, direction or a recognised leader; where a Premier resigns or dies and leaves a disputed succession. Such cases are common wherever cabinet government exists, with the result that the discretionary power of the Crown is more than a fiction.[34]

You may recall this view was shared by Ronald Fraser, as he too felt the monarch's discretion was needed when there was doubt about the choice of a Prime Minister – when a Prime Minister dies in office, when they resign at once for personal reasons or when there is a complex political situation that defies conventional practices.[35] This is a reality that is further highlighted by the fact that there is an established convention in the UK and the principal Commonwealth realms that the monarch or their representative is not required to ask for or accept the informal advice of their outgoing Prime Minister on whom their successor should be and are able to seek informal advice from other, wider sources.[36] This is because once a Prime Minister has resigned, they cease to have any official position and are only able to offer personal and informal advice that can in no way be constitutionally binding.

In Canada, the principle has been expressed as:

If there is one firmly established point in British constitutional practice, it is that the retiring Prime Minister has no right even to offer advice as to his successor, let alone have it accepted. He can advise only if asked, and even then, the Crown need not follow the advice.[37]

In New Zealand, this similarly applies:

[A] defeated Prime Minister is not constitutionally competent to advise the Governor-General, and Prime Ministers are appointed in exercise of the Governor-General's personal judgement under the reserve powers. Their appointments are logically prior to the tendering of advice.[38]

It also applies in Australia:

The commissioning of a person to form a government is entirely the Governor's prerogative and it is not within the gift of any political leader to hand over or cede to another political leader the right to form a government, whatever the result of the election.[39]

Whilst considerable effort has been made in recent years to limit and remove the Queen's discretionary powers as a means of protecting her neutrality, we must remember that this discretion has an important constitutional function and that any attempt to limit it may also cause significant harm to the monarchy and constitution. As David Butler points out, there would be a considerable degree of danger to the monarch if they were obliged to act only on the advice of a 'lame-duck' Prime Minister: 'It would be widely seen as outrageous if, in an essentially adversarial situation, the umpire had to act on the advice of one of the protagonists.'[40] Any attempts to establish a convention that required the monarch to act on the advice of an outgoing Prime Minister would be a dangerous one indeed. The creation of such an expectation, whilst at the same time obeying the fundamental constitutional convention that the monarch must appoint the person most likely to command the confidence of the House of Commons, could potentially place the sovereign in an impossible position should the two conventions find themselves in conflict with one another.[41]

That said, I hold that it is solely within those types of situations outlined by Ronald Fraser that this discretion should be considered active, and when it does become live, only the Golden Rule can provide a safe guide as to who should be appointed when a vacancy arises.

There are three primary circumstances where this discretion may become live. These are:

1. when an election outcome is unclear or a majority collapses in Parliament;
2. when there is a vacancy as a result of a Prime Minister either dying or choosing to resign without waiting for the election of a new party leader;
3. where the leader chosen by the party membership may not enjoy the confidence of the parliamentary party.[42]

All three of these circumstances came close to being triggered in the final years of the Queen's reign. We will go on to examine them here.

ELECTION OUTCOME IS UNCLEAR OR A MAJORITY COLLAPSES

In 2019, the newly installed government of Boris Johnson lost its parliamentary majority after the whip was withdrawn from twenty-one Conservative MPs. This raised the very real prospect of a vote of no confidence being carried. As the Fixed-Term Parliaments Act was in force at the time, it was unclear what would happen if Johnson resigned.[43] Under these circumstances, would the Queen automatically send for the Leader of the Opposition to form a government even though they could demonstrate less support than Johnson? Would a coalition be needed and, if so, of what kind? These are questions which by their very nature raise the spectre of George V in 1931. If the parties could not have agreed a way forward, the Queen would have been compelled to act with a wide degree of discretion as she lacked a Prime Minister to advise her. However, no vote was compelled and so the issue failed to arise.

NO LEADER

A problem will arise if there is a sudden vacancy in office, as almost happened in March 2020 when Boris Johnson's life hung in the balance. We now know that Johnson came within hours of being the first Prime Minister to die in office since 1865 and there were intense discussions about what would happen if this event occurred. As the Conservative Party would need to conduct a leadership election to find a new leader, there was no ready successor in place, a fact that would have left the Queen with no political adviser. To solve this, a caretaker Prime Minister would need to be appointed until such a time as the party could conclude its internal election. In such a situation, the monarch would have played a role in deciding who that person should be.

PARTY MEMBERSHIP VERSUS PARLIAMENTARY PARTY

The adoption of internal party elections that include the wider membership has raised the possibility of a conflict developing between MPs and the national membership, an event that has occurred in the last few years in both main parties.

Firstly, Jeremy Corbyn emerged as the surprise winner of the Labour leadership election in 2015 with 59.5 per cent of first-preference votes in the first round of voting.[44] This was in spite of the fact that he had only won the backing of 15 per cent of the Parliamentary Labour Party, the bare minimum needed to get on the ballot. This shallowness in parliamentary support came to a head when on 27 June 2016, twenty-one shadow Cabinet members resigned.[45] This led to a motion of no confidence being tabled in Corbyn's leadership, which he went on to lose by 172 to forty votes on the next day. Had this event happened in the Conservative Party, Corbyn would have found himself deposed.[46] Instead, he contested the subsequent leadership election and won with a higher level of party support.

Secondly, when Liz Truss was elected leader of the Conservative

Party in September 2022, she secured 57 per cent of the party membership vote despite having achieved the support of only 31 per cent of the parliamentary party.[47] When her economic policy was challenged by the markets, she found she lacked the support in the Commons to remain Prime Minister and had to resign forty-eight days after taking office.

These events raise a dangerous possibility for the future – that of a party leader not enjoying the support of the majority of their parliamentary colleagues. A Prime Minister's claim to office rests on their ability to command the support of a majority in the House of Commons. If a significant split occurs between the party's membership and its MPs, a situation could arise where there are multiple candidates for office, the national leader and a possible parliamentary leader. Constitutional convention would require the monarch to favour the individual who can command the support of the Commons and act accordingly. Such as situation would, however, be politically controversial and bring the monarch within the bounds of party politics, something that would be inevitable if the party leadership could not resolve the crisis internally.[48]

All of this matters because the late Queen or her representatives exercised her right to appoint three British, two Australian and one Fijian Prime Ministers between 1955 and 1977.* It must be stressed that each of the appointments in Britain took place before the political parties had developed their own formal internal leadership election rules, followed accepted historical practice and involved the appointment of a successor Prime Minister. In fact, these appointments took place at a time when the Conservative Party accepted a role for the monarch in the selection of their leaders and supported

---

* These were Anthony Eden in 1955, Harold Macmillan in 1957, Sir Alec Douglas-Home in 1963, John McEwen in 1967, Malcolm Fraser in 1975 and Kamisese Mara in 1977.

her interventions.[49] Despite this, the Queen and her advisers had an overwhelming interest in being seen to act as impartially and uncontroversially as possible. This became increasingly harder to do as her reign progressed, and so the crown has tended to require the relevant political actors at any given time to present the monarch with a solution rather than exercise any independent action, an act that has only been possible due to the relative political stability of the post-war period. Given the increased instability of modern politics and the three recent examples we have just examined, we should be mindful to how the Queen approached each appointment, as they hold lessons for the future.

Before we progress into that discussion, however, we should take a few moments to understand the basis on which her decisions and views were made. This is because they were founded on the precedents that had been set by her father and grandfather. As such, they form the historical basis that will inform any future actions by the King.

Given the relative strength of the political parties in the House of Commons during the 1930s, it is fair to say that had Stanley Baldwin wished to remove Ramsay MacDonald from office after the formation of the national government, he could have done so at any time after the general election of 1931, an election which saw the Conservatives, as part of the national government alliance, win an astounding 470 seats, making them by far the largest party in the House.[50] This was a number that stood in stark contrast to the National Liberal and National Labour groupings within the coalition, which were a fraction of the size of the Conservatives with thirty-five and thirteen seats respectively. Baldwin was, however, driven by a sense of decency that prevented him from seeking to remove the Prime Minister, as he had agreed to serve at the King's request.[51]

This acceptance of duty before self-interest ensured that the coalition was a highly effective combination of talents. Baldwin and MacDonald formed a powerful partnership that drove forward government business. As time went by, the pressures that exist within all coalitions began to exert themselves and the balance between the two men began to degrade throughout 1934. The catalyst for this transformation of the political scene was the steady deterioration in MacDonald's health that could no longer be ignored by the spring of 1935.[52]

Despite attempts to deny it, it was increasingly clear to not only the Cabinet but also the wider country that the Prime Minister was no longer fit for office due to the decline of his mental faculties. This loss of support was reflected in Fleet Street's coverage of the government, which began to slowly turn against MacDonald. His personal standing in the country, which had once been the government's greatest asset, was now becoming a liability.[53] He also faced increasing difficulty in dealing with the right of the Conservative Party, which was becoming more vocally opposed to his policies.

Although MacDonald was not eager to resign the premiership, he recognised that, as he could not lead the government through another general election, a change would have to be made soon. Determined to ensure the coalition's survival once he had stepped down, MacDonald entered talks with the National Liberal leadership on 13 March to find out if they would accept Baldwin as leader of the government, a premise that leader John Simon said his colleagues would be willing to support so long as MacDonald continued to be a member of the government as well.[54] In this way, Simon sought to ensure that the Cabinet did not become wholly Conservative in its composition. Recognising this strength of feeling in the Liberals and hoping to still be active in government in some way, MacDonald consented to their terms. Armed with the support of the National Liberal group, he then discussed the transfer of power with Baldwin, whom he felt should prepare himself to assume office shortly. MacDonald felt that the forthcoming celebration of George V's Silver Jubilee provided a fitting occasion for the transfer of power to take place. And so, with Baldwin's agreement, he informed the King of his intention to resign.[55]

To ensure a smooth transfer between MacDonald and Baldwin, the King met with Baldwin prior to his appointment as Prime Minister on 20 May to discuss the shape of the proposed new Cabinet. He felt its composition to be of extreme importance, given that MacDonald's agreement to remain in the government and thus retain the support of the National Liberal party was dependent on the administration retaining a national government character to the ministry.[56] Baldwin's claim to the premiership in this instance rested on his ability to maintain the existence of the national government and to ensure a broad coalition of support in the Commons. The King therefore needed to be sure that he could form a government that met these conditions. Had he failed in this aim, Baldwin's claim to office would have rested primarily on his control of a majority in the House.

As it was, this situation did not arise, as MacDonald agreed to serve as Lord President, replacing Baldwin in the role, and Simon accepted the role of Home Secretary, ensuring all three leaders held a senior position in the Cabinet. Although the King's hesitation in accepting Baldwin's elevation may at first appear to suggest there was some royal concern over his suitability for the role, nothing could be further from the truth. George V was just as determined that Baldwin should succeed as he had been that MacDonald should not resign in 1931. His primary concern was not about

Baldwin's ability to be Prime Minister but rather the need for the coalition to continue. As such, little discussion was held over the future of the administration outside of the three men concerned.[57] Reassured on this point, the way was clear for MacDonald to chair his last Cabinet meeting on 5 June and then to formally offer his resignation to the King two days later, on the grounds that he had been advised by his doctors that he was no longer fit enough for the burdens of office. With little fanfare, Baldwin once again assumed the premiership and the transition was complete.[58]

To the outside world, Baldwin appeared to be the very epitome of health and vigour and so seemed to bring a new sense of energy to a government that had been missing it for some time now. However, this was nothing more than a mirage, as Baldwin well knew.[59] The new Prime Minister did not enter his third term of office with any illusions of greatness ahead but with a firm, rational understanding that his best days were behind him. Having worked so closely with MacDonald and seen his decline at first hand, Baldwin was only too aware of his own failing health. He felt he had little left to offer the nation and saw his third term as being a short one. He expressed his thoughts to MacDonald's wife, Edith, just six weeks after assuming office:

It is a curious thing coming to office here for the third time. If my health lasts, I hope to do a couple of years, but I don't want a longer time. I think by then I shall have given all that I have got to give, and I should like to retire while in possession of such faculties as I have. So I shall do my best for the time left.[60]

The fact that Baldwin assumed office in such a quiet way whilst recognising his physical unsuitability for the role highlights just how much he was the King's candidate. It had been widely assumed in Westminster that Baldwin and MacDonald would have resigned together, making way for younger men to assume the reins, but this did not turn out to be the case. Had the Cabinet or the Conservative backbenchers had any say in the matter, this is indeed what would have happened, but they were not consulted.[61] The Cabinet showed no ardent desire to revolt and so the King, who liked and was used to Baldwin, simply acted on the assumption that he was to succeed and appointed him without question or consultation.[62]

This was a reality that found expression in the new driving dynamic of the government, which transferred from a MacDonald/Baldwin axis to a Baldwin/Neville Chamberlain one, in which Chamberlain, the Chancellor of the Exchequer, began to take on more and more responsibility for overall governmental policy. As Baldwin's health began to deteriorate, Chamberlain's grip on the entire range of policy decisions began to tighten. As he informed his sister Hilda shortly after Baldwin's elevation, 'You will see I have become a sort of acting PM – only without the actual power of the PM.'[63] Throughout 1935 and 1936, Chamberlain not only led on economic policy but was also the lead member involved in the reform of the Unemployed Assistance Board, the development of a new meat policy, the reform of ministerial salaries and the creation of a White Paper on physical training.[64]

His duties were not confined to domestic concerns alone, as he also led on collective security at the League of Nations, the reform of the government's sanctions policy towards Italy following the invasion of Abyssinia, improving relations with Japan and the government's policy with regards to the Spanish Civil War.[65] It therefore came as no surprise to the denizens of Westminster that he was increasingly seen as heir apparent to both the leadership of the

Conservative Party and the premiership. Nowhere was this reality more conspicuous than during the party's conference in Margate in 1935, in which Chamberlain took Baldwin's place to such a degree that he was sending for 'people and endeavouring to conduct business as if I were in fact PM'.[66]

George V's death on 20 January 1936, just eight months after his Silver Jubilee, created two scenarios that were of immense importance to the future of the government. The first was that the coronation, due in May 1937, created a fortuitous opportunity for Baldwin to announce his retirement in much the same manner as MacDonald had done during the Silver Jubilee. The second was that the new King's private life raised the possibility of a constitutional crisis that could bring the government down. For much of that year, Baldwin's time and energy would be focused on dealing with what would come to be called the abdication crisis. The situation was only resolved when Edward VIII announced his abdication, thus freeing himself to marry Wallis Simpson, on 11 December 1936. Such was the magnitude of this crisis that all of Baldwin's energy was taken up with it, a situation that was only made possible because Chamberlain took up the task of managing the day-to-day running of the government. The successful conclusion of the crisis brought Baldwin a late flowering of achievement that would crown his political career, as all sides were united in their belief that he was the man who had saved the nation and the monarchy.[67]

With all the skill of a seasoned actor, Baldwin recognised that now was the best time for him to leave the stage and intimated that he would resign following the coronation in May. Ever the consummate politician, he did not go so far as to explicitly state his intention to his colleagues.[68] His hints were strong enough, however, for Chamberlain to begin discussions with the Chief Whip about how the transfer of power could best be achieved. They accepted that 27 May would be an ideal date for the transfer and Chamberlain began to turn his attention to the many issues that had to be dealt with, to ensure things ran smoothly when the time came.[69]

His colleagues could also sense the way the wind was blowing and so they began to seek Chamberlain out for his advice and to lobby for their personal advancement. MacDonald himself was one such supplicant, as he felt that with Baldwin's retirement, it was now time for him to leave the government as well. He met with Chamberlain on 10 March to discuss how this could be accommodated and to secure his son Malcom's future in the Cabinet. Chamberlain assured him that Malcolm would have a place in the new government whilst also offering MacDonald a peerage when he retired, which MacDonald declined.[70]

Baldwin's lack of openness about his intention to stand down probably had something to do with his concerns about Chamberlain as his potential successor. The Chancellor was by no means the unchallenged choice of the party to succeed to the premiership, as the most recent Budget had not been a success and his personality left many of his colleagues cold. Chamberlain was not a man who could work well with others. He sought to dominate policy discussions, which did not bode well for the future of the coalition. Yet despite these concerns, Baldwin did not feel he could come out and actively encourage a challenge to Chamberlain's position, as he had for so long supported the assumption that Chamberlain was his choice. Instead, he created an air of expectation, allowing for a challenger to emerge should the party feel a contest was needed.[71]

There is some evidence to suggest that Baldwin intended Anthony Eden to succeeded him at this time, but as Eden showed no wish to do so, he was left with little choice but to support Chamberlain.[72]

Although nothing was ever said between the two men, Baldwin's actions affected Chamberlain deeply and potentially coloured his future relationship with Eden. This was a mood which infected his correspondence with his sister Ida following the death of his brother Austen, when he told her:

> I am not a superstitious man and indeed I should not greatly care if I were never to be PM. But when I think of Father & Austen and reflect that in less than 3 months of time no individual stands between me and that office I wonder whether Fate has some dark secret in store to carry out her ironies to the end.[73]

Given the history of his family and the failed attempts of both his father and brother to achieve the prize, Chamberlain was right to be wary of a potential challenge at the last moment. However, none came. Baldwin saw out his final term of office, culminating in the grandeur of the last great imperial coronation, in which the world gathered to honour the new King-Emperor. A fitting end to his political career. With nothing left to achieve, he resigned on 28 May, fourteen years after he had become leader of the Conservative Party.[74]

As with Baldwin before him, there had been no discussion about Chamberlain assuming office. The King had merely accepted him as the obvious choice. George VI was acutely conscious that he had lacked the formal training to be king and was inexperienced in the affairs of state. As a result, he looked to Chamberlain to provide the support and reassurance he needed in the early days of his reign as he looked to heal the wounds of the abdication crisis.[75] Due to this, the King and Prime Minister would form an especially close relationship over the next few years, in which Chamberlain would come to be seen as part of the family.[76] Chamberlain was thus the choice of George VI just as much as Baldwin had been the choice of George V before him, and so he had no need to worry about any challenge to his authority. His position was secure and the party accepted the King's decision. At a special party meeting in Caxton Hall on 31 May, Chamberlain was formally nominated for the leadership of the party. This motion was seconded by Winston Churchill, who would once have been seen as an obvious challenger but for his role in opposing the government's India policy and the abdication. Recognising this fact and seeking to build a positive relationship with the new Prime Minister, Churchill told his colleagues that day, 'Mr Chamberlain stands forth alone as the one man to whom at this juncture this high and grave function should be confided.'[77]

At sixty-eight years of age, Chamberlain became the second-oldest man to hold the premiership for the first time since 1900, and he did so without any of the usual struggles that accompany such an achievement. In fact, he would have the distinction of never having to face an election during his entire premiership, a rare feat for a modern politician. To his credit, Chamberlain was aware of the hand of fate in his elevation, as he disclosed to his sister Hilda shortly afterwards:

You will be wondering what my own feelings are on actually taking up this post which ought to have come to the two senior members of the family and only failed to do so because the luck was against them in forcing them to choose between natural ambition and their principles. It has come to me without raising a finger to obtain it, because there is no one else and perhaps because I have not made enemies by looking after myself rather than the common cause. But there is another contributory factor which is perhaps more important. I should never have been PM if I hadn't had Annie to help me. It isn't only that she charms everyone into good humour and makes them think that a man can't be so bad who has a wife like that. She has undoubtedly made countless friends and supporters ... and she has kept many who might have left me if I had been alone but are devoted to her.[78]

As all things find their balance in the universe, only history can judge if such an effortless elevation was worth the price he would eventually pay, given his fall from office and his historical reputation.

The appointments of MacDonald, Baldwin and Chamberlain formed the historical precedents that would confront the Queen when she would similarly seek to exercise the prerogative of appointment. As such, they would point her in the direction of her duty as she sought to manage the first meaningful transfer of power in her reign and would guide her actions in the days to come. We cannot therefore fully understand her actions during this period unless we recognise the precedents that shaped the palace's thinking at the time.

4

THE KING'S KNIGHT APPARENT

The retirement of Winston Churchill in 1955 presented the new Queen with the first political test of her reign, which required the skilful use of her prerogative of appointment. The transfer of power is always a moment of supreme importance for the monarch, but none is of such emotional intensity as the resignation of their first Prime Minister. The support and guidance that an experienced Prime Minister gives to a new sovereign should never be underestimated or overlooked, and this was very much at the heart of Churchill's relationship with the Queen.

Born in the nineteenth century, Churchill had been first appointed Prime Minister by her father when she was fourteen and had been leader of the Conservative Party since the death of Neville Chamberlain in November 1940. His retirement from office marked a period of profound transition. As the Conservative Party, at this time, had no formal process by which a new leader could be chosen, the Queen's choice would have a profound effect on the nation and was anything but symbolic.

Before 1965, leaders of the Conservative Party were not elected as such but rather 'emerged' following private discussions amongst leading Conservative MPs, a system which has been described by academic Paul Webb as 'an opaque process of negotiation and "soundings" involving senior party figures'.[1] There was no agreed formula on how the will of the party would be sought and the last time the party had been formally involved in the selection of its leader had been in 1922, when Andrew Bonar Law had been elected to the post prior to his appointment as Prime Minister.[2] Such were the opaque instruments of party management that confronted the young Queen as the elder statesman born in the reign of her great-great-grandmother finally announced it was time for him to leave the stage.[3]

It is perhaps for this reason that in his final audience with the Queen, Churchill chose to take a very formal and constitutionally proper approach to his dealings with her over the succession. When asked if he could recommend a successor, Churchill remained silent and instead said he preferred to leave it to the Queen. A pause then ensued, to be broken when, according to Churchill, 'she said the case was not a difficult one and that she would summon Sir Anthony Eden'.[4] In so doing, the Queen indicated that Eden would be her choice for the premiership, for his appointment made eminent sense from her point of view. Eden was undoubtedly the next most senior member of the government and had under his belt a tremendous amount of political experience that could be of immense help to the Queen as she navigated her way through her new role. Added to this, Eden had been regarded by many in Westminster as the next Prime Minister since the 1940s, with Nigel Fisher going as far as to state that 'no rival candidate existed and so there was no discussion or controversy of any kind' about his appointment.[5] Yet despite this assumption, Eden's elevation to the premiership was not as straightforward as many political observers then or now have assumed.

Churchill himself had significant doubts about Eden's ability to lead the nation and these concerns were evident on his last day in office, for even at this late stage he could not bring himself to recommend Eden for the post.[6] Lord Swinton, Secretary of State for Commonwealth Relations, bluntly told Churchill that Eden would prove to be 'the worst Prime Minister since Lord North' and that it had been a great mistake to have chosen him as a successor ten years before.[7] And these concerns were not only held by those within the party – Sir Alan Lascelles, as the Queen's private secretary, had shared his anxiety with Sir Evelyn Shuckburgh, Eden's private secretary at the Foreign Office, in early 1953. Lascelles felt that if Churchill died, Eden would undoubtedly have been the preferred candidate, but he also recognised that the mood within the party was slowly changing. This led him to believe that by the end of the year the situation would be considerably altered, with 'at least 50 per cent opinion in the Party and in the City by that time in favour of [Rab] Butler'.[8] Additionally, for those in the know, Eden's health, which had always been poor but had worsened following a series of operations, seemed to indicate he lacked the stamina needed for the premiership.[9]

The issue before the Queen, however, was not just one of who would make the best Prime Minister but also of who ought to lead the Conservative Party. In this distinction, we can see the constitutional issue that Eden's appointment raised. The Conservative Party found itself in an odd political position, in that its MPs were able to select their leaders in opposition but lacked the ability to do so whilst in office. As such, it was often assumed that whoever the monarch sent for to succeed an outgoing Conservative leader and Prime Minister would be appointed as the next leader. This had been the case with Arthur Balfour, Stanley Baldwin, Neville Chamberlain and Winston Churchill in recent times.

As early as 1947, palace officials had recognised that this was an uncomfortable position for the monarch to find themselves in now that party political structures were far more developed than was the case in the nineteenth century. This realisation led to Sir Alan Lascelles positing that

> a clear advance indication by the members of the party in power as to the man they want to be their leader is, it seems to me, a help to wise ruling by the Sovereign rather than a derogation of the Sovereign's power. It has been obvious for many years that it is no use the Sovereign sending for somebody who cannot command Parliamentary support; therefore, it is better that the Sovereign should have clear proof of who can command it ... In fact I should say that the definite and public adoption by the party concerned of a new leader is more satisfactory, and a more dignified way of doing business.[10]

Although they reflect a high degree of political pragmatism, Lascelles's words should not be taken to indicate that he believed that the monarch now had no role in the selection of the Prime Minister. Rather, he simply felt that it was no longer acceptable for the monarch to be involved in the internal selection process for a party leader. He felt that the private internal issues of a political party should be ones for them and them alone, whilst the monarch should confine themselves to the constitutional realm.

During earlier transfers of leadership when the outgoing Prime

Minister had declined to indicate a possible successor, the monarch had taken a close interest in the choosing of a new leader, seeking a wide range of advice before making their choice. Yet in this instance the Queen acted as though Eden's elevation was a foregone conclusion.[11] If any form of consultation had taken place during the five days between Churchill's notification of his intention to resign and the actual event, it was extremely discreet and has left no historical record. Eden and his biographers are reticent on the matter, treating it as the inevitability that many at the time saw it as being, given his undoubted levels of support amongst a significant section of the party. But what were the foundations on which this assumption was based and were they as strong as Eden's supporters felt them to be?

The central pillar of Eden's claim was that Churchill had indicated both publicly and privately for some time that he considered Eden to be his natural successor should anything happen to him during and after the war. The first of these indications was made exceedingly early on, after the resignation of Chamberlain from the government due to the cancer that would end his life a month later. Churchill knew his position in the party was weak and that Eden was a rival.[12] By making this claim, he was hoping to ensure Eden did not challenge him for the leadership at this time, but in so doing he made a Faustian bargain that would tie his hands in the future.

This was the first but not the last such statement by Churchill on the matter over the next fifteen years. The next and by far the most constitutionally significant sign of Eden's status as 'crown prince' came in 1942, when Churchill had cause to say who should succeed him if he was killed en route to America in June to discuss the progress of the war with Roosevelt.[13] In a discussion with the King, Churchill informally advised him that should he be killed during his journey, the King should send for Eden to form a government rather than Attlee. Given the significance and vital importance of Churchill to the government and the war effort, George VI took the unusual, yet necessary, step of asking the Prime Minister to formally provide him with this advice in writing before he left the country – a request that sought to ensure there could be no confusion as to the King's actions in such a situation.[14]

The letter produced by Churchill is a constitutionally unique document, as it contains official and formal advice provided by a Prime Minister on whom the King should send for in the event of the Prime Minister's death. As such, it must be seen as binding and is, therefore, a potential infringement on the King's sole right to decide who should form a government. Conscious of the significance of the moment, Churchill informed the King:

> In case of my death on this journey I am about to take, I avail myself of Yr Majesty's gracious permission to advise that He shd entrust the formation of a new Government to Mr Anthony Eden, the Secretary of State for Foreign Affairs … who I am sure will be found capable of conducting Yr. Majesty's Affairs with the resolution, experience & capacity which these grievous times require.[15]

What are we to make of this letter? On the face of it, this note seems to disprove the rule that a monarch cannot be bound in their use of the prerogative of appointment. Our enquiry is complicated further still when we realise that this was not the only time that Churchill tried to nominate his successor during the war. In 1945, he wrote to the King the day before he left for the Yalta Conference to once again state that Eden was his chosen replacement.

This time, however, he went further and said that Sir John Anderson, the Chancellor of the Exchequer and an independent member of Parliament, should be called on to form a government if Eden should also be killed. On this occasion, Churchill's letter stated, 'It is the Prime Minister's duty to advise Your Majesty to send for Sir John Anderson in the event of the Prime Minister and the Foreign Secretary being killed.'[16]

No longer content with nominating a successor, Churchill was now creating a line of succession to the premiership, which would have bound the King's hands should Churchill have been killed whilst out of the country. So how can we reconcile Churchill's actions with the mechanisms around existing constitutional processes?

Firstly, we must examine the times in which these actions take place. With the country at war and given the centrality of Churchill's place in the government, it stood to reason that the King would have needed some confidence that in the event of Churchill's death, a new Prime Minister could be found. Secondly, due to the effect Churchill's death would have had on the morale of the country and the fighting effectiveness of British forces, the King would need to be able to appoint a successor at once to reassure the nation that there was still a government capable of waging war. Given these important considerations, it makes sense that Churchill would nominate Eden as his successor given his importance in the government and Conservative Party at that time.[17]

Sir John Anderson, on the other hand, is a more interesting choice given he was an independent member of the government. His qualifications rested primarily on the vital role he played in coordinating home defence and his role as Chancellor of the Exchequer, which nominally placed him in the second most senior ministerial post in government. His inclusion in the line of succession may still have surprised many at the time, but it had been agreed with Clement Attlee beforehand. As both Churchill and Attlee planned to be out of the country at the same time, Sir John was selected as an alternative. He was a neutral candidate that both Labour and the Conservatives could support, thus ensuring the continuance of the war coalition.[18]

On both occasions, the King had informally discussed with the Prime Minister the procedure to be followed in the event of his death and was aware of Churchill's views. These messages were not therefore spontaneously generated by Churchill but were provided in direct response to royal requests. George VI had exercised his right to seek binding ministerial advice and requested that the Prime Minister formally present him with the advice he had provided informally during their conversations, in order to protect the Crown should Eden ever be appointed.[19] In the event of Churchill's death, the King's prerogative to consult widely would have remained in force but would have been greatly limited by the realities of war. To ensure the widest possible political support for an Eden premiership, the King formally asked for advice from his Prime Minister. In so doing, the advice became binding, thus preserving the political neutrality of the crown. Seen in this light, these letters do not represent a unique exception to the rules around the prerogative of appointment, as Churchill did not seek to bind his sovereign's actions. Rather the King exercised his right to request formal advice from the Prime Minister.

Although these letters were only ever envisioned as operating within a specific circumstance and were never meant to be a long-term statement of intent on Churchill's part, they nevertheless came back to haunt him. Eden and the rest of the Conservative leadership knew of their existence and their views on the future leadership of the party were influenced accordingly. Churchill had, by his actions, created an expectation that so long as Eden remained in frontline politics, he would succeed to the leadership on Churchill's retirement.[20] This expectation would harden into an article of faith as the years progressed, considerably restricting Churchill's room for manoeuvre in the process.

Subsequently, when Churchill returned to office in 1951, he once again showed his support for Eden as his nominated successor by proposing he be appointed Deputy Prime Minister. Eden felt that R. A. (Rab) Butler's appointment to the post of Chancellor of the Exchequer provided him with the means to become a rival for the leadership of the party and so he pressured Churchill into giving him the title of Deputy Prime Minister to bolster his long-standing claim – an understandable request given the fact that Butler was already being spoken of as a future leader amongst certain sections of the party. It was a degree of political chatter that would only increase in intensity as the government aged, greatly vexing Eden in the process. As there was always the possibility that the party may look to skip a generation for the next leader, Eden was taking no chances.

Recognising that the title was constitutionally meaningless, Churchill indulged Eden's vanity and duly made the recommendation. The King did not agree, however, with Churchill's opinion of the title's significance, as he felt that its use in this instance would limit his royal prerogative of appointment. As a result, he refused to accept the nomination.[21] In coming to this decision the King was well aware of the belief that Churchill would not remain in office long and that the use of the title could well indicate a natural line of succession. He therefore emphasised to Churchill and the government as a whole that he and he alone had the power of appointment and he would not be bound by any internal party agreements that may exist.[22] In other words, the King did not accept that Eden had an unassailable right to be appointed Prime Minister when Churchill eventually stood down but instead reserved his right to consult widely as to whom he should appoint when the time came.

Both men knew that the title of Deputy Prime Minister had been created by Churchill in 1942 as a means of highlighting the central importance of Clement Attlee to the wartime government and to allow for the introduction of the politically contentious Stafford Cripps to the Cabinet.[23] Due to his support for the Popular Front, a group that sought to coordinate left-wing opposition to fascism by cooperating with the Communist Party, Attlee had expelled Cripps from the Labour Party in 1939 and was not keen to see him join the government. His position as Ambassador to the USSR during the German invasion and the subsequent agreement of the Soviet Union to join the Allied war effort had, however, seen his popularity rise to a point where it briefly rivalled Churchill's own in the latter part of 1941.[24] In recognition of this fact, Churchill felt he had no choice but to include him in the government as Leader of the House when he returned from the Soviet Union in early 1942. Yet at the same time, he was also acutely aware that he could not afford to alienate Attlee.[25] To balance out Cripps's appointment, Churchill proposed to the King that Attlee be granted the newly created title of Deputy Prime Minister and be appointed Secretary of State for the Dominions, where he would coordinate the British war effort with that of Australia, Canada, South Africa and New Zealand. The King, recognising the importance of the Labour Party to the coalition, agreed to the title.[26]

What was necessary in war and what could be tolerated in peace, however, were vastly different things, as Churchill found out when he tried to award the title to Eden. George VI informed his Prime Minister that the 'office … does not exist in the British constitutional hierarchy' and that to confer such a title on Eden at this time might create an impression of an attempt to determine the succession to office, which would interfere with the King's prerogative of appointment. Aware of the pressure on the Prime Minister from within the government and not wishing to undermine its cohesion, the King did, however, accept the principle that Eden would effectively deputise in the Prime Minister's absence. Churchill accepted this compromise.[27] The net result of this episode was that Eden's probable succession, which he had sought to guarantee by his appointment as Deputy Prime Minister, had been transformed into but one possible option by the King's defence of his prerogative.[28]

Eden thus found himself with all the burdens of being Churchill's unofficial deputy with none of the benefits, which was a less-than-ideal position from his perspective as it increased his obligations whilst doing little to secure his overall position. In reviewing the actions of the King at this time, we gain a greater understanding of his motives during the war. This episode highlights that Churchill's advice as to Eden's succession was an extremely specific device for an extremely specific purpose. In normal circumstances, the King refused to be bound by ministerial attempts to dictate succession to the premiership, as he was adamant that this was an issue for the monarch alone.

Despite this royal impediment to his status as recognised heir apparent, the bonds of political connection and dependence between Churchill and Eden would be further strengthened in 1952. When Eden married Clarissa Spencer-Churchill, Churchill's niece, he was brought within the very bosom of the Churchill family itself. In

Westminster, the message seemed clear to all concerned: Eden was the coming man.

Although Eden was indeed in receipt of many undoubted marks of distinction and favour from the Prime Minister, we must not forget that he was a significant minister in his own right whose claim to the leadership was supported by others within the party and he was not solely dependent on Churchill's favour alone. Eden had, after all, been a leading politician before the war, a position he had only strengthened with his resignation from the government over the issue of appeasement in 1938.[29] Brought back into office by Churchill in 1940, he had been close to the centre of power throughout the war, ensuring his survival in the Conservative electoral defeat of 1945. In opposition he – far more than Churchill – led the party in the Commons and alongside Butler and Macmillan helped develop the policies that would return the Conservatives to office in 1951. All of which meant that by 1955, he was, according to his biographer Robert Rhodes James, 'after Churchill, the most famous face in Britain'.[30] His public support was tremendous, with Gallup listing his approval rating as a commanding 73 per cent.[31]

Eden was undoubtedly both a glamorous and cultivated politician, but his charm and competence disguised the reality that lay beneath this facade – someone who was 'an extremely tense, lonely and shy man'.[32] This inner flaw would prove to be his great undoing, for Eden had few friends in the Commons and he lacked the gregarious nature that thrived in the tea rooms of the Palace of Westminster. As a result, he lacked a support network of his own and found himself more dependent on Churchill's support than he had hoped – a defect he clearly recognised. He well knew he lacked the dynamism needed to succeed as a master politician, for he was both timid and vain.[33] He had, therefore, largely succeeded in political life due to the patronage of others, first Baldwin and then Churchill, rather than through his own political heft, with the result that he was respected but not loved.[34]

This may have been enough for him to succeed in the past, but from 1953 onwards he suffered from an unceasing string of ailments, from appendicitis to migraines and gallstones. All of this led to a series of disastrous operations from which he never quite recovered and that sapped his vigour, his patience and his imagination to such a degree that many questioned whether he could physically manage the office. Whispers of discontent could be heard in the recesses of the Commons, but this sense of unsuitability had yet to reach the Cabinet, where the majority of his supporters could be found.[35] This fact was expressed by Harold Macmillan within the diary where he recorded the views of his Cabinet colleagues. In a passage on 17 January 1953, he said:

> I think he [Eden] notices that we all want him to succeed to the Throne, and that no one is intriguing to supplant him … There is no doubt at all that, if and when Churchill goes, Eden will succeed. Even Eden believes that. But when *will* Churchill go? At one moment, he seemed inclined to lay down the burden. At another, he clings to the job like a leech.[36]

Macmillan's recollection of his conversations with his colleagues provides a strong indication that Eden was indeed the preferred choice to lead the party after Churchill left office. But we should not just take this assertion at face value, as Macmillan was hardly the impartial observer of the leadership succession he presented himself as being. Macmillan, as much as Eden and Butler, had a very personal interest in who would take over from Churchill when the time came, as all three men had ambitions for the premiership themselves. Macmillan hoped that Eden would take over as soon as possible as this would enable him to have a chance at the leadership at some point in the future, given he was of a similar age to Eden. Butler, on the other hand, represented the next generation in the party and so desired for Churchill to stay on for as long as possible in the hopes that the torch would be passed to him and thus bypass Macmillan, who would then be considered to be too old.[37] Churchill was well aware of the ambitions of Eden and Butler and engineered events during his premiership so as to keep both men guessing, ensuring a rivalry came into existence between them. He further stoked the flames by giving his support to Eden in his request for the title of Deputy Prime Minister whilst correspondingly appointing Butler to the Treasury.[38]

The succession was not, therefore, as clear cut as it may have seemed at the time. There were both concerns as to Eden's suitability for the role and other people who could have had a claim to leadership of the party.[39] Moreover, George VI had deliberately ensured that the options of the monarch remained open when the time came for Churchill to retire.

Given Churchill's reservations and the ambitions of younger men, few would have been able to object if the Queen had reached out to other members of the government to ascertain their views as to the succession. After all, there was no other leadership election process to which the monarch could defer. These consultations may well have and probably would have confirmed that Eden was the best choice to succeed Churchill, but the fact they were not undertaken was a sign that Eden's appointment was the choice of the Queen alone, acting on her own authority free from advice.[40] Her actions at this moment in time would have far-reaching repercussions, for when exercising their discretion, the monarch must not only consult widely but be seen to consult widely to ensure their reputation for political independence remains intact.[41] As Ben Pimlott has highlighted in his biography of the Queen, 'The smoothness of the first prime ministerial changeover of the reign, and the absence of even a token assertion of royal independence helped establish the expectation that, at any future moment of transition, the Palace would not seek an active role.'[42]

He argues that the lack of royal engagement with the process at that time has led to an assumption in the political class that the monarch has no independent role to play in the appointment process, to the detriment of our politics.[43] Such an assumption fails to recognise that an active role by the monarch is not only acceptable but that it may be necessary in the right circumstances. The emergence of a belief in the passive role of the monarch during the transfer of power has unfortunately led to a weakening of the constitution. This is because the delegation of the decision on whom to appoint to an ever-widening group of party-political members runs the risk of the monarch finding themselves in difficult and contentious waters if disagreements occur within the party. Notwithstanding these concerns expressed at the time and ever since, the Queen appointed Eden on 6 April 1955.[44]

With that, Eden achieved his life's ambition and the Queen concluded the first transfer of power of her reign. Eden's elevation can only ever be seen as a royal appointment, as no other process was undertaken or soundings held to determine his suitability. He was not nominated by his predecessor nor by a vote of the Cabinet or parliamentary party. He was merely summoned by the Queen who offered him a commission to form a government, unadvised and by her authority alone. There is no evidence for why she made this decision without consulting widely – though, of course, there is nothing to prevent the monarch choosing anyone they like for the role, but the political reality is that their choice must be able to command the confidence of the Commons.

As was the accepted practice, Eden was then duly elected unopposed as leader of the Conservative Party at a special meeting of the party on 21 April 1955, fifteen days before the dissolution of Parliament and the start of the general election campaign. This meeting was attended by a wide representation of the party, including 320 Conservative MPs, 280 peers in receipt of the whip, 250 parliamentary candidates and 150 members of the Executive Committee of the National Union. Presided over by Lord Salisbury, the august event nominated Eden and the motion was carried unanimously, freeing the way for the national contest to come.[45]

In this way, Eden is unique amongst modern successor Prime Ministers. He called an election within a month of assuming office and his subsequent victory, with an increased majority of sixty, would provide him with an electoral mandate to govern. This would subdue any concerns around his appointment until the eruption of the Suez Crisis a year later. Eden therefore combined the benefits of succession with those of an electoral victory, which went a considerable way towards mitigating the flaws in his appointment. He was also helped by the fact that he had achieved the considerable political feat of being the first Prime Minister in the twentieth century to win an election that saw his party's majority rise in its second term of office.[46] The historical record, however, makes it clear by reference to Eden's actions and those of his successors that the monarch involving themselves personally with the selection of new Conservative Party leaders was clearly one that was losing favour in the hallowed halls and tea rooms of Westminster. As such, Eden embodies a turning point in British political life, for he was both the last of the pre-war style of Prime Minister and the first of the new.

5

THE KING'S DILEMMA

In 1957, the Queen found herself once again confronted with the need to appoint another Prime Minister, far sooner than she had anticipated. Confronted by both his collapsing health and his loss of support amongst Conservative MPs, Eden was forced to resign following the Suez Crisis. After receiving definitive advice from his doctor that his life was in danger if he remained in office, Eden reluctantly arranged to see the Queen at Sandringham to inform her of his decision on 8 January 1957.[1] His decision to resign as Prime Minister against the backdrop of the Suez Crisis, which had deeply divided the nation, the government and the Conservative Party, left the Queen in an extremely exposed position.

In such a fluid and explosive political environment, two things immediately confronted the Queen. The first was that as there was no clear successor to Eden at this time, she would be required to be more involved in the selection process than she had been on the last occasion in 1955, a situation which had the potential to drag the crown into a bitter political crisis. The second was the problem of the Queen's location. She had taken the view since her accession to the throne that all official business, such as the resignation and appointment of the Prime Minister, should only take place at Buckingham Palace and not at the other royal residences such as Sandringham.* As such, it was decided that they would have to return to London and meet again formally the next day. This was a decision which neatly solved the Queen's second issue but did little to assist with the first, which would prove to be far more complicated and would have long-lasting implications for the crown.

Upon first glance, it would have appeared to the Queen and others in Westminster that the choice for the succession lay between Butler and Macmillan. But as there was no officially recognised way of deciding who should be chosen in such a situation, save by royal intervention, the Queen faced the most difficult prime ministerial succession since 1923.[2] In the intervening years, the need for political guidance for the monarch over the succession had only increased in importance, but the political mechanisms used to achieve that guidance had failed to materialise.[3] The political environment of 1957 starkly highlighted this fact. Should the Queen be seen to be favouring one candidate over the other without any external guidance, a case could be made for her personal intervention in the political arena, which could only harm the monarchy in the long term. This was especially true because her decision at this particular moment could potentially be interpreted as indicating her views on the government's wider Suez policy, given Macmillan and Butler's opposing positions on the issue. The loss of her Prime Minister at this time, therefore, could potentially place the Queen on a collision course with her own government.[4]

Courtiers understood this danger acutely and so let it be known

---

* A position the Queen would be compelled to abandon for her final transfer of power in 2022 as she was too ill to leave Balmoral, with both Boris Johnson and Liz Truss meeting her in Scotland.

that the politicians would need to provide a solution that insulated the Queen from these dangers. As Sir Edward Ford recalled, 'We took the view that it was for the Conservative Party to select its leader and that the Queen should not do anything until she was sure what the Party had decided.'[5] This statement should be recognised for what it was – namely, a desire by the Queen and her advisers to remove the crown from the internal selection process of the Conservative Party. It should not, however, be seen as an attempt to limit the Queen's wider role in the appointment of the Prime Minister generally or her more active role in disputed successions specifically.

To aid the Queen in resolving the succession, Eden met with Sir Michael Adeane, the Queen's private secretary, later that day. At the meeting, Eden made the historic suggestion that the Cabinet should be canvassed for their opinions to allow a considered view to be provided to the palace ahead of his resignation. Eden thought that Lord Salisbury, as an elder statesman and peer, would be the best person to arrange this, as his authority would ensure he was acceptable to all interested parties, especially as he would not wish to be a candidate himself.[6] Through this suggestion, Eden was proposing a change to the process of the past, which had involved the monarch's private secretary conducting the canvass directly and informing the sovereign of the outcome free from political interference. Adeane, however, liked the suggestion as it placed the onus on politicians to find a solution, and so he approved its use. He felt it would form a mode of advice that could guide the Queen's actions whilst preserving her political neutrality.

At first glance, this may have seemed to all parties to have been a perfectly acceptable process for the Prime Minister to suggest. After all, it was his responsibility to ensure that the monarch was able to appoint a successor once he had notified her of his intention to resign. But as Victor Rothwell points out, the solution was not as clear cut as it may at first have appeared, for Eden had his own views about the role and place of the monarchy in British politics. Eden, Rothwell states, favoured a Japanese- or Scandinavian-style monarchy that was not involved in politics and sought to keep the Queen at a distance from governmental decisions during his premiership. This was an approach that had already caused tensions between Downing Street and the palace over the Suez Crisis.[7] However, Eden was supported by palace courtiers in his desire to keep the monarch out of politics, who also saw a benefit in distancing the monarch from internal party matters.[8]

Buckingham Palace and Downing Street therefore collaborated to remove the consultation process from the hands of the Queen's staff and placed it instead in the hands of a party grandee to distance the crown from the process, insulating the institution from the toxic political environment of the time. In hindsight, however, this decision held a fatal flaw. It may have removed the monarch's direct role in the identification of a successor, but it still left the crown open to charges of becoming involved in politics, as later events would highlight. In any leadership contest accusations of corruption tend to arise, with claims of cheating or else foul play being levelled at the victor by the loser. In placing the monarch's decision solely in the hands of grandees, Adeane had created a situation in which the crown could be accused of political favouritism, which would come to haunt the Queen's actions to this day.[9]

However, as this outcome was not foreseen at the time, Adeane sought to implement the procedure he had agreed with Eden when he went to see Salisbury the next day to discuss how the party should be canvassed. Salisbury expressed his opinion that the members of the government should be consulted on an individual basis following that day's Cabinet meeting and said that Winston Churchill's views should be asked for as well. He also felt that Lord Kilmuir, the Lord Chancellor, should aid him in canvassing opinion to ensure no one could claim he had gerrymandered the result. Adeane agreed with these suggestions and authorised Salisbury to continue along these lines at once so he could inform the palace of the Cabinet's decision in the afternoon.[10]

So instructed, Salisbury reached out to Kilmuir to inform him of what had been decided and to seek his opinion on whether the consultation process should be widened further to include MPs as well. Whilst Kilmuir accepted the offer to help Salisbury in the consultation process, he did raise objection to the suggestion that Conservative MPs should be included in the consultation, as he felt to do so would jeopardise the Queen's prerogative in any future leadership process. His fear was that such a meeting – tantamount to a Labour-style leadership election – would end the viability of the Queen's prerogative with a correspondingly negative impact on the constitution that he felt could not be justified.[11] It was decided that only members of the Cabinet would be formally asked to express an opinion, but to ensure there was some input from the wider party, the views of the Chief Whip, party chairman and the chairman of the 1922 Committee would be sought as well, a precaution adopted to ensure that any new leader could be confident they enjoyed a wide degree of support in the party rather than just the Cabinet. Both Salisbury and Kilmuir felt that such a process would not be too difficult to manage in the timeframe proposed as it was widely accepted that there were only two possible candidates for the job – Harold Macmillan and Rab Butler.[12]

Following the Cabinet meeting on 9 January, at which Eden

informed his colleagues of his intention to resign later that day and the process he had implemented for the choosing of his successor, Salisbury and Kilmuir conducted a canvass of Cabinet members one by one in Salisbury's room in the Privy Council Office. Upon entering the room, individuals were greeted with a simple question made famous by Salisbury's speech impediment: 'Well, which is it? Wab or Hawold?' Their answers were recorded on a single sheet of paper drawn up by Salisbury, with two columns representing the support each candidate received. It was officially recorded by Salisbury and confirmed by Kilmuir that everyone had voted for 'Hawold', except for Patrick Buchan-Hepburn who voted for 'Wab' and Selwyn Lloyd, who refused to vote.[13] Although a seemingly decisive result in Macmillan's favour, it was at this point that the inevitable accusations of electoral maleficence started to enter the story, for Salisbury was not the impartial umpire that Eden had presented him as being to Adeane.

Salisbury had never been a Butler supporter. The two men had been on opposing sides of the political argument since the appeasement debates of the 1930s and it was felt by many staunch Conservatives that an appeaser should never be allowed to lead the party.[14] To ensure this outcome did not come to pass, it was alleged that Salisbury decided not to summon Cabinet members in order of seniority but rather in accord with their known support for Macmillan. In so doing, he engineered a situation in which Cabinet members were confronted by a sheet of paper on Salisbury's desk that clearly showed the mounting number of votes for Macmillan, a process which ensured that any individuals who might have supported Butler chose not to do so in the hopes of being seen to back the winning candidate.[15] In this way, Butler's supporters claimed, their man was robbed of the premiership, which he would have won had Salisbury not rigged the vote in Macmillan's favour. This was an accusation that was, unsurprisingly, dismissed by Macmillan's supporters, who felt it was merely sour grapes expressed by the defeated team.[16]

Unaware of such concerns with the process at this stage, Salisbury followed up his meeting with the Cabinet by interviewing Edward Heath as Chief Whip, Oliver Poole, chairman of the party, and John Morrison, chairman of the 1922 Committee, who provided him with their understanding of the views of the backbenchers and wider party members. Heath said that the right of the party would not accept Butler's leadership under any circumstances, but the left, who favoured Butler, would serve under Harold if he emerged as the Cabinet's choice.[17] Poole felt that as Butler had been unfairly seen as a scapegoat for Suez, he was now unpopular with rank-and-file members in the country. He would not be a popular choice to lead the party at this time, despite his potential to be acceptable at another time in the future. They both, therefore, said that Macmillan would be the better choice. This view was confirmed by John Morrison, who had seen both men perform in front of backbenchers at recent 1922 Committee meetings and so was able to weigh their merits accordingly. Armed with these insights, Salisbury met with Lord Home, deputy Leader of the House of Lords, the next day, who confirmed that the peers also took the view that Macmillan was the best choice.[18] So although some detractors would claim in the days to come that the consultation process was limited in scope, Conservative politician Bob Boothby would challenge this assertion when he argued:

The party was consulted extensively, and at every stage ... There is no doubt the overwhelming majority of the party preferred

Macmillan to Butler. If there had been a vote it would have been exactly the same.[19]

Armed with the results of the first ever consultation exercise of Conservative Party opinion ahead of a prime ministerial appointment, Salisbury made his way to the palace on 10 January to inform Adeane that Macmillan was the man to send for.[20]

Courtiers felt the Queen would now be insulated from the political controversy that Eden's resignation might entail, as the Conservative Party had implemented a consultation process that fell somewhat short of an election but involved a greater degree of engagement by the party's leading members than had ever been the case before. Such a process ensured that Salisbury was able to meet with the Queen and offer her his opinion on the views of the Cabinet and the party to aid her in making an appointment. Having sought this advice in the first instance, the Queen was now bound by the recommendation in a way that her predecessors had not been during similar consultation processes as the result was presented as the considered opinion of the Cabinet, which could not be ignored. The palace could have accepted this limitation if the primary aim of the consultation had been met, namely that it had insulated the Queen from any political controversy over the appointment, but this was not to be the case as the validity of the consultation was questioned almost immediately.[21] The resulting controversy would come to haunt the Queen in the days to come, but more importantly, it would also profoundly affect the Conservative Party, which at this stage did not consider itself to be an internally democratic institution, causing it to reassess its views on how its leaders were chosen.

Party members had long felt that it was right to defer some

matters to rank and authority and so they had accepted that the choice of who should be the Prime Minister was for the Queen alone. The process of consultation, however, had begun to change this assumption and had allowed for a conversation around the internal democratisation of the party to begin.[22] This development was triggered by the distrust Butler's supporters had in the consultation process. Those opposed to Macmillan believed that the consultation had been designed in such a way as to engender an inbuilt level of support for Macmillan, to Butler's detriment, and so could not be said to have been a fair process. Yet this view is itself only sustainable if your mind lends itself to an acceptance of conspiracies at the heart of government, which is seldom the case.

Butler's supporters chose to ignore several key facts in their interpretation of the events leading up to Macmillan's succession on 10 January. The first was that unlike Butler, Macmillan was actively seeking the leadership from the moment Eden left for Jamaica to recuperate on 20 November. As soon as Eden's plane took to the skies, Macmillan began to court his fellow MPs with a focus and energy that conveyed his serious ambition to lead the party.[23] Macmillan at all times ensured he was seen as a passionate defender of the government and its policy, whilst Butler, during the same period, often came across to his fellow MPs as apologetic about the use of force and as someone who was hedging his bets. 'The whole time he was saying "on the one hand, on the other." It did him a lot of harm,' recalled Anthony Head, a Conservative MP at the time. Nowhere was this more apparent than during a meeting of the 1922 Committee on 22 November. Butler talked in generalities, but Macmillan expressed himself in an emotionally uplifting and optimistic manner.[24] So, whilst Macmillan was busy making friends, Butler was only antagonising his colleagues by his actions. All of this led to a feeling that he was, according to a newspaper report of the time, 'an intellectual without the grace to pretend that he is not ... a master of the dubious phrase and uncertain compliment'.[25] What the party wanted in these dark times was a man of action, who knew the outside world and could rebuild the transatlantic alliance that had been so disrupted by Suez. Macmillan, with his long friendship with Eisenhower, was the man who most embodied that need and so there was little support for Butler.[26]

Such advantages, however, can appear more defined in hindsight than they were perceived at the time. Far from believing the succession was being managed in his favour, Macmillan and his supporters felt Butler had all the innate advantages. When Eden announced his resignation to the Cabinet, Macmillan was alarmed by the swiftness of the transfer being proposed as it appeared that Eden would resign and his successor would be appointed that evening – a prospect that Macmillan felt could only benefit Butler as the presumed frontrunner. It was, therefore, with a considerable feeling of relief that Macmillan welcomed the news that the Queen would follow the precedent laid down by Churchill's resignation and wait till the next day to appoint a new Prime Minister – a decision, incidentally, made necessary by the extension of the consultation process beyond the Cabinet that Salisbury had outlined to Adeane earlier in the day. With more time now available for the consultation process to take place in, it appeared to Macmillan that he was still in the running and he was determined to make best use of the time available to him.[27] Macmillan's response stands in stark contrast to Butler's actions. As he and his team felt that the race had already been won, Butler busied himself that evening preparing for his planned broadcast to the nation the next day rather than courting support for his claim.[28]

Macmillan, meanwhile, ensured he was a visible presence around Westminster that night. He was followed by photographers and journalists as he walked through Whitehall, ending his sojourn at the flat of Lord Woolton, the former party chairman, where he stayed for the next three hours.[29] Given the fact that Eden's final Cabinet meeting had ended around 6 p.m. and it was clear to the Cabinet members questioned that Macmillan was in the lead, it strains our credulity to believe that this information had not begun to rapidly spread throughout Westminster and the wider party. This ensured a growing bandwagon for Macmillan, which Butler was unable to prevent given his early retirement to his home that evening. Butler's passivity during these crucial hours ensured that the process became simply one of form, as it had become an accepted fact throughout the evening that Macmillan would succeed the next day. Rather than being an act of conspiracy, Butler's failure had more to do with his lethargy and the sense of entitlement that prevented him being active in the selection process, whilst Macmillan remained focused until the very end.[30]

Due to the controversy generated by the contested choice of Macmillan, the consultation process failed to insulate the Queen as intended. The decision to allow Salisbury, rather than Adeane, to conduct the consultation allowed the impression to be formed that the process was manipulated to favour one candidate over the other by partisan members of the party and so distorted the true views of the membership. This accusation would undermine the Queen's perceived neutrality and weakened support for the involvement of the monarch in party matters.[31] The issue for many Conservatives at the time was not so much that the Queen should not have a role in choosing the leader of the party but that any consultation on the issue should be conducted by her or her officials alone and not by partisan members of the party. By removing a neutral referee in the form of the Queen's private secretary from the consultation process, the monarchy had made itself more vulnerable to political controversy and criticism.[32] Such was the emotional heat generated by this debate that to this day the legitimacy of Macmillan's appointment continues to divide academics and political pundits, who persist in arguing over the facets of a battle long since fought.

With the consultation for his successor underway, Eden was at last free to see the Queen and his resignation audience took place in the early evening of 9 January. Thankfully for us, Eden left behind his record of this meeting, which aids us in shedding some further light on the events of the day. Eden recounts:

> Her Majesty received me in Audience on the evening of the January 9 when I told her that the doctor's report which The Queen had seen left me in my judgement no choice but to be asked to be relieved of the duties of Her First Minister. I did this with the greatest possible regret. Her Majesty was good enough to signify that she shared this regret and understood how painful the decision must have been. She also expressed the wish that I would accept an Earldom, not necessarily now if I did not wish to, but perhaps a little later.
>
> Her Majesty spoke of the future and of the difficult choice that lay before her. I agreed that it was certainly difficult. The Queen made no formal request for my advice but enabled me to signify that my own debt to Mr Butler while I have been Prime Minister was very real and that I thought he had discharged his difficult task during three weeks while I was away in Jamaica very well. Before I left I thanked Her Majesty for the kindness and for the gracious words she used towards me.[33]

Several interesting details are revealed to us through this statement. The first is that despite his own views as to the effective operation of the monarchy, Eden accepted in the end that it was the Queen's sole choice as to whom she should invite to form a government. The second is that Eden does not record if he was asked directly and informally by the Queen whom he felt she should send for, as tends to be customary at such meetings. Instead, he covers himself rather cleverly by saying that the Queen made no formal request of him on the day but leaves out any mention of informal conversations that might have taken place between the two of them during this meeting or on the day before. Although Butler's name is only mentioned in regard to his contribution to the running of the government in the last few weeks, it could be seen that this comment is indeed a type of recommendation on Eden's part that demonstrates his support for Butler's candidacy. Why else would he raise this matter in a conversation about the succession?

This could be explained as a mechanism Eden deployed to cover himself. He was aware that the consultation process he had initiated was taking place at this time and so he was no longer able to notify the Queen of any opinion other than his own personal preference. Eden later stated when this point was raised with him that as he regarded the communications between the Queen and Prime Minister to be confidential, he would not reveal what might have been said that day, which further suggests that Eden may have sought to promote Butler's candidacy.[34] This has led some to argue that Eden did in fact recommend Butler as his successor, which may have seemed appropriate to him as Eden still believed at this time that only the Cabinet, which he felt favoured Butler, would be consulted on the succession, further fuelling the speculation surrounding the process. As only the Queen and Eden knew for sure what was actually said that day, it will forever remain a mystery. All we know for certain is that Eden explicitly said he made no formal recommendation as to his successor.[35] That said, in the end it does not really matter if Eden was for Butler or Macmillan because, as we have discussed, this would only have been his opinion and as such could not have bound the Queen once he had resigned.

Following Eden's departure, Adeane duly phoned Macmillan's office in 11 Downing Street the next morning to set up a meeting and arrived to find the Chancellor of the Exchequer reading *Pride and Prejudice* underneath a portrait of Gladstone whilst waiting to discover if he would be appointed Prime Minister.[36] A more English scene is hard to imagine. It has a whiff of Shakespeare's *Richard III* about it that no doubt occurred to Macmillan at the time. With such palpable tension in the building, it says much about the Macmillan marriage that when Dorothy Macmillan had lunch with him on the day of his appointment, she failed to notice his formal dress or even his air of nervous excitement. It was only when he had finished his meal and rose from the table that she commented, 'Oh, you've got your tailcoat on. Where are you off to?' To which the reply came, 'I have got to go to the Palace to see the Queen.' Such was her disengagement with the events of the previous few days that it was only at this point that Dorothy realised her husband was about to become Prime Minister and their life was to fundamentally change.[37] Faced with such a revelation, she chose to leave London at once and return to the family home of Birch Grove to do some gardening and protect her grandchildren from the press, who were bound to intrude into their lives. As Alexander Macmillan recalls, he was told by a nursemaid hiding in the bushes on his return from a day out, 'The Press has arrived. Your grandfather is

Prime Minister' – the first indication he had of the transformation in the family's fortunes.[38]

Meanwhile, back in London, Macmillan arrived at the palace at 2:30 p.m. and was ushered into the royal presence to be asked by the Queen to form a government, having achieved at long last his life's ambition. Although delighted to have been appointed Prime Minister, Macmillan was only too aware of the burdens that awaited him in Downing Street. The Suez Crisis was still raging and could bring down his administration at any moment.[39] From his privileged position within government and due to his involvement with the key decisions around Suez, Macmillan was aware that Eden had lied to the Commons about British collaboration with Israel and he could have no confidence at this time that the truth would not come out in the forthcoming debates. It was for this reason that he would inform the Queen of his concerns at his first audience. 'I could not disguise from her the gravity of the situation,' he recalled. 'Indeed, I remember warning her, half in joke, half in earnest, that I could not answer for the government lasting more than six weeks.'[40]

Once he left the palace, however, the joy of the occasion began to set in. He arrived back in Downing Street having reflected on the return journey about how unfortunate it was that his mother had not lived to see his success, given her instrumental role in his rise.[41] Rather than succumb to the depression that regularly stalked him, Macmillan chose to celebrate his achievement in a way unimaginable by today's standards. Far from returning to Downing Street to begin the steady work of government, he instead headed out to the Turf Club with Edward Heath to enjoy a dinner of oysters, game pie and champagne.[42] Heath records his astonishment at Macmillan's behaviour that night. He recalled Macmillan announcing to him, 'I think we had better go to the Grill Room at the Savoy,' following their discussions around Cabinet appointments. In reply to this, Heath spluttered:

> 'Don't you realise that you are now the Prime Minister and wherever you go in public tonight you will be besieged by the press, radio and television, as well as large crowds? … The exit is surrounded with press and Downing Street is packed with people.'
>
> He insisted we had to have some food and then suggested the Turf Club off Piccadilly as a quitter [sic], more private, alternative. I arranged for his car to be backed from the front of No. 10 to the door of No. 11. When we got to the hall, the door-keeper flung open the door. Macmillan took two paces across the pavement and disappeared into the car … I fell into the car, half dragging myself and half being pushed by the doorman, and scrambled into the seat beside the Prime Minister. He told his driver to get away and up Whitehall as quickly as he could, then to the Turf Club, where we arrived without anyone having caught up with us.[43]

Upon being seated, the new leader of the nation set about enjoying a well-deserved treat for having achieved the ultimate political summit. The venue was an ideal choice as there was but one other patron in the bar that night, who was reading the *Evening Standard* with the banner headline 'Macmillan Prime Minister'. Looking up from his paper, the man was confronted by the Prime Minister sitting next to him. He called out without missing a beat, 'Have you had any good shooting recently?' Macmillan replied 'No', eliciting the response, 'What a pity.' As Macmillan and Heath finished their drinks and started to move towards their table, the gentleman again looked up and languidly exclaimed, 'Oh, by the way, congratulations.' That was the sum total of the intrusion Macmillan would receive over his dinner that night.[44]

The meal, although designed to present an image of aristocratic elan to the wider political world, only further highlights the precarious state of the Macmillan premiership in these first few days, as Heath was more than just an amusing dinner guest. In fact, many would argue he was quite the opposite. Heath was the Chief Whip, and as such, he was going to be one of the most – if not the most – important members of the government in the short term, as management of the party's MPs would be crucial to ensuring its survival. So, although the food was celebratory, the conversation was in all likelihood very much business, with stabilising the government the main topic.

His repast finished, Macmillan began his preparations to leave. The club manager approached to inform him that he had made arrangements for Macmillan to exit by the back door for his convenience. This suggestion was met with the comment, 'How very kind, but I think it is perfectly all right for me to leave by the front door. I am not ashamed of being Prime Minister, you know.' A statement that neatly sums up the comedy of the evening entirely.[45] Upon exiting, he found his car was waiting for him by the door along with the assembled mass of the nation's press, which had tracked him down and now requested details of what the two men had been discussing. The response came: 'Oh, just the future.' With that, Macmillan returned to No. 10 and the forming of his government.[46] His image for aristocratic calmness was firmly established by the reports of the nation's press the next day.

Despite the consultation exercise that had been instigated by Eden and Adeane and carried out by Salisbury, Macmillan is the second man in our study to be appointed as the monarch's choice, as he was not the leader of the Conservative Party at the time. Just as with Eden before him, his elevation to the leadership of the party would occur after his appointment as Prime Minister – on 22 January at a meeting in Church House, Westminster, attended by 1,000 people drawn from the party's membership in the Lords, Commons, National Union and adopted candidates. Presided over again by Lord Salisbury, Macmillan was proposed for the vacant office and approved unanimously by those present.[47]

By examining these two appointments, we can see the degree to which Macmillan's appointment as Prime Minister was the result of his selection by the Queen to be her chief minister rather than by overt party choice, much as it had been with Eden before him. Had the Queen sent for Butler, he would have been elected leader instead. As *The Times* informed its readers, this was the first time since Baldwin's appointment in 1923 that the royal prerogative was no empty formality and the Queen was able to exercise some degree of discretion.[48] Yet Eden's innovation of holding a consultation exercise would mark the beginning of the end for the monarch's role in directly choosing a Conservative Party leader and has led to the modern view that they have no role in the selection of the Prime Minister, which is not always the case. Unfortunately, the failure at this time to actively use the prerogative of appointment has created the impression that it is a doubtful instrument, which could have significant repercussions in any future crisis in which it needs to be deployed.[49]

Despite his concerns as to the stability of the new government, Macmillan would go on to hold office for a far longer period than Eden, winning the 1959 election handsomely and confounding the views of many in the country that the party was bound to lose support following the Suez debacle. Macmillan's appointment did, however, engender enough concern within the political class at the time that it led to the instigation of a significant constitution-al innovation. It compelled the Labour Party to publicly state for the first time that the parliamentary party would expect no one to accept office from the Queen before they had duly been elected leader of the party.[50] In this, they were following in the footsteps of the precedent set by Bonar Law in 1922 when he had required the Conservative Party to formally elect him leader before he would accept a commission from the King – a precedent his own party went on happily to ignore in 1923, 1938, 1955 and 1957.[51]

In doing this, the Labour Party made it clear that the monarch was to have no role in the internal selection process of their leader, whilst at the same time ensuring that party members were aware they were not to accept a commission to form a government with-out the support of the wider party, as MacDonald had done in 1931. By this statement, the Labour Party compelled the palace to recognise the existence of an internal process for the selection of a party leader prior to any offer to form a government being made, an innovation which greatly hampered the constitutional freedom of movement the monarch had enjoyed to this point. This would have repercussions for the next transfer of power and would compel the Conservative Party to move towards a similar process of internal selection.

6

THE KING'S FRIEND

Macmillan's turn to resign came in October 1963, when an impending prostate operation finally convinced him it was time to leave office. Driven by the considerable amounts of pain he was experiencing, Macmillan reluctantly informed Butler and Lord Home that he would have to stand down, and the palace was duly informed. His resignation had been long suspected by the palace, given the fallout from the Profumo affair, and steps had been taken to insulate the Queen from any appearance of impropriety ahead of a new selection process. Sir Michael Adeane had, for instance, refused an invitation to a shooting party at which the Prime Minister would be present in August to avoid any speculation occurring in the press as to the possible topics the two men may have discussed at such a meeting.[1] The decision now made, however, Buckingham Palace looked to the Prime Minister to handle the announcement.

As luck would have it, his decision to resign corresponded with the party's national conference, taking place in Blackpool that year. In a letter read out by Lord Home, Macmillan told the party faithful and the nation at large:

It is now clear that … it will not be possible for me to carry the physical burden of leading the Party at the next General Election … In these circumstances I hope that it will be possible for the customary processes of consultation to be carried on within the Party about its future leadership.[2]

With these simple words, Macmillan turned what had been up to that point a fairly quiet and low-key conference into an exciting unofficial beauty contest, in which the heirs to the throne vied for the support of party members in a manner more reminiscent of an American political convention.[3] The reason for such a heightened sense of excitement was the sheer scale of the challenge that now faced the party, as there was no agreed successor waiting in the wings to assume the leadership. This fact more than any other illustrated the degree of dominance that Macmillan wielded over the organisation during his premiership, for unlike in 1953 and 1957, the choice of successors was not limited to one or two but had widened to at least five principal candidates. None of them were in any way strong enough to stand above the rest as an heir apparent in the way Eden, Macmillan and Butler had done. This time round, the contenders would be Butler, returning for his third tilt at seizing the crown; the mercurial Quintin Hogg, Lord Hailsham, Lord President of the Council and Leader of the House of Lords; the respected Reginald Maudling, Chancellor of the Exchequer; the talented Iain Macleod, Leader of the House of Commons; the steady Edward Heath, Lord Privy Seal; and the surprising Lord Home, Foreign Secretary. Alongside these principal five, there were also another three less likely contenders.[4]

Such a large list of candidates had come about due to the most surprising of events. The line-up of runners and riders had been significantly increased due to the recent changes to the law that had been spearheaded by Tony Benn – changes that allowed hereditary peers to renounce their titles and free themselves to seek election to the Commons. This revolutionary innovation created a brief moment in time in which Conservative peers such as Home and Hailsham could seek the party leadership, a fortuitous outcome that miraculously coincided with just such a vacancy occurring due to Macmillan's announcement of his retirement. This quirk of history is one of the most remarkable features of the transfer of power in 1963, as it created an opportunity for both men that was only possible at this precise moment in time. The Act allowing them to renounce their titles required them to do so within six months of it coming into force on 31 July 1963. And so it was that a measure that had been created to allow Benn to re-enter the Commons would now have the profound effect of allowing a peer to be appointed as Prime Minister for the first time since 1902.[5]

In recognition of this wide field of contenders, the palace chose to formalise the process used during the last succession and requested that the party inform the Queen of its choice of successor to prevent her being involved in a politically contentious act. The thought of the monarch having to choose between five candidates was not at all a pleasing one for her officials, who could see no upside to such a situation.[6] As such, the Queen's motivations during this period were entirely understandable, as she wished to avoid constitutional impropriety and felt the best way of achieving this was to place the onus on the Conservative Party to resolve the problem. Had Macmillan chosen to wash his hands of the situation as Bonar Law did in 1923, chaos would have ensued as the monarch would have been drawn into a bitter struggle for the leadership of the party.[7] She needed one name that could be agreed upon and the palace let

Macmillan know that it was his responsibility as Prime Minister to ensure she received it. Although formal advice was not usually sought on these occasions, Macmillan was informed that it would be this time, in much the same way as Churchill was so informed in 1942. He summarised the situation to his biographer:

> It was intimated to us quite clearly from the Palace that the Queen would ask for advice … it therefore became necessary for me to do what I would have preferred to avoid and become involved in the situation as it was after my colleagues had returned from the Blackpool conference.[8]

Accepting his duty to the Queen, Macmillan took control of the process in a way Churchill and Eden had failed to do, as he believed it was his task to preserve the prerogative of appointment, free from the interference of party machines. It is thus a supreme irony that in trying to preserve the prerogative, Macmillan would do the most to undermine its use, as we shall go on to see.

To achieve his goal, Macmillan wrote a 'minute of instruction' from his hospital bed regarding his proposed consultation procedure, for the Cabinet to formally discuss on 15 October, a document that has become known to history as the 'Tuesday Memorandum'.[9] In that document, he laid out a four-stage formal process to assess the views of the party, which seemed to build on past consultation exercises that the Cabinet duly approved with little debate. Under this process Lord Dilhorne, the Lord Chancellor, was delegated to sound out the Cabinet's views about whom they supported; Sir Martin Redmayne, the Chief Whip, was to sound out MPs and junior ministers; Lord St Aldwyn, the Chief Whip in the House of Lords, was to sound out the peers; and Lord Poole, joint party

chairman, assisted by Mrs Shepherd, chairman of the National
Union of Conservative Associations, and Lord Chalmer would
determine the views of the extra-parliamentary party. In this way,
all sections of the party would be formally consulted and have a
say in deciding the new leader – unlike in 1957, when only Cabinet
members were directly involved.

Here, we should just pause for a moment and examine what exactly was being proposed by Macmillan at this stage, as it will be
crucial for us to understand the process if we are to make sense of
the result, which was far from simple. First and foremost, we need
to accept that this was not a process of election but rather one of
consultation, which would be held in private and would result in
the Prime Minister recommending the name of the individual who
was considered to have the widest level of support in the party. As
the process would only recommend an individual, it was accepted
that the Queen could still appoint another candidate if she chose,
a choice the Conservative Party would accept.[10] This means that in
accepting the Tuesday Memorandum, the Cabinet was agreeing a
process to determine the views of a private institution – namely,
the Conservative Party – on whom they would find acceptable as
a leader, prior to that individual potentially being appointed Prime
Minister and by extension leader of the party – in that order. The
ease with which this process was accepted by both the palace and
Downing Street not only highlights the degree to which the monarch was involved in the choice of Conservative Party leaders but
also the degree to which public and private institutions had become
interwoven in the British political system by this time.

As advice would be sought by the Queen on this occasion and
relied on the exercise of her prerogative of appointment, it was accepted by Macmillan that the consultation had to be as thorough

as possible to ensure that there was no significant opposition to the recommended candidate, as had appeared in 1957. To achieve this outcome, Macmillan ensured that everyone consulted was asked three questions: 1) who their first preferred candidate was, 2) who their second choice was and 3) most importantly, was there anyone they absolutely opposed? The questions were designed to not only determine who the most popular contender for the leadership was but also – and most importantly, as events turned out – who the least unpopular candidate was.[11] Once this process was officially accepted, Adeane and Lord Swinton met to arrange how Macmillan would resign when the time came. They agreed that 'when Harold was ready to advise HM on his successor, the Queen would visit him in hospital and accept his resignation and receive his advice'.[12]

Lords Dilhorne, Redmayne, St Aldwyn and Poole met with Macmillan on the afternoon of 17 October to discuss the results of the consultation. Their conversation quickly determined that the contest had narrowed itself down to a fight between Home and Maudling, as Butler did not have enough support from the MPs or the grassroots members to be a challenger.[13] Upon closer examination of the responses, it was found that although Maudling had considerable support in the Cabinet and the country, there was a significant section of the party that was strongly opposed to his claim. Home, on the other hand, had support in all four areas and his candidacy was not strongly opposed by any section of party, making him the least unpopular candidate. The group, led by Macmillan, therefore decided that Home would be the preferred nominee. In making this decision, it was accepted that for Home to succeed in his claim, he would need to show he would have the backing of the Cabinet, where Maudling had the strongest level of support.[14]

As this news began to spread to the wider party, Macmillan

drafted the 'Thursday Memorandum', which contained his formal advice to the Queen on the succession. This memorandum is a rare document in modern British history. As with Churchill's correspondence with the King during the war, it is a rare example of the Prime Minister tendering formal advice to the monarch on whom to appoint as their successor ahead of their loss of office. However, this example is far more significant. Churchill's advice had dealt with a future theoretical situation, whereas in this case the situation was far from theoretical. The Queen, through her officials, had requested written advice on the succession ahead of the event, which was something altogether unprecedented.[15] This fact must be borne in mind while we consider the events as they unfolded.

The political reaction in Westminster to the news of Home's elevation was swift. Maudling's supporters met within hours and let it be known that they objected to the choice of Home and they would refuse to serve under him, with Hailsham, Macleod and Enoch Powell calling on both Macmillan and Home to express their opposition.[16] This refusal to serve in government was a threat that was taken very seriously by Macmillan and his advisers, as it would not only have weakened Home's claim to being able to form a government but would ultimately have undermined the Prime Minister's ability to recommend one name to the palace as requested. In an attempt to increase the pressure on Macmillan further, Powell held a meeting at his home in South Eaton Place with Macleod, Maudling, Fredrick Erroll (President of the Board of Trade) and Lord Aldington to discuss how they should proceed. After much discussion, it was decided that they would all support Butler's candidacy should he wish to push his case as, in their view, he was the man that could command the most support.

This decision was then promptly relayed to both Martin

Redmayne as Chief Whip and Butler as potential leader. The group hoped that, reinforced with their support, Butler would hold out and refuse to serve under Home, thus ending any hope that Home could be Prime Minister.[17] To ensure their views were known at the highest levels, Macleod, Powell and their supporters took the precaution of phoning the palace to lodge their objections to Home's appointment, in the hopes that such a clear sign of opposition would prevent the Queen making the appointment. The response they received from Adeane was surprising to politicians used to the active involvement of the monarch in their internal affairs: 'You're the party. Choose your undoubted leader and we will inform the Queen.'[18]

In recognition of the growing levels of opposition to Home's appointment but still wishing to push ahead with it, Macmillan raised, in an addendum to the 'Thursday Memorandum', the possibility of using the Aberdeen process of 1852, whereby Home would be asked to see if he could form a government prior to being formally appointed Prime Minister.[19] This suggestion appealed to Macmillan not only for its sense of history but also for its simplicity, as it created a mechanism whereby if Home failed to form a government, the Queen could send for someone else free from any binding advice. He felt this was the best way to proceed in the circumstances. If those opposed to him held their ground, then Home would not be able to form a government, but if they broke then the Golden Rule would be Home's ally. Macmillan's understanding of history and constitutional practice provided him with the means to defuse the political crisis and bluff out his opponents by placing the onus on Butler and his supporters to see if they had the courage of their convictions. Confident in the viability of his plan, this advice was formally presented both in a letter and verbally to the Queen by Macmillan in his hospital bed on 18 October.[20]

The Queen's visit to Macmillan was a unique event in modern constitutional history and highlights the importance of the occasion, as this would be the only resignation of a Prime Minister to date where the Queen visited her Prime Minister rather than the other way round. This anomaly would not, however, prevent the event proceeding smoothly. She arrived promptly at 11:15 a.m. and after some initial chit chat asked if Macmillan had any advice for her. Macmillan responded:

> 'Ma'am do you wish me to give you advice?' and she said 'Yes I do'
> ... so then I said 'Well, since you ask for it, ma'am, I have, with
> the help of Mr Bligh, prepared it all, and here it is.' And I just
> handed over my manuscript ... then I read it to her, I think.[21]

Recognising that his recommendation of Home was becoming unfortunately contentious, Macmillan advised the Queen in person not to appoint Home Prime Minister immediately but to instead ask him at their first meeting to see if he could form an administration, thus allowing Home the possibility of consulting his colleagues before agreeing. He explained his thinking to the Queen by highlighting how such a process would insulate her from political controversy whilst allowing Home time to establish his claim. Macmillan outlined:

> I advised the Queen, both verbally, and in the second part of the
> written memorandum, not to appoint Home as PM at his first
> audience, but to use the older formation and entrust him with

the task of forming an administration. He could then take his sounding and report to her.[22]

In this way, Macmillan highlighted the importance of the first part of the Golden Rule and demonstrated that it is not a foregone conclusion that an individual can meet the requirements for office. If an individual is in doubt, they can always seek time to determine whether they have the level of support needed to form a government before agreeing to assume office. This process could have been implemented in 2010 when David Cameron was seeking to build a coalition with the Liberal Democrats, but the failure of Brown to resign meant that it was not used at that time. Yet for all this, we cannot escape the fact that Macmillan's advice was a constitutional oddity. It was prepared before he resigned with the full knowledge of the fact that, at the request of the crown, it would be presented on his resignation.

Macmillan's actions highlight the consequences that flow from any attempt to remove the monarch from the consultative process and instead transfer that responsibility onto political actors, who are far from unbiased. In order to 'protect' the monarch from the political fallout of the succession, royal advisers were forced to breach the central convention of the constitution: the outgoing Prime Minister cannot bind the monarch as to their successor. The result was that the monarch was presented with advice that was anything but uncontroversial. To be fair to the Queen's advisers, however, the issue only arose because the Conservative Party had failed to develop an internal process for the selection of its leaders up to this point that did not require the active engagement of the monarch. It was for this reason that the palace was so insistent that the party alone determine who should succeed Macmillan.

The linking of the official and political in such a way caused a significant systems error, which has to some degree corrupted our understanding of the process to this day. Now that the monarch has been removed from internal political party processes entirely, we can confidently return to the constitutional principle that the monarch acts upon their own prerogative in the appointment of a Prime Minister, free from advice, allowing us to view this moment as a historically fascinating aberration.

Adeane, in his capacity as her private secretary, suggested to the Queen on their journey back to the palace that she did not have to accept Macmillan's advice. She was not bound by it, he explained, as Macmillan had resigned and as such she had no obligation to act upon his advice.[23] This late counsel from her secretary stands in sharp contrast to the events leading up to the appointment of Home. Adeane had deliberately requested that Macmillan provide this very advice in order to insulate the Queen from the internal politics of the Conservative Party, in the full knowledge that it would be binding. The proposal of Home was so extraordinary, however, that it was clear that royal officials recognised a threat to the Queen's position if she acted on it. So Adeane sought to backtrack the process and took steps to inform the Queen that she did not have to appoint Home, despite being in receipt of written advice from the Prime Minister and Cabinet.

Although the advice offered was no doubt contentious, had the Queen followed her secretary's advice at this stage, she would have found herself in a position whereby she had refused official advice when requested and offered – a far greater constitutional issue than the one she now faced. Instead, Macmillan had presented her with a way out of any political impasse by also advising her to simply offer Home the chance to see if he could form a government as a way of determining if he could indeed command the support of the party, as Macmillan believed he could. The Queen was wise enough to recognise the importance of that advice. If Home could build a government, then so much the better. If not, the Queen would have tried, and with Home ruled out she would be free to pursue another candidate through more traditional methods, as Macmillan's advice would no longer be binding. Seen in this light, the Queen's instincts on this occasion were more proper than those of her advisers, and in exercising her own judgement she protected the crown more effectively than might otherwise have been the case.[24]

Not only was the nomination of Home therefore constitutionally correct, but it also seems to have pleased the Queen personally. There is evidence to support the idea that she found Butler too remote a figure and too intellectually complex for her tastes, whereas Home was her cup of tea entirely. They were old friends, they were neighbours in Scotland, they shared passions for dogs and shooting and they were of a similar class who mixed in the same social circle.[25] In possession of such supportive advice from her former Prime Minister, the Queen was free to support a candidate who was very much to her taste, and as such, Home can be seen as the last person who can be said to have gained office through royal favour.[26] As Adeane and a section of the Conservative Party were urging her to consult more widely as to Macmillan's successor, the option lay open for her to ignore the advice, but her actions in sticking to the constitutional path at this moment appear to have been motivated by the happy confluence that both duty and personal desire merged in the recommendation of Lord Home.

Her decision made, Home was duly summoned to the palace at 12:30 p.m. As the royal announcement stated, 'The Queen has received the Earl of Home in audience and invited him to form an administration.' Home responded to her invitation by saying that he would try to do so and would return later to inform the Queen of the outcome of his discussions with his colleagues. As Home recalls of this meeting in his memoirs:

> On October 18 I was sent for by Her Majesty and invited to form a Government. I expressed my gratitude, but explained to the Queen that I must ask leave to go away to see if I could form an administration. I was by no means sure, after the drama of recent weeks, what the attitude of some of my colleagues would be. I had to enlist Butler, Maudling and Hailsham at the very least, to have the foundations on which to build a Cabinet and Government which could command support in the country and respect overseas.[27]

These simple words bely their importance upon first reading. In my studies to date, I have yet to find any other statement by a former Prime Minister that more clearly highlights the Golden Rule in action. Home did indeed need the support of his colleagues and the wider party if he was to be able to exert his claim on the premiership and there was no time to lose if he was to seize the initiative.

On arriving in Downing Street, Home swiftly held a series of meetings with colleagues that were so complex and numerous that Downing Street's staff struggled to keep track of them, with the result that the timetable of the day's events is confused. But one thing was clear to all concerned. As Martin Charteris, the Queen's assistant private secretary, said, 'We all understood that Alec could not form a government unless Rab agreed to serve and, if not, the

Queen would have had to call for Rab.'[28] Butler was, therefore, the first person that Home met. Armed with the support of Macleod, Maudling and Powell and with Home's political life in his hands, Butler had a loaded gun, as Powell put it, that he could have used to end Home's premiership at that meeting once and for all. If Butler had refused to recognise Home's claim and instead stood by his own, it is likely that Butler would have been sent for shortly afterwards to form a government himself. Yet rather than press his claim at this pivotal moment, Butler, for unknown reasons, equivocated, allowing Home to hold onto the political momentum that his visit to the palace had given him.[29]

Home's next meeting was with Maudling, who, true to his word to Butler, held out from accepting office and so weakened Home's position. Yet as the day progressed, things began to ease for Home. Hailsham became the first of the objectors to accept office and, in so doing, shattered the unity of Home's opponents.[30] As word leaked out that Hailsham had joined the government, other members of the Cabinet decided to jump ship and began to accept offers of office. The lure of power proved too great and the ruthlessness and conviction of Butler and Maudling proved too little to hold out for long. The next day, both accepted office as Foreign Secretary and Chancellor respectively.[31] Home had done it! He returned to the palace to inform the Queen and be appointed Prime Minister.

With his appointment, Home became the first peer to hold the office since 1902. He would continue to hold this record for four more days before he renounced his peerage and sought election to the House of Commons for Kinross & West Perthshire on 8 November.[32] It was only after this that Sir Alec Douglas-Home, as he was now known, was finally elected leader of the Conservative Party at a meeting on 11 November, thus formally assuming control

of the party machine.* Every Conservative MP was summoned to
the meeting at Church House, Westminster, to ensure that they had
each played some part in electing Macmillan's successor. Although
a number of his supporters did not attend the meeting, which they
saw as a fiction, Butler for the third time nominated his rival for the
leadership, which was approved by the members present.

As events over the next few days unfolded, it became clear that
this installation was only the beginning of Home's historic premiership. It was swiftly followed by another extraordinary moment on
12 November, when the country and the House of Commons witnessed the unique event of a Prime Minister being introduced to
the House as a new member. As such, there was not a vacant seat
to be had in the Chamber. Because two by-elections had been held
recently, the Speaker, as is tradition, summoned the new members
in order of election. On this day, the first to be called was William
Howie. The man who had won Luton for Labour was greeted by
loud cheers from the opposition benches. Yet this greeting would
pale in comparison to the one Home received. As his name was
called and he began his march up the green carpet towards the
Speaker's chair, the entire government side of the House rose to
its feet, cheering, waving their order papers and, to the surprise of
some present, even singing in acclamation of his return to a chamber he had left in 1951 when he became the 14th Earl of Home.

Such was the rapturous acclaim that greeted Home's return to
the Commons after a twelve-year absence. It left its mark on all
those who were present that day but most especially on Home
himself. But joyous as such a reception might have been, it did not

---

* My thanks to Anabel Farrell, the Conservative Party archivist at the Bodleian Library, for
confirming the dates on which Eden, Macmillan and Home were elected leader of the
Conservative Party.

mark the end to Home's duties that day. Before him lay the burden of making the first major government speech in the debate on the Loyal Address, an event that would, amazingly, be the first speech he had ever made from the front bench in the Commons.[33] At no other point in history has such a confluence of events taken place, and the chances of such events occurring again are so remote as to be unimaginable today without some type of reform to our political system. No matter what else can be said about his time in office, one thing is certain – Sir Alec Douglas-Home's premiership was a historic event that tells us much about how our constitution operates.

Through the cases examined here, we can see that the Queen, through her own authority, appointed three men who were not the leaders of their party, the choice of a coalition or the victor in an election to the office of Prime Minister. In fact, all three men were appointed leader of the Conservative Party expressly because they had been appointed Prime Minister, with the party leadership being awarded only once office had been reached. These circumstances were, however, unique to the times in which they took place. The lack of any form of internal election process for leaders of the Conservative Party allowed for the involvement of the monarch in the selection process, which was not seen as ideal by either the palace or the party in the end. An internal process was, therefore, introduced as one of Home's last acts as Conservative leader and adopted in 1965, ending this particular and peculiar form of selection for Prime Ministers. Home understood that the old ways of selecting a leader of the party were no longer fit for the times in which he lived, and so it fell to the last hereditary peer to be appointed Prime Minister and leader of the Conservative Party to finally internally democratise the party, severing once and for all the role of the monarch in its internal affairs.[34]

PART III

THE PREROGATIVE
OF DISMISSAL

7

THE KING'S COMMISSION

In the summer of 1831, all of London society was awash with the rumours of the troubles and splits that beset the government and speculation was running rife as to how long the Prime Minister, Lord Grey, and his colleagues would remain in office. Discontent between William IV and his ministers had been growing ever since he assumed the throne from his brother, but the foundations of this current crisis had been laid by the government's attempts to push through a series of reforms – the Great Reform Act 1832, the Slavery Abolition Act 1833 and Catholic emancipation – that were causing significant opposition within Parliament and the country. Although the King agreed that reform was needed, he felt the government was moving too far and too fast for public opinion and as such, a little prudence may have been called for.

Faced with such obvious royal reticence and significant public opposition, the government had found it hard going in the Commons. The opposition was successfully resisting the introduction of the proposed reforms, a situation which had compelled the Prime Minister to request a dissolution of Parliament in the hopes that a fresh mandate would solve his problems. The gamble had paid off and the Whigs now luxuriated in a large majority in the Commons, which ensured the passage of their legislation. The election, however, had not improved the government's position within the House of Lords, where the Tories continued their opposition by blocking the proposed reforms. Parliament thus found itself gridlocked between the forces of reform and continuity. Hoping to end this stalemate, the Prime Minister requested that the King consent to the appointment of enough new peers to guarantee passage of the legislation, thus overcoming the last remaining opposition to the government's agenda.

This fresh appeal for royal support was to prove to be a bridge too far for the King, who, despite his sympathy for the proposed reforms, was incensed by the actions of his ministers, whom he felt were deliberately causing considerable civil unrest by insisting on pushing forward with their agenda despite the obvious parliamentary resistance and public unease. Such was the state of the kingdom, he was deeply concerned that there was a very real possibility that social disturbance could erupt, which had the potential to lead to civil war within the realm. He felt it was his duty to do all in his power to ensure that this did not happen and therefore refused the request to create the new peers in the hopes this outcome would force the government to seek the path of compromise rather than conflict. Recognising that he no longer had the support of the King, the Prime Minister resigned in protest and the government duly collapsed.

The power vacuum thus created forced the monarch to approach the Leader of the Opposition, the Duke of Wellington, to see if he would be willing to form a government, but much to his dismay, he discovered that the Tories were unwilling to do so. This left him with no alternative but to reappoint Lord Grey as Prime Minister, who only agreed to accept the appointment on the condition that the King would create the peers needed to pass the proposed legislation. Faced with no other choice, the King reluctantly agreed and the government won the day, ensuring the reforms were passed. But this was an achievement that had only been attained at the cost of the irretrievable breakdown of the relationship between the monarch and Prime Minister.[1]

When Grey chose to resign for the final time in 1834 due to parliamentary disagreements over the government's Irish policy, the King saw his opportunity to once again reach out to the Tories to form an administration, in the hopes that they would be more amenable to work with. Due to their inability to form a majority in the Commons, the Tories once again had to refuse the King's commission, forcing William to appoint the Home Secretary, Lord Melbourne, as Prime Minister instead. Accepting the political reality he faced, the King was nevertheless still concerned by what he saw as the political extremism of Whig reformers such as John Russell and Henry Brougham. He was, therefore, keen to find an excuse to dismiss his Whig ministers at the earliest opportunity. Sadly for Melbourne, his first ministry was to be plagued by personality conflicts, rows over Ireland and tensions between radicals and the more conservative elements of his party over the ongoing issues of social and constitutional reform.

The delicate balance that Melbourne had established to manage these conflicts was finally shattered by the death of the Earl Spencer, an event which forced his son, Lord Althorp, who was serving as Leader of the Commons, to assume his father's title and place within the House of Lords, necessitating a restructuring of the government. Sensing an opportunity in the unfolding chaos, William argued that due to Althorp's elevation, the Cabinet was no longer viable and should be replaced. Melbourne acknowledged that this may indeed have been the case, as he felt the loss of Althorp had significantly weakened his administration. He too was deeply irritated by his own party's squabbling and was clearly looking for a way to leave office with dignity, a fact he chose to hint to the King at the time. Accepting his Prime Minister's desire to leave office as a gift from the heavens, William promptly dismissed the government on 14 November 1834.[2] Writing to his predecessor, Lord Grey, in the aftermath, Melbourne laid out what he understood to be the King's reasons for dismissing his ministry. The King's great mistrust for the majority of Cabinet members, the conduct of the Lord Chancellor Henry Brougham in engaging in a public row with the Earl of Durham over details of the Reform Bill and apprehension at measures to reform the Church were all cited as reasons by Melbourne for William IV's bold decision.[3]

Once again in need of a new government, the King swiftly looked to replace Melbourne with the Tory moderate Sir Robert Peel, who had previously shown a dislike for the Whig reformers. Unfortunately for him, Peel had left the country on a long holiday the month before. He was swiftly summoned back and Wellington agreed to act as an interim caretaker until he returned, being appointed First Lord of the Treasury on 15 November. The duke's second administration was to be short-lived, however, as Peel arrived in Britain on 9 December, having made a mad dash across Europe to return home.[4] Yet despite his considerable efforts to assume office, the Whigs continued to outnumber the Tories in the House of Commons, a fact which ensured Peel's grip on the reins of power was precarious in the extreme as he struggled to hold his government together in the face of a hostile Commons. Only an election could break the deadlock and one was duly called in January 1835. Although Peel greatly increased the number of Tory MPs returned to the new Commons, his achievement was not enough to secure the desperately needed majority. Recognising the political reality of his situation, Peel resigned, having served a mere 120 days in office. As a result, Melbourne assumed the premiership once more.[5]

William IV's attempt to dismiss the Melbourne ministry and replace it with a more conducive one under Robert Peel marks the last time in British history that a monarch has attempted to dissolve an administration that enjoyed the confidence of the Commons and replace it with one they personally found more to their liking – although, given the fact that Melbourne was highly sympathetic to the King's actions, it can be argued that William did not exercise his power of dismissal on an unwilling Prime Minister. That being the case, the last truly unequivocal instance of a government being dismissed from office by the King rather than the Commons or the people of the United Kingdom was in 1783 when George III dismissed the Fox–North coalition.[6] Given the considerable length of time between this last use of the royal power and today, it has understandably been suggested by some constitutional scholars that it must now be unconstitutional for the sovereign to dismiss the Prime Minister, and by extension their administration, in all but the most exceptional circumstances.[7] An example of this line of reasoning can be found in the work of Basil Markesinis, who directly challenges the assertion that the prerogative of appointment, and by extension the prerogative of dismissal, still rests in the monarch's hands, arguing that the power of dismissal is, to all practical purposes, dead.[8]

This is a view supported by the arguments of Rodney Brazier, who affirms that although the personal prerogatives of the monarch exist in law, they have been superseded by modern political realities. Brazier feels that because our parliamentary system has ensured through legislation that governments are forced to seek the support of the electorate at regular intervals, the monarch's role in the dismissal of a government is now superfluous: 'The use of the sovereign's reserve powers has ceased to be a weapon of first resort against politicians who might be tempted to depart from the constitutional straight and narrow.'[9] This view is further supported by the convention on ministerial advice, which reassures politicians that the king would not seek to act on his own personal discretion.

This is not, however, a universal view. There are a number of constitutional historians who believe that the power to dismiss remains just as valid today as it did in 1834, an assertion that is based on the logical assumption that if the monarch is the only person empowered to appoint a Prime Minister, then they must, by extension, be the only person capable of dismissing one.

Their arguments have, however, tended to take place over other jurisdictions where the powers of the crown have needed to be more clearly defined when a specific constitutional issue has arisen. We can clearly see this in the judgment of Lord Radcliffe in the Privy Council case of *Adegbenro v. Akintola* in 1963, a case which required him to resort to analogies on how the Queen's prerogative of dismissal in the UK applied to the ability of the Governor of Western Nigeria to dismiss his premier. Radcliffe stated:

> British constitutional history does not offer any but a general negative guide as to the circumstances in which a Sovereign can dismiss a Prime Minister. Since the principles which are accepted today began to take shape with the passing of the Reform Bill of 1832, no British Sovereign has in fact dismissed or removed

a Prime Minister, even allowing for the ambiguous exchanges which took place between William IV and Lord Melbourne in 1834. Discussion of constitutional doctrine bearing upon a Prime Minister's loss of support in the House of Commons concentrates therefore upon a Prime Minister's duty to ask for liberty to resign or for a dissolution, rather than upon the Sovereign's right of removal, an exercise of which is not treated as being within the scope of practical politics.[10]

The dismissal of a Prime Minister is thus the most controversial exercise of the royal prerogative and, as a result, this will be the most controversial chapter of this study. The dismissal of a government is, by its nature, a positive exercise of power that actively removes a Prime Minister from office by the direct action of a head of state that is presumed to be politically neutral in their role and therefore raises questions as to the true nature of the monarchy in the UK. The use of such a power would by definition bring the monarch into the realm of politics, which could potentially damage the trust and confidence that is placed in the institution by the political class.

To avoid this situation occurring, a constitutional convention has developed that requires a Prime Minister who has lost the confidence of the lower House to either resign or else seek a dissolution to allow an election to be held.[11] Should they go on to lose the resulting election, a secondary convention applies that requires them to offer their resignation so as not to place the monarch in the position of having to dismiss them from office. This position is officially laid out in the *Cabinet Manual*, which states:

Historically, the Sovereign has made use of reserve powers to dismiss a Prime Minister or to make a personal choice of successor, although this was last used in 1834 and was regarded as having undermined the Sovereign. William IV dismissed Lord Melbourne's government that had majority support in the House of Commons.

In modern times the convention has been that the Sovereign should not be drawn into party politics, and if there is doubt it is the responsibility of those involved in the political process, and in particular the parties represented in Parliament, to seek to determine and communicate clearly to the Sovereign who is best placed to be able to command the confidence of the House of Commons. As the Crown's principal adviser this responsibility falls especially on the incumbent Prime Minister, who at the time of his or her resignation may also be asked by the Sovereign for a recommendation on who can best command the confidence of the House of Commons in his or her place.[12]

The view enshrined in the manual was later confirmed to me by Jeremy Heywood when he was principal private secretary to Gordon Brown. In our conversation, he said that he felt it was the role of the civil service as the principal advisers to the monarch, the Prime Minister and the Cabinet to ensure a situation never develops whereby the Queen is placed in a position where she is required to actively use her discretionary powers.[13]

In short, what Jeremy was outlining here is what has become colloquially known as the 'good chap' theory of government – that is, the good chaps know what a good chap is expected to do and will never push things too far.[14] Or to put it another way, as Sir Kenneth Stowe, another former principal private secretary to the Prime Minister, once said, 'The "good chap theory" is shorthand for saying that there is a consensus among everyone with responsibility for the governance of the United Kingdom – that the government shall be carried on in a certain spirit and an orderly way.'[15]

If this may at first sight appear to be a strange way in which to run a government, you should cast your mind back to those special rights and responsibilities that we discussed earlier, which the sovereign can expect to enjoy from their ministers. You may recall that these were set out as:

1. The sovereign must act on the advice of ministers in the exercise of most but not all executive functions.
2. Ministers must accept all the political consequences for their decisions.
3. The monarch must be politically impartial.
4. Ministers must not act in a way that draws the monarch directly into the political process.
5. The sovereign must accept the advice and support of their ministers, thus ensuring the sovereign cannot have an independent policy.

Now, if we examine this list in more detail, we can see that the 'good chap' theory lies at the heart of it, for the system depends on individual actors always conducting themselves with the best interests of the state in mind. This is a situation that was well known to William Gladstone, who in 1879 outlined that the British constitution 'presumes more boldly than any other on the good sense and the good faith of those who work it'.[16]

Not much has changed since Gladstone's time, at least as far as high constitutional principles are concerned. Points two, three and four of this list underpin the 'good chap' theory, as ministers must accept the consequences of their actions, which in this case means either losing an election or the confidence of the House of Commons. Should such an event occur, the Prime Minister of the time must uphold the convention by offering their resignation to the monarch, which frees them to appoint new ministers who can command the confidence of the Commons. This relies on the monarch and their ministers to ensure the monarch always remains politically impartial and ministers must not draw the monarch directly into the political process by their actions or lack thereof. Should a Prime Minister attempt to cling to office without the support of the people or the House of Commons, they would compel the king to act in a way that would be perceived as political by dismissing them and so would have failed in their responsibility to the monarch. In short, they would not have been a good chap!

It is for this very reason that I cannot agree with those legal and political commentators such as Rodney Brazier and Basil Markesinis, who argue that the power of appointment, and by extension dismissal, has now atrophied to such a point that it no longer exists.[17] It may be the case that the vast majority of the time no discretion is used, but that does not mean the power does not exist nor that its use in the future would be somehow unconstitutional. This is because the crown's power of independent action in terms of both appointment and dismissal only becomes live when our constitutional processes are threatened or, in other words, when the 'good chap' theory breaks down.

This fact has led some commentators to liken the personal powers of the monarch to those of a 'constitutional fire extinguisher'.[18] Just because they are very rarely used does not mean that they are not real. And this is a fact that politicians and civil servants are acutely aware of, as they work hard to ensure a political fire never breaks out in the first place, which is why there have been so few attempts at constitutionally illegal acts in modern British history and very few cases of dismissal in the principal Commonwealth realms.[19] In short, the mere existence of the monarch's ability to act independently compels political actors to uphold the constitutional principles that lie at the heart of our political system. Seen in this light, the power of dismissal keeps Prime Ministers honest, as they are always compelled to recognise that they are the servants of a higher power, not the masters they like to portray themselves as.

A couple of quick examples can highlight my point. The first is probably the most notorious example and comes from Australia in 1975. So significant is this event that I shall return to it in more detail later, but a brief overview would be helpful for our discussion at this point. In the summer of 1975, the Australian Parliament hit an impasse when the House of Representatives and the Senate failed to agree on a Budget. To break the deadlock, the Governor-General, Sir John Kerr, dismissed Gough Whitlam as Prime Minister and appointed the Leader of the Opposition, Malcolm Fraser, in his stead. A politically controversial move to say the least, as Whitlam still enjoyed the support of a majority of MPs, but his inability to secure a Budget was held to be a constitutionally valid reason for his dismissal by Sir John. The Australian Labor Party, Whitlam's party, naturally saw things in a different light and argued that the Governor-General had by his actions shown a lack of political neutrality, thereby damaging the standing of the crown in the process.[20] In the end, the political controversy was resolved, as Fraser was able to pass a Budget and, importantly, requested an election that he subsequently won, a result that appeared to vindicate the actions of the Governor-General.

Nevertheless, the political repercussions of this seminal event have continued to ripple out through Australian politics to this day, fuelling the Australian republican movement in the process. Kerr became a hate figure for the political left and was forced from office prematurely due to the controversy he created, an outcome that led one commentator to observe that 'the exercise of the prerogative powers of the Crown does not require gratuitous political bloodletting' but 'it should at all times, if possible, be conducted gently and in a spirit of constitutional comity'.[21]

This brings us to a more recent example and one that is closer to our own experience. You may recall that the British government experienced a little local difficulty as it tried to implement the removal of the UK from the European Union – a situation that was brought to a head when Boris Johnson attempted to prorogue Parliament for a significant period in the latter stages of the process. Following the result of Gina Miller's legal case, in which the Supreme Court found the government to have been in error and Johnson's advice to the Queen to have been unlawful, speculation was rife as to Johnson's future.[22] Westminster gossip mills went into overdrive as politicians tried to figure out whether Johnson could be dismissed if he lost a vote of confidence, given that the Fixed-Term Parliaments Act was then in force.[23] Speculation revolved around the hypothetical question of whether if the Prime Minister had lost a vote of confidence but refused to resign, which he would have been entitled to do during the fourteen-day waiting period under the Act, or else delayed calling an election, the Queen could have dismissed him?

Experts were divided, with some arguing that the Queen could have done so provided the House of Commons had indicated a suitable successor and others arguing that the situation was not yet extreme enough to trigger the intervention of the monarch.[24] How the Prime Minister might choose to act in this situation was a matter of conjecture, but this did not prevent rumours appearing in the press that Johnson preferred to challenge the Queen to dismiss him rather than resign.[25] Yet what did emerge from this debate, in some parts grudgingly, was the agreement that in the event of the House of Commons being unable to demonstrate which individual was able to form a government the House had confidence in, the choice to dismiss the Prime Minister would be one for the sovereign alone.[26] This situation is a concrete demonstration of the fact that the power of dismissal is far from a defunct part of the constitution.

Situations of this kind are thankfully rare indeed and often highlight a deep division within society generally, but we would be remiss in not recognising the role the prerogative plays in lessening these tensions. As Norman Ward argues, 'The mere existence of the power will, in fact, tend to prevent the need for its exercise arising.'[27] This is a point that critics of the personal prerogatives often tend to overlook and one that has been more strongly argued in Canada, and to a lesser degree Australia, than in the UK in recent years. Take, for example, the statement made by David Lam whilst Lieutenant Governor of British Columbia: 'The lieutenant governor exits to deny the government absolute power.'[28] If we merely substitute 'lieutenant governor' with 'the king', this provides a succinct statement of the purpose of the personal prerogatives of the crown.

Given all this, why is it so hard for academics and politicians to accept the existence of the power of dismissal? Well, largely this has to do with the fact that social scientists either miss or do not understand the significance of rarely invoked or rarely infringed constitutional limits and powers. This is particularly true with regards to formal power that may be rarely exercised, precisely because, as Dennis Baker asserts, 'it is significantly clear and powerful that those subject to its constraints generally prefer to avoid its actual implementation by *limiting themselves*'.[29] If this all sounds familiar to you, that is because it is just a more technical way of outlining the 'good chap' theory of government. The existence of the power compels political actors to conform to accepted constitutional rules to such a degree that the use of the power becomes rare enough for commentators to argue about whether it exists at all.[30]

In recognising this essential truth, we are confronted by the realisation that our constitutional settlement relies on a far more active and involved monarch than we have been led to believe by the Bagehot theory of government. The constitution requires the active engagement of the king and at times his direct intervention because he is responsible for identifying the person who can best occupy the office of Prime Minister at any given moment. He then has the constitutional responsibility of ensuring that the Prime Minister possesses and continues to enjoy the confidence of the House of Commons and does not look to govern without it, a fact embodied in the Golden Rule governing the use of the power of appointment that we discussed in a previous chapter.

This is a grave responsibility and one that should not be lightly dismissed. As the defender of the constitution, the king ensures by his actions that the principles of parliamentary democracy are observed and honoured. In the final analysis, it falls to the king to stand against any unprincipled political action that threatens the survival of our constitutional settlement, for he is the ultimate protector of the constitutional order.[31]

This is a view that was best outlined by Eugene Forsey when he stated:

The danger of royal absolutism is past; but the danger of Cabinet absolutism, even of Prime Ministerial absolutism, is present and growing. Against that danger the reserve power of the Crown, and especially the power to force or refuse dissolution, is in some instances the only constitutional safeguard. The Crown is more than a quaint survival, a social ornament, a symbol, 'an automation, with no public will of its own'. It is an absolutely essential part of the parliamentary system. In certain circumstances, the Crown alone can preserve the Constitution, or ensure that if it is to be changed it shall be only by the deliberate will of the people.[32]

Quite so, and a timely reminder of why we should not give too much power to our Prime Ministers at the expense of the monarch. When discussing the roles of the dignified and efficient parts of the constitution, we must always keep in mind the fact that the Prime Minister may not always be a neutral agent in any political crisis that may arise. It would therefore be rather bizarre and outrageous if the supposed umpire of the process were also one of the protagonists, as David Butler has highlighted, for it would strike at the principles of natural justice.[33] If the crisis was caused, for instance, by a Prime Minister's refusal to resign following their defeat in an election and their loss of the confidence of the House, why should the monarch continue to accept their advice that they should remain Prime Minister when constitutional precedents indicate that they should resign or else be dismissed? For these reasons, I feel, the *Cabinet Manual*'s statement in this regard can only ever be a guide in normal political times but not in periods of emergency, when a degree of flexibility may well be needed.

This brings us on to an interesting aspect of the king's power of dismissal and its effect in a crisis. As you may recall, the dismissal of the Prime Minister is the dismissal of the government, an act which robs the monarch of the benefit of ministerial advice. It is by its nature a positive exercise of power, which is why its existence is so controversial for some constitutional experts. But it does raise the question of whether the monarch can use their power of appointment and dismissal in a more passive way and refuse to accept the resignation of a Prime Minister when it is offered?

The resignation of the Prime Minister creates a moment in time when the executive ceases to be effective, which lasts until the appointment of a new ministry. In most normal circumstances this is only a matter of hours, but in certain moments of crisis it can last days. To cover this eventuality, our political settlement accepts the existence of the 'caretaker principle', which outlines that a minister continues to remain in office following their resignation until such time as a new minister can be appointed. The reason for this is that it is a constitutionally accepted axiom that 'the king's government must be carried on' and so there cannot be an interregnum between one government and the next. This was a view expressed by Sir Donald Somervell whilst Attorney General, when he observed:

> The long-established constitutional practice in this country is summarised in the following passage from a Privy Council Memorandum on Change of Government: 'There can be no interval between Administrations. The outgoing Ministers remain technically responsible and can exercise their functions until the new Ministry is appointed.'
>
> In a case therefore in which the Sovereign accepts the resignation of a Prime Minister … there is no gap in the Executive authority. No doubt in this interval Ministers would not take major decisions but they remain in their offices.[34]

In the UK, we tend to refer to this by the term 'purdah', which is used to indicate the time, usually during the period between a general election being called and it taking place, when the ability of ministers to use the resources of the government for political purposes is restricted. So, although ministers remain in office during these times, they do so with certain restrictions placed upon their actions, the most important of which for our purposes is that they lose the ability to formally advise the monarch of what actions they should take. This could leave the monarch politically exposed if the 'purdah' period coincides with a national crisis that prevents the easy formation of a new government. Such a situation would leave the sovereign without the benefit of ministerial advice for an extended period of time, which is a far from an ideal situation.

This is where the negative power to reject a resignation comes in, as the monarch could engender a situation in which the Prime Minister is compelled to remain in office to ensure the king has the benefit of the advice of his ministers. This is founded on the 'old common law rule that a person cannot legally refuse service under the Crown'.[35] That said, however, in more modern times the monarch has largely relied on their powers of persuasion to prevent their Prime Minister resigning at inopportune moments, a feat that has most often been achieved by arguing that either their resignation is unnecessary at this moment in time or else that it would be damaging to the country if they did so. An example of this can be found when Britain faced a hung Parliament in 1964. Confronted by this unwelcome outcome, the Prime Minister's Office noted that if the Prime Minister tended his resignation, the Queen could act in one of three ways. She could:

1. press him to stay on until defeated in the House;
2. press him to stay on in the hope that he may form a coalition;
3. send for someone who was not the leader of either major party in the hope that some sort of compromise government could be carried on until it was feasible to have another general election.[36]

It should be noted, however, that the monarch cannot formally compel a person to remain as Prime Minister if they are determined to resign. They can only seek to persuade a Prime Minister not to do so.[37] You may recall the example we discussed in a previous chapter of Ramsay MacDonald and the formation of the national government in 1931. In that scenario, the King persuaded MacDonald to remain in office and attempt to form a coalition government, which he duly did, thus ending the Labour administration in the process.[38] Similarly, George V refused to allow Stanley Baldwin to resign until he had submitted his government's fate to the Commons following the inconclusive election results in 1923. In the wake of the government's subsequent defeat on the King's Speech, the King relented and allowed him to resign in MacDonald's favour, creating the first Labour government in the process.[39]

This brings us to the most recent example of when the monarch's influence has been brought to bear on a Prime Minister to prevent their resignation at an inopportune moment. As one surveyed the political tea leaves of the 2010 election, it became clear that a hung Parliament was going to be the most likely outcome. This filled the mandarins of Whitehall with concern as they had become used to very stable governments and worried how the nation would cope with an unstable political landscape and an economic crisis at the same time.

Gus O'Donnell, in his role as Cabinet Secretary, had game-played likely outcomes with Edward Young, the Queen's deputy private secretary, and Heywood, the Prime Minister's principal private secretary, to determine how events may unfold after the election in January 2010. When the 'three wise men' came to the scenario of the Conservatives emerging as the largest party but still a considerable way short of a majority, they recognised that the Liberal Democrats would become the key players. Both Gordon Brown and David Cameron could claim office with their support, but as the role-playing progressed, they realised that Nick Clegg would spend more time talking to Cameron than to Brown, an outcome that would increase the very real possibility of Brown resigning before the talks had concluded. If that was to happen, what were officials – and, more importantly, the Queen – to do when faced with the prospect of a Prime Minister who wanted to resign and a coalition not yet formed?[40]

The answer would lead to the creation of the *Cabinet Manual*, which would set out the main rules and practices that support the actions of officials. Key to this was the assertion that come what may, Brown could not resign until the coalition was formed, as he had a constitutional duty to remain in office until the end of the political negotiations.[41] Events, as they would transpire, would show that things are never quite as clear cut as they may appear to be in the real world. Although a laudable endeavour, this implied duty imposed a responsibility on Brown that simply contradicted accepted constitutional practice. As the talks progressed, it became clear that the Liberal Democrats would demand Brown's immediate resignation from office as the price for conducting coalition talks with Labour. Peter Mandelson relayed this message to Brown, who immediately saw a problem with the Lib Dems' position. If he resigned at once, the Queen would have been required to appoint Cameron, thus preventing the formation of a Labour-Lib Dem administration. In the hopes of breaking the impasse, Brown announced his resignation as leader of the Labour Party, an act that kickstarted political discussions between the two parties.[42]

Come the next day, however, the general view in No. 10 was that Clegg was simply using Brown to secure his preferred terms from Cameron and the feeling grew amongst his advisers that Brown should resign immediately. It had become clear that as Brown could not resign whilst the talks were ongoing, Clegg could use this fact to gain more time to pressure the Conservatives to soften their position. Outraged by the way in which he was being used, Brown at last decided to withdraw himself from the auction. He felt he could no longer wait in Downing Street whilst Clegg sought to extract better terms from either Cameron or himself, and so he began to plan his exit.[43] When they were told that Brown was now intending to resign, O'Donnell, Heywood and Christopher Geidt, the Queen's private secretary, all placed pressure on him to stay until an agreement was reached. Brown resisted, saying in response that he would only remain in office if this was the express wish of the Queen. By 3 p.m., official opposition to Brown's resignation collapsed as Geidt confirmed that the Queen would accept his resignation, opening the way for his announcement a few hours later.[44]

O'Donnell, Heyward and Geidt had all placed pressure on Brown not to resign during this period until the coalition talks had finished, telling him it was his duty to stay on and not to place the Queen in a difficult position. As Geidt informed O'Donnell, 'The Prime Minister has a constitutional obligation, a duty, to remain in his post until the Queen is able to ask somebody, either Gordon or an alternative, to form an administration. He'll have to wait a bit longer until things become a bit clearer.'[45]

In this way, the system was used to produce the preferred outcome of a coalition government.[46] Far from ensuring the political neutrality of the civil service, this decision clearly favoured the Liberal Democrats and made their negotiating position that much stronger, a fact which enabled them to get more concessions out of the Conservatives than would have been the case if they had been negotiating with a sitting government. The Lib Dems also benefited from being the only political party who knew what everyone else was saying and offering, giving them a huge strategic advantage over the other negotiating teams. In this way, they were able to play both Labour and the Conservatives off against each other.[47] This is confirmed by Paddy Ashdown, who, at the time, told Andrew Adonis that Labour 'needed to stop thinking like a government and start thinking like a supplicant for power' in a clear indication of his party's mindset during these talks.[48] The terms the Lib Dems were thus able to extract from the Conservatives were more significant than either party would have agreed in other circumstances and so mark a real success for them – a success that ultimately doomed the coalition, however, as Cameron agreed to more on voting reform than he could deliver.[49]

To summarise, the monarch holds the prerogative of dismissal and can use their powers of appointment and dismissal in a more passive way by refusing to accept the resignation of a Prime Minister at opportune moments to ensure political stability. But given the fact that the power of dismissal has not been utilised in Britain for more than two centuries, we will be forced to look further afield to find the guide that we need to help us through any such emergencies that may occur in the future. If we look to the most comparable jurisdictions to ours, the other Commonwealth realms that share our monarch as their head of state, we will see that the ability of the monarch, through their representative Governor or Governor-General, to dismiss a Prime Minister who refuses to resign is indeed well established and based on the solid foundations of British constitutional practice. So, what do these jurisdictions have to tell us? Well, Patrick Monahan, for instance, has noted that if a Prime Minister refuses to resign in Canada, 'the governor general would be justified in refusing to accept advice from the prime minister and could, instead, dismiss him or her and appoint a new first minister, or else dissolve Parliament and call an election on her own motion'.[50]

In the context of New Zealand, Philip Joseph has expounded the same premise with regards to a potential situation where the Prime Minister has lost the support of their party or the coalition of parties that they lead. In this case, it is accepted that they are constitutionally obliged to resign and if they do not do so in a timely manner, they can be dismissed from office. He observes:

> Constitutional convention obliges the Prime Minister to resign in certain situations. A Prime Minister must do so if his or her government is defeated at the elections, or he or she is replaced as party leader ... or a government nominates another party leader from within the government as leader. The Governor-General would be compelled to dismiss a Prime Minister who refuses to resign in any of those situations. Should a Prime Minister be dilatory, the Governor-General may summon that person's attendance and 'request' his or her resignation. Refusal to vacate would leave no alternative but peremptory and ignominious dismissal.[51]

So, although it may appear strange to us in Britain today, the fact remains that other Commonwealth realms are far more at ease with the intervention of the monarch in the forced dismissal of a Prime Minister than is the case in our own country, where modern practice has been to shield the sovereign from any appearance of involvement in the political process. Yet despite this tendency by civil servants to minimise the potential of royal intervention within the political realm, the power to dismiss a premier still exists and is capable of use in the right circumstances within the UK. Logically, if the monarch is the sole authority that can appoint a Prime Minister, they must also be the sole authority that can dismiss one too.

I am, therefore, confident in asserting that dismissal by the monarch is a potential way in which a Prime Minister can be removed from office, even if it is an extremely rare and unorthodox possibility within our current political system. There are several accepted grounds on which action can be taken, and I will discuss each one in turn in the following pages.

Before we proceed, however, a word of warning is perhaps required at this stage as to the use of this power. As the act of dismissal is of such a serious nature and has such profound potential consequences for the monarchy, it should not be contemplated, let alone undertaken, unless there is no other constitutional option available. It is and must be seen as a power of last resort that can only be used in an emergency when all other possibilities have failed but a decision must be made. Any monarch who contemplates such an act must first provide a fair warning of their intention to do so to their Prime Minister to allow them the opportunity to either resolve the situation themselves through accepted political means or else by resigning before they are dismissed. That being said, everything we will discuss here flows directly from the principle that the monarch is the ultimate guardian of the constitution and proves how, in extreme situations, they can act to uphold our collective constitutional freedom from improper use by political actors.

8

THE KING AND PARLIAMENTARY PROCESSES

As the sovereign is the guardian of our political settlement, it naturally flows that they can exercise the power of dismissal when a political actor tries to breach a fundamental principle of our parliamentary process. In a situation where the House of Commons has clearly demonstrated that the government no longer retains the confidence of the chamber, but the Prime Minister insists on continuing to govern, a crisis can develop in which the monarch becomes the sole actor capable of resolving things. Should this event arise, it would be the king's job to mitigate the conflict by advising their Prime Minister that as they can no longer meet the requirements of the Golden Rule, they must either resign or request a dissolution of Parliament to allow the people to resolve the crisis.

To understand why this should be the case, we need once more to return to the revolutionary settlement of 1688. This seminal moment did not outwardly create a new form of monarchy within the three realms of England, Scotland and Ireland, as most of the powers of the crown were left intact.[1] The monarch was still able to determine all issues of policy, choose their own ministers, veto parliamentary legislation and dissolve Parliament, but the changing financial position of the country affected how these powers were used. William and Mary's continental wars against Louis XIV necessitated the creation of a national debt, which in turn needed to be serviced by regular grants of taxation from Parliament. This, more than anything else, guaranteed the continual sitting of Parliament from 1689 onwards and the decline of the monarch's veto power over legislation.[2]

This increasing need for a steady supply of revenue derived from taxation ensured that parliamentary management became much more of a priority for ministers than had been the case in the past, as they needed to ensure that not only were taxes raised but also that important legislation required by the crown was introduced and passed by Parliament. To ensure this outcome, Treasury officials and other departmental heads were increasingly drawn into parliamentary sittings to serve as intermediaries between the legislature and the executive. As a result, ministers had to develop new skills. They were increasingly required to present government policies, explain the government's financial needs, account for how money was spent and negotiate with Members of Parliament to ensure the support of a majority. Their presence in the Commons Chamber became so regular, in fact, that they were given reserved seats on the front bench to the Speaker's right, and to this day, these seats are referred to as the Treasury bench. It was on this bench on any sitting day that government ministers were to be found and it is from this bench today that the Prime Minister rises to answer the questions of the House every Wednesday. As a result of this continual attendance, authority began to accrue to ministers, who found that, little by little, they became the institution's leading members.[3]

Ministerial power over the House was further increased when

they managed to wrest control of the order of business away from ordinary members. As the Commons was the sole body that could authorise the collection and spending of money following the revolution, the government faced the constant threat that non-ministerial Members of Parliament would ruin the country's finances by proposing ill-considered money bills. To prevent political chaos and ensure their own position, ministers sought to establish their sole right to propose such bills. In 1706, they gained a considerable advantage when the Commons informally declared, 'This House will receive no petition for any sum of money relating to public Service, but what is recommended from the Crown.'

This announcement, in hindsight, marked the moment in time when the government, rather than backbench MPs, became the primary agents and implementors of parliamentary business. The non-binding rule was then made a permanent feature of the House on 11 June 1713 when Standing Order 66 was passed, stating that 'the Commons would not vote money for any purpose, except on a motion of a Minister of the Crown'. This order has remained unchanged for 300 years and is still in force today as Standing Order 48. It is the rock upon which the modern executive's power has been built.[4] When this order was combined with Standing Order 14(1) in the 1880s, which states, 'Save as provided in this order, government business shall have precedence at every sitting,' governmental primacy over legislative business was firmly established.

Between them, these two orders uphold and embody the centrally important and basic constitutional principle that Parliament must have its say, but government business must get its way. It is due to this concept that the UK is a parliamentary monarchy in which Parliament holds to account but does not rule. It is for the ministers of the crown to administer the country, not Parliament, but to do so, the government must retain the confidence and support of Parliament. This is a classic example of the harmonious principle that lies at the heart of our constitutional settlement – which was stretched as never before during the Brexit debates, as we will discuss below.

Standing Order 66 had an instantaneous and lasting impact on our political process; it empowered ministers with the sole right of financial initiative and in so doing transferred the leadership of the Commons from prominent members to the servants of the crown. Pre-eminent amongst them was the Lord Treasurer, who had responsibility for all fiscal matters and so assumed a leading position amongst the rest of the government's ministers.[5] This new power of financial initiative was not, however, absolute but was itself moderated by parliamentary oversight. It was true that only ministers could initiate money bills, but they still needed to submit their proposals to parliamentary enquiry and seek parliamentary consent before raising the funds. In this way, Standing Order 66 was not just the beginning of executive primacy in parliamentary business but also marked the foundation of ministerial responsibility and accountability to Parliament. Through it, both Houses established their right to question ministers and hold them to account when government policies failed. As a result, ministers now had to make themselves available to be questioned by Parliament and to answer for their performance – ministerial question time was thus established.[6]

Out of this settlement came the Golden Rule, which requires all candidates for the premiership to demonstrate that they can form a government that has the confidence of the Commons. An individual can acquire and retain the premiership only so long as they can show they meet this rule. Should they fail to meet either condition – that is, they must be able to form a government and secure the confidence of the Commons – they must resign or else face the possibility of dismissal by the monarch. Everything we will go on to explore in this section flows from these parliamentary assumptions and ensures that Prime Ministers cannot become over-mighty subjects who threaten our parliamentary democracy. So long as the 'good chap' theory operates, the sovereign need not be involved in the political process, but should the system break down, the possibility that they might have to intervene increases. So, what are the potential grounds for dismissal that fall under this category?

LOSS OF A VOTE OF NO CONFIDENCE

The first ground for dismissal is the failure to resign after a defeat on a vote of no confidence by the House of Commons. The fundamental principles of responsible government have given rise to the convention that a Prime Minister who is defeated in the lower House on a matter of confidence must either resign or else request a dissolution, leading to an election.[7] This is such a fundamental part of our constitutional system that it has almost universal compliance within the UK and abroad.

This issue, somewhat surprisingly, became a subject of live debate within the UK following the appointment of Boris Johnson to the premiership with a policy of leaving the European Union with or without an exit agreement on 31 October 2019. MPs who were opposed to this eventuality indicated that they would seek to hold a vote of confidence in the new government, which had a majority of one, to force a change of administration. It was argued by Jeremy Corbyn and others at the time that such a vote would force the Prime Minister to resign, allowing for an alternative candidate who could demonstrate that they had the support of the Commons to be appointed in his place, thereby preventing Brexit from occurring on 31 October without an approved exit agreement in place.[8] Superficially, this approach seemed like it had a solid basis in constitutional precedent and may well have had a chance of success before 2011, but it ignored two fundamental issues. The first was that the Fixed-Term Parliaments Act of 2011, then in force, did not require the Prime Minister to resign in such circumstances. The second was that established custom has always accepted the right of a Prime Minister who has lost the confidence of the Commons to seek the support of the people through an election. After all, this is what Jim Callaghan chose to do in 1979 after he lost a confidence vote.[9]

John Bercow, the Speaker of the House of Commons at the time, was reported as having stated that if a vote of confidence were to take place and the government lost the vote, he would have sought to place pressure on the Queen to dismiss the Prime Minister in favour of someone else who could command the confidence of the House.[10] As we have seen, any attempt by him to do so would not have been constitutionally acceptable. The monarch should not engage in such a political crisis as it would require them to take sides in a political debate. If the Prime Minister had lost the vote of confidence, he would have been well within his rights to inform the Queen that he would now seek a mandate from the people for his actions, and she must have accepted such a decision and allowed her premier to do so. Should Johnson have failed to win that election, he could either have resigned immediately or chosen to remain in office to face the House. If the Commons again registered its lack of confidence in the government and he still refused to resign, only at this stage might the right of dismissal have become live.

Retaining the confidence of the House of Commons is a central tenent of the British constitutional settlement and it is the foundation upon which modern governments base their legitimacy. Since 1782, the most clear-cut way to show this support is through votes of confidence, such as the motion triggered by Lord North's conduct of the war in North America, which resulted in a vote of no confidence and brought down his administration. Since that time, there have been twenty government defeats on a vote of confidence, all leading to either a dissolution or resignation. This was a fact that confronted Harold Wilson in 1974. Since he did not hold a majority in the new House following the February election, Wilson faced the possibility of losing the vote on the Queen's Speech, which outlined the proposed government's legislative agenda. As this vote was the first occasion on which the government could show the confidence of the House, a defeat would have ended Wilson's government before it began. Confronted by this possibility, officials made it clear to the Prime Minister that if he lost, he would have to either request a dissolution of Parliament or resign. If he failed to do either, the Queen was required to dismiss him and appoint someone who would so advise her. As it was, the government won the vote with the support of opposition parties, but the fact remains that Wilson could have been dismissed had he failed to achieve the result.[11]

For the sovereign to proactively remove their Prime Minister from office in this way, the issue that confronts them must not be one of politics but rather one of law. As the guardian of the constitution, the monarch can only intervene to uphold constitutional principles and must never be seen to enter into matters that are purely political in nature. Should the Queen have acted in the way that the Speaker suggested in 2019, she would have been found to have been expressing a political opinion and taking sides in a political conflict, which would have endangered her position and the institution of the monarchy. For the monarch to act, the issue must therefore be one that is a breach of a constitutional principle and that fact must be widely accepted by both the political class and the public at large.

FAILURE TO ACHIEVE SUPPLY

The second ground for dismissal is where a government fails to achieve supply. The primary duty of a government is to ensure the provision of supply, or in other words revenue through taxation, to the crown.[12] The crown cannot tax its citizens; only Parliament can do that. The crown cannot draw money for the purposes of governing from the Treasury without Parliamentary approval, which can only be done by an appropriation Act. This is the foundational belief on which our system of representative and responsible government is based and where the office of Prime Minister springs from.

As First Lord of the Treasury, the Prime Minister was originally a creature of the Treasury, and it was through that role that the head of government developed to ensure that the crown was able to secure taxation from the people. Although this is not in question, the issue of whether there is a separate ground for dismissal due to a failure to gain supply is. It is felt by most academics that the issue would instead be one of confidence as a government that could not pass an appropriation Act would not have the confidence of the House and would need to resign in any case. It is generally felt, therefore, that this issue would only apply to bicameral Parliaments where the upper House has the right and ability to block supply.

Although the British House of Lords held this power till 1911, it no longer enjoys such a right, leaving the Canadian and Australian Senates as the primary chambers with this power today. Both continue to exercise their right to oversee the passage of finance bills, but of these two examples, only Australia's Senate, which has an elected upper chamber with an equal democratic mandate, has sought to block a finance bill outright, with the Canadian Senate confining itself to offering amendments. However, it has said as recently as 2017 that it can and will reject a Budget if needed, raising the spectre of a potential clash with the Canadian House of Commons at some point in the future.[13]

United Kingdom

It is, therefore, not surprising that our examples for the use of this ground for dismissal primarily come from Australia, but this must not blind us to the fact that the UK also has the potential for this conflict to arise should we see further parliamentary reform. The House of Lords historically had the ability to block money bills, but it traditionally did not seek to introduce or amend them. Correspondingly, there was no way in which disagreements between the two Houses could be resolved when a deadlock occurred except through the creation of new peers, as was the case over the passage of the Treaty of Utrecht in 1713. To pass the treaty, Queen Anne created twelve new Tory peers to allow the government a majority in the Lords.[14] From that point onwards, the mere threat that the monarch would create new peers to pass a bill saw the Lords eventually back down – as they did over the Reform Act in 1832 for fear that their chamber would be diluted with new peers. This created an informal convention that the Lords would give way when the public was behind the House of Commons and so resolved the issue of deadlock between the two Houses.

Although seemingly to the benefit of the Commons, this convention gave the Lords a corresponding right to demand proof that this public support was present and so they took onto themselves a right to decide the timing of general elections.[15] What this meant in practice was that the House of Lords would seek to delay the passage of specific money bills that it disagreed with until either the government withdrew them or called an election to test the support the government enjoyed amongst the people. As governments did not wish to have to face an election every time they needed money, Gladstone made the decision to consolidate the process. From 1860 onwards, the Budget was introduced as a single item that held all the separate fiscal requests and spending commitments of the government, in order to limit the scope of opposition to a specific provision contained within it.[16] This innovation had the merit of denying the Lords the ability to veto specific proposals whilst simultaneously allowing the majority of money bills to pass unhindered, rendering, in the process, the opposition of the upper House less likely. The inherent flaw in such an approach was that although it made an overall challenge far less likely, it raised the stakes considerably when a clash did occur, as any rejection would now be a rejection of the whole Budget since the Lords lacked the ability to amend fiscal bills.[17]

Just such an occasion occurred in 1909 when Lloyd George introduced the People's Budget, which proposed several tax increases on income and land value to fund Liberal welfare reforms. These taxes hit directly at the aristocracy as a class and they were, unsurprisingly, unwilling to let them pass without some form of opposition. The result was that the House of Lords, for the first time since the passage of the reform acts, rejected the whole Budget by 350 votes to seventy-five.[18] The government cried that this was a breach of the constitution, but the Lords countered that it was for the government to prove public support for the Budget by calling an election. Faced with such determined opposition in both the House of Commons and Lords and unwilling to amend their proposed Budget, the Liberal government was left with no choice but to call an election.

The election of January 1910 saw the Liberal Party lose its majority but remain in office with the support of the Irish Parliamentary Party. As per their own rules, the House of Lords recognised the verdict of the polls and duly passed the Budget. Things may well have ended there had it not been for the fact that, as part of their deal to support the government, the Irish Party required the government to enact Irish Home Rule. Both parties recognised that the House of Lords and its veto over legislation was the primary obstacle to achieving this ambition and so sought a way to ensure the veto was never used.[19] They proposed an Act that would remove once and for all the Lords' power to veto money bills and limit their ability to do more than delay legislation for two years. These proposals set off a titanic political battle between the government and the opposition that threatened to split the country apart, with the Conservative and Liberal Unionist parties using every ruse they could think of to block the passage of the bill. The Act was eventually passed but only after a further election in December 1910 and a public pledge by the King to create enough new peers to pass the Act, which finally convinced the Lords to approve its passage.[20]

With this Act, the ability of the Lords to prevent supply ended in the UK.[21] Should the Parliament Act 1911 and its sister Act in 1949 ever be amended or revoked, however, then the possibility of a conflict between the two Houses will again arise, an eventuality that becomes more likely if the House of Lords is reformed to make it more democratic. The limits on the powers of the upper House flow from its lack of democratic accountability, but should this limitation ever be removed, it will be hard to continue to impose such limits upon it. The year 1910 was, therefore, the last time a British Prime Minister enjoying the support of the Commons faced the possibility of being dismissed from office because they could not secure supply to the crown. Notwithstanding the fact the government continued to enjoy the confidence of the Commons, had the Lords continued to block the passage of the Budget the King may well have been compelled to dismiss H. H. Asquith and summon Arthur Balfour to form a government to ensure taxes could be collected.

The possibility of dismissal for failure to secure supply is still an active consideration for minority governments, however, as they cannot guarantee the Commons will support their Budget. If a situation arises in which a minority government cannot pass a Budget but tries to remain in office, this issue may become live once more.

Australia

Were this situation to arise, we can look to the Australian experience for help. The Australian Senate has found itself in very much the same position as the House of Lords did in 1911 – the Australian constitution did not provide it with the power to introduce or amend money bills, but it did give it the power to reject them. The reasons for this are twofold. First, the powers of the Senate reflected those of the House of Lords in 1901 when the constitution was created. Second, as Australia was a federal country, the House of Representatives was regarded as representing the people in aggregate whilst the Senate was seen as representing the Australian states. To ensure the more populous states did not dominate the smaller states, the principles of federalism recognised that both chambers should be balanced by allowing them to hold each other in check.[22]

As a result, Australian governments have continued to operate under a burden that has been unknown to their British counterparts since 1911. What this means in practice is that although a majority in the Senate is not needed for the government to show it has the confidence of Parliament, it is needed to secure supply. To govern, a government must secure supply, but if it cannot do so, it must resign or else call an election. This has led William Harrison Moore to state:

> The responsibility of the Ministry to the Upper House, if it exists, is of a very indirect kind; but a check upon the Ministry and the Lower House lies in the fact that the Upper House might in an extreme case refuse to pass the Appropriation Bill, and thereby force a dissolution or change of Ministry. These are the conditions recognised by the Constitution.[23]

Just such a situation arose in 1975 when Gough Whitlam was dismissed by the Governor-General, Sir John Kerr, on 11 November. In his dismissal, Sir John made it very clear that it was the failure to secure supply alone that was the grounds for dismissal, not illegality or the loss of confidence. Although supply had technically not been refused by the Senate but rather deferred 'until the Government agrees to submit itself to the judgement of the people', the effect was the same as the government faced the very real possibility that it would run out of money by 11 November. If an election was to be held before the Christmas period, it needed to be granted by 13 November at the latest, but this could only be done once supply had been secured. In choosing the date for the dismissal, the Governor-General had left it to the last possible moment to dismiss his Prime Minister.[24]

The politics of this crisis were rather straightforward in that the Labor Party had a majority in the House of Representatives,

ON HIS MAJESTY'S SERVICE

but the Liberals held a majority in the Senate. Malcolm Fraser, as leader of the Liberal Party, wanted to force the government to call an immediate election as he felt he would win it, but Whitlam rejected this as he wished to call the election at a time more favourable to his own party. A series of scandals and poor decisions had weakened the government's standing in the polls and left the opposition outraged. To place pressure on the administration, Fraser used the power of the Senate to defer debate on the Budget and force a political crisis. Either the Prime Minister would have to call an election or he would be dismissed, with Fraser being installed as premier.[25] It was no small coincidence that Fraser was from the state of Victoria, which had a long history of using the issue of supply to force the dismissal of unpopular governments. He was thus intimately familiar with the use of this parliamentary tactic in a way that Whitlam, who hailed from New South Wales, was not.[26] Whitlam, for his part, was strongly opposed to the principle that the Senate could force an election in any capacity and so sought to break its power once and for all by creating a crisis similar to that which surrounded the People's Budget in 1909. In a clash between federalism and responsible government, Whitlam believed the principle of responsible government was the most important, and as such, the government should only be answerable to the House of Representatives as the 'people's House'. So long as he had the confidence of that House, he could govern and did not need to call an election.[27]

Legally and politically, things were more complicated than both men realised. To put pressure on the Governor-General, the opposition released a legal opinion by Robert Ellicott QC, a former Solicitor General and a shadow minister at the time, which said that a government without supply cannot govern. Ellicott argued that the refusal by Parliament to grant supply to the government, whether by the House or the Senate, was a clear indication that the government could not fulfil its primary function and so the Governor-General should send for new ministers. In response to this legal opinion, Kerr asked that the government provide him with advice from the crown law officers to outline how he should act in the current situation and whether he had the power to dismiss for failure to secure supply. In an incredible lapse of responsibility, the law officers did not provide Kerr with this formal advice but offered instead to provide an informal draft of their advice, which confirmed he did have the power to act but questioned if he had a duty to act.[28]

This constitutional lapse in not providing suitable advice to the Governor-General that he had specifically requested created a vacuum that others looked to fill. A joint opinion by Keith Aickin QC, Murray Gleeson QC and Professor Pat Lane stated:

> What is the position of the Governor-General whose Ministers are unable to procure supply from Parliament, who are supported by a majority in the House of Representatives, and who are not prepared to advise the Governor-General to dissolve the House and call an election?
>
> There is precedent to support the view that in such a case it would be within the power of the Governor-General to dismiss his Ministers and to seek the advice of other Ministers if it is available. By the time such a state of affairs has been reached the political situation could be so fluid that it is difficult to predict the source of such alternative advice. If, however, the Governor-General were advised by the new Ministers to dissolve Parliament he could act on that advice.[29]

With supply running out and Whitlam refusing to call an election, instead looking to find extra-parliamentary sources of funding, Kerr decided to act. At 9:55 a.m. he called Fraser's office for what would turn out to be one of the most historic phone calls in Australian history. He confirmed he was considering dismissing the Prime Minister, but before he could do so, he needed several assurances from Fraser. If he was appointed Prime Minister, would he agree to do so as a caretaker and undertake no policy changes, would he obtain supply straight away, would he advise a dissolution that day and would he guarantee no action was to be taken against Whitlam or his ministers for any of the scandals that had rocked the government? Fraser responded that he was happy to accept all these conditions.[30]

The conditions outlined are all highly relevant, as they ensured the Governor-General's actions were in line with expected political practice. In asking that Fraser guarantee he would recommend an election, Kerr was ensuring that the people would ultimately determine the validity of the outcome. For as Eugene Forsey highlights, 'It all boils down to this. Save under very exceptional circumstances the King can appeal against his responsible advisors to Parliament, or against Parliament to the electorate, only if he can induce an alternative Minister to accept responsibility for the step contemplated.'[31]

Kerr had ensured that this would be the case in 1975 and so had secured the crown's position within the crisis because:

the Crown cannot act without the advice of Ministers. If it refuses the advice of Ministers in office and they refuse to back down, it must find other Ministers who will take responsibility for the refusal; and the new Ministers must secure the support of either the existing Parliament or of the new Parliament.[32]

By agreeing to Kerr's terms, Fraser was accepting that responsibility. Although Whitlam was right that the principle of responsible government does depend on the government having the consent of the lower House, he forgot why the principle exists in the first place – to ensure supply. By exacerbating the crisis and not calling for an election, Whitlam left Kerr with no choice but to dismiss him. Although Kerr handled the situation well, he did fail in one significant way: he did not provide Whitlam with the chance to face the election as Prime Minister rather than be dismissed. Kerr, famously, is believed to have given no warning to Whitlam when he dismissed him and so prevented him from bowing to the inevitable and preventing the use of the dismissal power.

This is based on Whitlam's account of the events, which Kerr strongly denied, saying if Whitlam had agreed to call an election, he would not have dismissed him. Whitlam's supporters have argued that had he known he would be dismissed unless he advised a dissolution, it is likely he would have remained Prime Minister for the election. The counterargument to this, as some have suggested, is that Whitlam thought the dismissal would help him at the polls and so he may have complied with Kerr's actions in the hopes of an electoral advantage. Such an explanation would account for why Whitlam made no attempt to prevent Fraser passing the Budget in the Senate. Had he done so, Fraser would have had to return to the Governor-General and admit that he could not meet the terms of his commission, forcing him to resign and placing Kerr in the embarrassing position of having to reappoint Whitlam. This lack of action can only otherwise be explained by Whitlam's clear antipathy to the Senate and his belief that control of the lower House was all that mattered.

Either way, Kerr is seen by constitutional experts to have erred by not warning Whitlam of his intentions and as a result was forced to retire from his post early, a warning to his successors on the dangers of using their power of dismissal.[33] A monarch in a comparable situation may at best find themselves driven from the throne or at worst be found to have endangered the monarchy itself if they have misjudged such a situation.

LOSS OF PARTY SUPPORT

The third ground for dismissal is if the Prime Minister has lost the support of their own party and has failed to replace it with a similar or greater level of support from elsewhere in the House.

Where a Prime Minister has lost the support of their own party and is acting against the wishes of their own Cabinet but refuses to resign, the issue arises as to whether the monarch should intervene or whether the issue is best left to a vote of no confidence in the Commons.[34] Should such a situation arise, it would be presumed that internal political pressure within the governing party and government would resolve the issue without recourse to the sovereign, as the *Cabinet Manual* envisages. If, however, the Prime Minister refuses to vacate their office after having been replaced as party leader, it can be argued that the Cabinet would be within their rights to advise the monarch to dismiss the Prime Minister, paving the way for the formation of a new government.[35]

Let us image, for instance, that in 1990, rather than choosing to resign and not contest the second round of the leadership contest, Margaret Thatcher had chosen to push on with her claim. Let us then imagine that she lost to either Michael Heseltine or John Major, who was appointed the new leader of the Conservative Party in her stead, but she still refused to resign as Prime Minister, arguing that she had won an election and this entitled her to stay in office. In such a circumstance, it would seem plausible that the party would be loath to either table a confidence motion against its own government or hold a vote of confidence in the Prime Minister themselves. There would have been considerable pressure within the party and government for Thatcher to resign, but we are left to wonder what recourse would have been available if she had simply refused to bow to that political pressure. Such a situation would have created a political crisis that only the monarch could have resolved. In this case, the Cabinet could have requested that the Queen dismiss Thatcher and appoint the new party leader in her place, as they alone could meet the requirements of the Golden Rule.

In this scenario, the monarch would have been acting to uphold the accepted political process rather than being drawn into a party-political issue. But before such action would have been taken, the palace would have placed considerable pressure on the Conservative leadership and Thatcher to resolve the issue without the involvement of the Queen. This would undoubtedly have taken the form of the Queen advising the Prime Minister that she was in breach of the convention and if she persisted in her actions, the Queen would have no alternative but to dismiss her. In so doing, she would provide Thatcher with the option of resigning rather than being dismissed.

This brings us neatly to the case of Ramsay MacDonald and the formation of the national government in 1931. In that case, MacDonald lost the support of his party and was expelled due to his actions in continuing to lead the new coalition. However, unlike the theorised situation we have just discussed, he was able to continue as Prime Minister because he had the support of a majority in the Commons who backed the national government. To preserve constitutional niceties, MacDonald first resigned as Prime Minister of the Labour government and then accepted a new commission as Prime Minister of the national government, which was and is an acceptable constitutional action.[36]

When discussing dismissal on the grounds of a loss of party support, we must be careful to bear in mind that the leadership of a political party and the ability to command the confidence of the House may often be one and the same, but this is not always the case. A Prime Minister can be dismissed when they have lost the support of their party because it is assumed that the confidence in the government flows from the party's control of a majority of the MPs. But just because a Prime Minister has lost the support of most of their own MPs, it does not always follow that they have lost the confidence of the House. In some cases, a new government may be constructed with cross-party support, allowing the Prime Minister to show they still have the confidence of the House even if their own party no longer supports them.[37] As in all things, the Golden Rule will operate to govern the situation at the time, so some examples may be useful for our discussion.

Garfield Todd

In 1958, Garfield Todd was Prime Minister of Southern Rhodesia, at the head of a reforming ministry that had begun to develop personnel problems. Todd's Cabinet colleagues found his leadership style to be too presidential and lacking in the degree of consultation they thought was required of the post. They had become restless with his leadership and had put pressure on him to change his approach to governing. Todd had repeatedly resisted their requests and so his Cabinet had decided to resign en masse, hoping to force Todd's resignation by their actions. At a heated Cabinet meeting on 10 January 1958, Todd was confronted by his Cabinet colleagues and informed that they intended to collectively resign if he did not immediately vacate the premiership. Unsure how to respond to this ultimatum, Todd discussed the issue with some friends and supporters and decided that he would fight it out to see what levels of support he held in Parliament and in the party. The next day, he officially announced the appointment of a new Cabinet, much to the surprise and fury of his colleagues who had assumed that he would bow to their pressure.[38]

Both sides were spoiling for a fight and confident of the justness of their cause, but the question remained as to where this battle was to be fought; was it to be in the parliamentary chamber or in the party caucus? As Parliament was in recess at the time, it would need to be formally recalled for a vote of confidence to take place, but for this to happen, the Speaker and the Prime Minister would have needed to jointly support the action. Unsurprisingly, the dissidents did not feel that Todd would be willing to allow Parliament to be recalled under the circumstances and so they focused their attention on the party caucus, the party congress and the Governor – in that order.

Following a caucus meeting on 14 January, it became clear that most of the party's MPs did not support the Prime Minister and as such, they urged him to resign. Todd refused to do so because he was still the leader of the party. Seeking to overturn this situation, the dissidents then moved on to the next stage of their rebellion by arranging for a special meeting of the party congress to be called for 8 February to formally discuss the issue of the leadership. With tempers running high on all sides, the meeting was ill-mannered and violent, with accusations of foul play flying thick and fast around the room, preventing any accord being reached. So heated, in fact, was the meeting that neither side looked like it would be able to land a knockout blow on the other until late in the day, when a surprise announcement was made that Sir Edgar Whitehead, the High Commissioner to Washington, would allow his name to be considered for the leadership.[39]

Whitehead's announcement transformed the situation profoundly because he was a serious challenger to Todd who could rely on strong levels of support in all sections of the party. When the vote was at last taken, late in the evening, Todd narrowly emerged at the top of the first ballot with 129 votes to 122 for Whitehead and seventy-three for Sir Patrick Fletcher, the man who had initially led the revolt in the Cabinet but who ultimately found he did not have the personal support in the wider party needed to unseat Todd. Accepting this reality, he swung his support behind Whitehead, who emerged victorious on the second ballot. Todd had been deposed as leader, but he still refused to resign as Prime Minister, to the outrage of his opponents. Faced with no other choice, Whitehead entered into negotiations with the Governor, seeking the formal dismissal of Todd from office.

Before he would consider such an act, however, the Governor made it clear he would need to be satisfied that an alternative candidate existed who could form a government that had the confidence of the House. Whitehead therefore set about forming a broad-based administration that could meet these requirements. Hoping to heal the wounds in the party, Whitehead reached out to Todd and offered him a place in the new government, but Todd refused the offer and made it clear to his supporters that they should refuse as well. When it became clear to him that his supporters were ignoring his directive and accepting office, Todd finally realised the game was up and agreed to resign. Had he failed to do so at this point, Whitehead would have been well within his rights to request that the Governor consent to dismiss Todd on the grounds that he could no longer form a government that had the confidence of the House.

In the end, Todd had discovered that the ability to form a government relies on the consent of your colleagues to abide by your leadership, and without that consent, you simply cannot meet the requirements of the Golden Rule. Todd had sought to fight his own party to stay in office, but in the end, he would have been dismissed by the Governor had he continued to fight on once he lost the party leadership.[40]

Sir Robert Muldoon

In 1984, New Zealand Prime Minister Sir Robert Muldoon similarly came close to being dismissed by the Governor-General. Faced with the need to secure the government's precarious position in Parliament due its two-seat majority, Muldoon decided to gamble on calling a snap election in July 1984, which he ended up losing.[41] The resurgent Labour Party had secured a commanding majority, but Muldoon did not immediately resign. Transfers of power in New Zealand are delayed somewhat following an election due to the requirement for the election results to be declared and the writs returned to Parliament before new ministers can be sworn in. Muldoon, therefore, remained in office as a caretaker Prime Minister until this procedural requirement had been met.

Events would conspire, however, to create a situation that almost precipitated a political crisis due to the immediate need to devalue the currency. During the election campaign, there had been much debate on the necessity of devaluing the New Zealand dollar, which Labour supported but which the National Party opposed. With the aim of reassuring the markets, David Lange, the presumptive new Prime Minister, met with Muldoon, the Treasury and the Reserve Bank following the election. At the meeting, Treasury officials revealed that the dollar had to be devalued at once or the country would default on its commitments.[42]

Muldoon would not accept this and refused to act on the advice he had been given, much to Lange's and the Cabinet's annoyance. Finding his actions indefensible, Muldoon's Deputy Prime Minister, Jim McLay, met with other senior members of the government and decided that if Muldoon would not act, they would remove him as leader of the National Party. They would then recommend that the Governor-General remove him as Prime Minister and appoint McLay as a temporary Prime Minister for the sole purpose of devaluing the dollar.[43] The Governor-General was alerted to this possibility and indicated that if he received advice from McLay that Muldoon no longer enjoyed the confidence of the National Party leadership and caucus, 'he would dismiss Muldoon and appoint McLay as temporary Prime Minister to effect the devaluation'.[44] Rather than face this outcome, Muldoon relented and agreed to devalue the dollar, thus ending the crisis. Had he not done so, the Governor-General would have had strong grounds for dismissing Muldoon because he had lost the election and thus did not command the confidence of the House and because the urgency of the financial crisis meant the Governor-General could not wait for Parliament to be recalled or a new government to be formed.

Sir Joh Bjelke-Petersen

In Queensland in November 1987, Premier Sir Joh Bjelke-Petersen lost the support of his ruling National Party due to the fallout from a corruption scandal that had engulfed him. The allegations of corruption were so bad, in fact, that the Labor opposition called on the Governor, Sir Walter Campbell, to dismiss Bjelke-Petersen from office. This, in turn, led to increasing opposition within his own party, to the point where Sir Joh had to announce he would retire on 8 August 1988, the date of his twentieth anniversary in power.[45]

Refusing to be placated by this attempt to delay the inevitable, his colleagues continued to reject his leadership. Bjelke-Petersen therefore chose to follow Todd's example by restructuring his Cabinet and dismissing his opponents, presenting the Governor with a new administration. His actions outraged the parliamentary party, which decided to hold a meeting on 26 November to declare all leadership positions vacant and to elect the recently dismissed Health Minister Mike Ahern as leader of the party. Ahern then sent a letter to the Governor asserting that he had the support of the ruling party and therefore a majority in the Legislative Assembly. The letter stated:

> As Leader of the ruling Parliamentary Party, I am able to form a government and assure supply to the Crown. No other Member of Parliament is in a position to give such an absolute assurance.
>
> I accordingly request Your Excellency issue me a Commission to form a government and withdraw any Commission existing at the time of receipt of this letter.[46]

Attached to this letter were the signatures of the entire parliamentary membership of the National Party, except for the premier himself, thus indicating the level of support Ahern held in the House. In making such a request to the Governor, Ahern was supported by the sound principle of the Golden Rule, as only Ahern could form a government that had the confidence of the Assembly. This was a view that was strongly supported by the Solicitor General. Giving the Governor legal advice, he said:

> In the event of the deposed Leader declining to resign the Governor's options would be to withdraw his commission or to recall Parliament. While it is entirely a matter for the Governor to decide which course to follow I would imagine that he may well consider the former if it was clear that the new Leader commanded a majority in the House, on the best information available to him. The latter might be done if the situation was sufficiently unclear.[47]

Faced with a political crisis, the Governor chose discretion and advised Bjelke-Petersen to ask the Speaker to recall Parliament so that it would be able to resolve the issue. This request allowed time for the pressure to build on the premier, providing him with the space to decide to resign in his own way and in his own time rather than being forced to do so by the intervention of the crown.[48] In this way, the Governor avoided the use of the power of dismissal, resolved a political crisis and ensured that political convention was upheld. Such was the skill displayed in this crisis that Sir Walter has been praised for his astute actions that preserved the prerogative and political neutrality of the crown.[49]

As all three of these examples highlight, it is impossible to apply any hard and fast rules to a political crisis, as any decision made must be done in the light of the factual context at the time. In

Southern Rhodesia, there was no clear successor for the Governor to appoint and so he refused to get involved until the politicians resolved this issue for themselves. In New Zealand, the country faced a political crisis that required immediate action. In Queensland, the Governor had the luxury of time. As a general principle, it is best that Parliament and the politicians should resolve a crisis without the intervention of the monarch in all but the most severe and extreme cases. In such moments it is the sovereign's role to ensure gridlock is avoided.

REFUSAL OF A DISSOLUTION

The final ground for dismissal that we need to consider revolves around the prerogative of dissolution, which we shall discuss in more detail in the next chapter. If the Prime Minister holds the confidence of the Commons at the time of their dismissal but is acting in a manner that breaches constitutional principle, such as attempting to govern without regard to electoral outcomes, the monarch may seek to intervene to force an election. To do this they would need to dismiss the current government and appoint a caretaker Prime Minister, whose sole purpose would be to advise a dissolution to the sovereign in order to allow the people to choose a new government.[50]

The inherent danger of this approach is that if no one is prepared to accept the king's commission, the monarch would be left politically exposed. It was for this reason that Sir John Kerr ensured that Malcom Fraser would accept the commission before he dismissed Whitlam.[51] In some cases, the Leader of the Opposition may feel compelled to support the king in accepting the commission, but that will depend on the political situation at the time. Usually, ambition or obligation will be sufficient to ensure someone is willing to form a government in the wake of a dismissal. However, this is not always the case, as was shown in 1936. Faced with the abdication crisis, all the main political leaders entered into an agreement that they would refuse such a commission if offered by Edward VIII should he try to force an election on the issue of his marriage.[52]

Likewise, the monarch refusing a dissolution may give rise to the effective dismissal of the government. This was explored by Andrew Heard when he noted that rather than 'remove outright a government from office' the King 'can induce a change of government by refusing its advice on some important matter, such as advising that an election should be held'.[53] If the government should lose a vote of confidence in the Commons and recommend a dissolution but the King refuses to grant one because there is someone else who can form a government, the Prime Minister is expected to resign. Should the Prime Minister refuse to resign, they may be formally dismissed by the monarch.[54] The only modern example of such an event occurred in Canada in 1926, when the Governor-General refused the Prime Minster's request for a dissolution and instead invited the opposition to form a government. Known as the King–Byng Affair, this event helped shape our understanding of not only how the power of dismissal can be used but also the power of dissolution, and we shall discuss it in greater detail in the following chapter.[55]

Such moves by the King or their representatives are indeed rare and the line between dismissal and resignation is often hard to identify. This is because, according to Thomas Penberthy Fry, 'a resignation forced by the Crown is in the same category as a dismissal by the Crown'.[56] One of the main aspects of a dismissal, as opposed to a forced resignation or dissolution, is that the act implies a degree of wrongdoing on the part of the dismissed administration, an impression that is likely to be noted by the electorate who will seek to punish the wrongdoers in any future election. For this reason, a Prime Minister invariably regards resignation as preferable to dismissal, with the result they often resign when faced with this choice. Likewise, the monarch prefers to let the people resolve a political crisis rather than becoming directly involved and so will agree to a dissolution rather than attempt to dismiss a government.

9

THE KING AND CONSTITUTIONAL PRINCIPLES

Alongside parliamentary processes, the king must also take note of key constitutional conventions, as they too can provide grounds for the dismissal of a Prime Minister. Unlike the premises which flow from parliamentary practice, these grounds deal with broad constitutional principles that provide the foundation for our wider political system and deal with issues that occur just as much outside of Parliament as within it. All revolve around the monarch's role as the defender of the constitution and have only been used to resolve the most severe of political crises. As such, they are mercifully rare occurrences both here and in the primary Commonwealth realms. The 'good chap' theory of government and an uncommonly stable political environment have ensured that the UK has not had to deal with issues of this kind for a considerable period of time, although events surrounding Brexit brought us close. To that end, we can take comfort in the knowledge that our constitutional monarchy is working as intended and the mere threat of the use of the king's prerogative powers is enough to ensure the wider political system checks any blatant breaches of accepted constitutional principles.

ILLEGALITY

That said, we can turn to our first ground for dismissal under this category, which is for illegality or corruption. As the sovereign is the ultimate upholder of the law, it is accepted that the monarch cannot be advised to break the law and if they had to choose between doing so and keeping their Prime Minister, they should dismiss their adviser. This assertion, however, brings the monarch's role into direct conflict with two other well-established pillars of our constitutional settlement. The first is the principle of responsible government, which requires the head of state to act upon the advice of their ministers, who in turn have the confidence of the House of Commons. This principle ensures that any negative results which flow from that advice are for the ministers to bear, not the monarch, who will not be held personally accountable for their actions. As ministers are responsible to the people, it will be for them to judge the value of the government's behaviour at the polls. The second is that the rule of law not only requires the head of state to obey the law but also prevents them from knowingly taking part in or authorising the doing of any unlawful act. In so doing, this has the potential to clash with another constitutional principle, that of the separation of powers, which states that it is for the courts, not the head of state, to decide what is and is not legal.[1] An issue involving the monarch can occur, however, if the alleged infringement of the law is non-justiciable in nature, thus preventing the involvement of the courts.

The clash between these principles has created an area of extreme ambiguity around when the sovereign can and cannot act when presented with advice that may prove to be illegal, which often reflects the degree to which a particular commentator places a greater value on one principle over the other. Peter Hogg, for instance, discussing the issue in relation to Canada, has taken a very narrow view of the role illegality can play in the dismissal of a government. He asserts that it is for the courts alone to decide whether an issue is legal, thus emphasising the central importance of the separation of powers.[2] He goes as far as to suggest this is the case even when the sovereign is fully aware that the proposed act is against the law.[3] Although sympathetic to this line of reasoning, Patrick Monahan does not go as far as Hogg, as he feels that the issue is one for the courts except where 'a government persists with a course of action that has been declared unconstitutional or illegal by the courts'. He further says that if the government seeks the Governor-General's participation in an action that has been declared unconstitutional, he has the right to refuse to take part.[4]

The only exception open to the head of state in Monahan's argument is where there is both a breach of the rule of law and an attempt to enlist the aid of the monarch or their representative in the unlawful act. Outside of that one example, there is no discretion for independent action by the sovereign at all. Such views are still controversial and have been challenged by the likes of Eugene Forsey and R. MacGregor Dawson. Both have taken a far broader view of the monarch's responsibilities, arguing that when the government has been shown to be corrupt or consciously acting in an illegal manner, the monarch must act. They argue that in such situations, it is not only the right but the duty of the monarch to either intervene by dismissing the government directly or to try to engineer a situation in which either Parliament or the people can remove the government instead.[5]

When considering this issue in 1987, the advisory committee to the Australian Constitutional Commission concluded that the head of state may dismiss the Prime Minister for:

persisting in grossly unlawful or illegal conduct, including a serious breach of the Constitution ... or when the High Court has
declared the matter is not justiciable, and the Governor-General
believes that there is no other method available to prevent the
prime minister or the government engaging in such conduct.[6]

To govern their actions, the sovereign can request written advice
from their ministers on any issue they feel may require them to act
in an illegal manner, to assure themselves that the act requested is
presumed to be legal. If requested to provide such an assurance,
the government must comply or it risks exposing the fact that it is
indeed suggesting an illegal act to the monarch. The provision of
such advice has the effect of allowing the sovereign to accept the
proposed action in the certain knowledge that should the action
be found to be illegal later on, it was not because the government
failed to provide grounds at the time. In this way, the monarch
would be able to balance the two competing principles outlined
above whilst simultaneously leaving the courts free to determine
the legality of an issue at a later date. It is not enough, therefore, for
the sovereign to merely suspect that a requested act may be illegal.
To act, they must be certain that an act is illegal, hence the right
to request legal advice and the duty of the government to provide
it. This distinction has led Andrew Head to conclude, 'If the right
to dismiss a corrupt government does exist, it would appear that a
governor could consider removing a government only when it was
found to have committed acts of corruption or conflict of interest
whose facts have been clearly established.'[7]

Historical precedent would seem to support this proposition, as
we will go on to discuss.

Edward Prior

In British Columbia, in 1903, Premier Colonel Edward Prior became the subject of corruption allegations, which led to the government losing a vote of no confidence in the House. Looking to rely on his right to seek an election following his defeat in the House, Prior sought a dissolution of Parliament and an election from the Lieutenant Governor. As the Budget had not yet been passed, the Lieutenant Governor was unwilling to grant this request until the government had secured supply, thus ensuring revenue collection. Whilst this was being carried out, a parliamentary committee was simultaneously investigating the alleged corruption and subsequently discovered that Prior was implicated in corrupt practices for personal gain. Upon investigation, it emerged that the premier had been involved in the granting of major government contracts to his own hardware business. When confronted by this, Prior argued that there was nothing wrong with his own company competing for contracts from a government of which he was the head.[8] Finding such comments legally untenable, the Lieutenant Governor dismissed Prior and called on the Leader of the Opposition to form a government. Once supply had been secured, a dissolution was granted, paving the way for an election, which Prior lost.[9]

Sir Rodmond Roblin

A similar case occurred in Manitoba in 1915, when it emerged that the Conservative government of Sir Rodmond Roblin was involved in a corruption scandal over the contracts for the construction of a new legislative building. The government refused to allow Parliament to investigate the allegations and used its majority to block any attempts to force it to do so. The Lieutenant Governor placed pressure on Roblin to hold a royal commission to investigate the allegations, informing him that he would expect his resignation if he did not.[10] Roblin agreed and the inquiry began. It was to find that the builder who had won the contract had been overpaid by the amount of C$892,098 (approximately C$19,314,629 by today's value) in return for a considerable sum being donated to the Conservative Party.[11] The evidence was of such a magnitude that the government at once resigned rather than await the dismissal, which was widely expected to occur if they did not do so. Interestingly enough for followers of the Hogg and Monahan school of thought, in the trial that followed, the jury was unable to reach a verdict on whether the actions were corrupt or not and all charges were dropped, which just highlights the difficulty the courts can have in dealing with political cases of this nature.

Jack Lang

Surely the best example of how this rule operates occurred in New South Wales in 1932, when the Labor government led by Jack Lang was dismissed on the ground of illegality due to a conflict that arose between the state and the federal government over their financial response to the Great Depression. In 1927, a financial agreement had been reached by the Australian government and the states, which was formally enshrined in the Australian constitution in 1929. The federal government would assume a state's obligation to bondholders if they defaulted on their payments, in return for the federal government's ability to recoup the money from the state. In 1931, this occurred in New South Wales and the federal government duly stepped in to assume the debt. The issue quickly became a constitutional matter when the state government refused to repay the sums when requested, despite legal attempts by the Australian government to force them to do so.

Determined to recover the sums owed, the Australian Parliament passed a law allowing the federal government to seize the sums directly from New South Wales's state bank accounts instead. The state government responded by instructing state officials to remove all such sums from these accounts and deposit them instead in the state treasury, thereby moving the state's financial transactions to a cash-only basis. Once this transfer was complete, New South Wales challenged the validity of the federal law in the High Court but lost its case.[12]

In response, the Lang administration issued a government circular to all state public servants on 12 April 1932, instructing them to keep all monies received and not to deposit any sums in the bank. State officials immediately raised concerns with this, as they felt this request breached the State Audit Act that required all such money to be deposited in a bank. Concerned with this development, seven senior lawyers wrote to Governor Sir Philip Game, telling him that this circular gave him grounds for the dismissal of his premier. He could do so because:

the Governor normally is entitled to accept his Premier's statement of a legal position if it is fortified by a formal legal opinion, but he cannot disregard the law of the land when finally declared by the High Court, and it is his right, and, indeed, his duty, to refuse to be a party to the illegal actions of the Premier and to decline assent to any Order in Council which, in substance, is illegal. Moreover, he will be under an obligation of considering whether it is possible for him to leave Mr Lang the authority of the Premier's office in order to defy the law of the Constitution.[13]

Despite receiving this letter from such eminent members of the state's legal profession, the Governor remained unsure of his exact capacity to act in this situation and so sought advice from the Chief Justice of New South Wales and the Secretary of State for the Dominions in London. The advice that flowed from London informed him that in the Secretary of State's opinion:

> there is no constitutional requirement that he [the Governor] should intervene to question the illegality of acts in which he is not personally involved. In such cases the only legal authority which he could be called upon to recognise is that of the courts. It is not for the Governor to hold that Ministers are acting illegally until the courts have so declared. If the courts have pronounced on the matter (without possibility of further appeal) and Ministers still persist, it might be necessary for the Governor to take action.[14]

The Dominions Office went on to advise the Governor that he should obtain legal advice from the law officers that that state government's actions were indeed legal. If such advice was offered to him, he would be deemed to have acted properly and it would be for his ministers to bear responsibility if they were proved to be wrong.[15] If Lang persisted in his action but did not provide the requested advice, dismissal would be possible but only if he was confident a new ministry could be found to carry on the government. In light of this direction, Game duly requested legal advice regarding the government's actions, but Lang refused to provide it. Game, therefore, requested that Lang resign and, following his refusal, dismissed him.[16]

The Lang case highlights that a disagreement over a particular policy between the sovereign and their ministers is not grounds for dismissal, but illegality can be. In this case, the Governor asked for legal advice from the government, but he was not provided with it. In his conversations with Lang on the issue, the premier pointedly refused to confirm or deny that his actions were legal when asked to do so directly by the Governor. The issue was tried in court and the state government's actions were found to be illegal. There were thus several acts of illegality before and after the issue was tried by the courts and the premier refused to give the required legal advice to the Governor, leaving Game with no choice but to dismiss Lang.[17]

The position of the Governor in relation to the constitution at the time was outlined in the *New South Wales Yearbook* in 1931, and all subsequent editions until 1986: 'The general nature of his position is such that he is guardian of the constitution and is bound to see that the great powers with which he is entrusted are not used otherwise than in the public interest. In extreme cases his discretion constitutes a safeguard against malpractice.'[18] On this basis, the monarch and their representatives could dismiss their ministers for illegality.

Interestingly, the issue of illegality arose in the UK for the first time in modern British politics over Brexit. As discussed earlier, to secure the exit of the UK from the European Union by 31 October 2019, the Johnson government proposed proroguing or formally ending the current term of Parliament and delaying the calling of a new Parliament for a long enough duration to ensure that the UK formally left the EU, thereby preventing MPs who opposed the UK's withdrawal without an exit agreement from delaying the process. Seventy-five MPs and peers launched a legal challenge in the Scottish courts, asserting that the prorogation was illegal.[19] As events unfolded, the government did seek a prorogation for a more limited term of five weeks on 28 August, which in turn led to legal cases being filed in England, Scotland, Northern Ireland and, ultimately, in the UK Supreme Court. On 24 September, the Supreme Court ruled unanimously that the government's actions were indeed illegal and Parliament was still considered to be sitting. At this point, the government accepted the court's ruling, and the crisis died down, removing the threat of dismissal by the Queen that some saw as a potential result of the government's actions.[20]

The prorogation crisis had pushed the civil service to the very edge, raising the real possibility that the government could collapse. Helen MacNamara warned ministers and their advisers that the civil service's first duty was to uphold the rule of law and constitutionality. There had been a very real possibility that officials were going to stop obeying orders given by ministers. As one observer stated, 'Helen thought it could end up with the Prime Minister having to resign.'[21]

BREACH OF CONSTITUTIONAL PRINCIPLE

Our second ground for dismissal flows from the first and is based on a breach of a fundamental constitutional principle. Much like the grounds of illegality, this is also something that may or may not fall within the purview of the courts to decide. Only if the action was found to be non-justiciable would the head of state have the ability to intervene.[22] Areas that could fall under this scope would be an attempt by the Prime Minister to undermine the system of democratic oversight, an attempt to negatively interfere with responsible government or an attempt to interfere with the rule of law in such a way that the damage could not be remedied in the courts.[23] Should this situation arise, there is an argument to be made that the monarch could dismiss the premier in response. In their study of the British constitution, Stanley de Smith and Rodney Brazier have argued that the Queen would be 'justified in dismissing her Ministers if they were purporting to subvert the democratic basis of the constitution – for example, by prolonging the life of a Parliament in order to avoid defeat in a General Election, or by obtaining an electoral majority through duress or fraudulent manipulation of the polls'.[24]

As the basis for royal intervention under these circumstances is the principle that the monarch is the guardian of the constitution, the alleged breach would have to be of such a significant and serious nature that there was widespread concern amongst the political class and public and intervention was required. In times of war, for instance, the constitutional foundations of our system have been suspended, with no obvious objections or calls for the monarch to dismiss the government. Nor can it be said that a proposed constitutional reform that is opposed by some but promoted by others could trigger this intervention.

So long as the political process is working within its normal framework, no grounds for a fundamental breach of constitutional principle can be raised. What would be needed would be a breakdown of the system caused by the systematic actions of a government determined to remove themselves from the limitations placed on them by the day-to-day constitutional order. If, for instance, a political party was able to win an election and assume power in the UK but then set about pursuing policies that were designed to perpetuate their power permanently and so establish a dictatorship, this grounds for dismissal would become viable. The government's actions in that instance would be classed as a breach of the constitution, enabling the intervention of the monarch, because the party's control of Parliament would enable the government to legalise their actions through legislation, thus preventing judicial oversight and so removing the ability of citizens to seek legal redress for the government's actions in the courts.

South Africa

This is, of course, an extreme case and luckily there are virtually no examples of such a situation happening within the UK or the other primary Commonwealth realms, although the same cannot be said for some Commonwealth republics. One of the closest examples would have to be the case of South Africa in the aftermath of the Second World War, when the government sought to implement the policy of apartheid and so fundamentally alter South Africa's constitutional framework to the benefit of the party in power. Before this could become an issue, however, the South African government moved to replace the monarchy with a republic and thus remove the Queen's oversight of the constitution in 1961. They did this because members of the government had become concerned that the monarch, and by extension the British Privy Council, which at that time acted as South Africa's Supreme Court, might seek to challenge the legality of the discriminatory laws within South Africa. The South African Cabinet was aware that royal assent could be withheld by the Governor-General under section 64 of the South Africa Act 1909 and wished to prevent such an event from occurring. Proposed laws that sought to disadvantage the black African population were capable of being reserved for the Queen's direct consent, which in practice meant the British government, and the South African government did not feel that such consent would be forthcoming, given the divergent views on race relations between the two governments.[25]

This suspicion was engendered by the speech Harold Macmillan had given to the South African Parliament in February 1960, in which he appeared to be critical of the apartheid policies of the South African government. This speech was widely seen in South Africa as instigating the Sharpeville riots that rocked the country a few weeks later.[26] Fearing both an internal political rising amongst the black population and external interference from the Queen and the British government, the South African government held a referendum under a new franchise system for the creation of a republic on 5 October 1960.

As strange as it may seem to us now in light of subsequent South African history, the African majority sought to keep the monarchy in South Africa precisely because it was known to be a barrier to the Afrikaner nationalists' agenda of full racial segregation and white political dominance. Had the monarchy continued in South Africa after 1961, it is extremely likely that the pressure on the monarch to directly intervene in the political affairs of South Africa would have grown to such a point that the Queen would have struggled to ignore it.[27] An echo of this can be seen by the fact that the Queen and Thatcher were to clash over the UK government's policy towards South Africa in the 1980s, with the Queen displaying her sympathies for the black African population. How much worse would such a crisis have been had she still been Queen of South Africa?[28]

Rhodesia

This neatly brings us on to the primary case where this ground has been used to dismiss a government. Rhodesia was a self-governing British colony until 1965, when the Rhodesian government under Ian Smith made a Unilateral Declaration of Independence (UDI) on 11 November following failed talks with the British government over the colony's future status.* This decision was not a sudden one and discussions had been ongoing between the Rhodesian capital, Salisbury, and Whitehall for some time. Considerable attention had been given by both sides to the role the Queen, and by extension the Governor of Rhodesia, Sir Humphrey Gibbs, would play should a UDI be declared. Fearing an illegal act was imminent, Prime Minister Alec Douglas-Home had written to Gibbs in 1964 to outline the constitutional position of the Governor, as the British government saw it, following a request from the Governor for such advice in the event of a UDI being announced. In that letter, he outlined:

> I consider that you, as Governor, would be justified in taking any measures which are open to you to secure respect for the Constitution of which you are the ultimate guardian. If, in that eventuality, you decide to dismiss your Ministers or dissolve the Legislature, on the grounds that they were infringing the Constitution, you could count on the full public backing of the British Government. In the exceptional situation which you envisage, we would regard ourselves as free to take whatever legislative or executive steps might be necessary to validate your actions.[29]

Confident that he now had the full support of the British government for any decisions he subsequently made, the Governor, with the assistance of Chief Justice of Rhodesia Sir Hugh Beadle, prepared a statement in June 1964 saying that in the event of a UDI, ministers would have forfeited their offices due to their unconstitutional actions.[30] This concept of forfeiture, however, was not

---

* Southern Rhodesia's name was shortened to simply Rhodesia in 1964 after Northern Rhodesia gained its independence as the new nation, Zambia.

considered appropriate by the Commonwealth Relations Office, which sought further legal advice from the crown law officers. Their opinion was that there were only two ways in which a ministry could be terminated and that was by either the resignation or dismissal of the Prime Minister. They asserted that should a UDI take place, the Governor, with the consent of the Queen, should dismiss his Prime Minister and government directly.[31]

This advice was then duly transmitted to Gibbs but was immediately challenged upon receipt by Sir Hugh Beadle, who argued that section 43 of the Rhodesian constitution only applied to the Governor's power of appointment of ministers and was silent as to whether the Governor had the power to dismiss them as well. Unlike other Commonwealth judges when faced with a similar issue, Beadle did not look to import accepted British constitutional practice into the scope of the Rhodesian constitution. Instead, he asserted a more complicated maxim that ministers would be legally considered to have resigned their offices by their illegal actions because they could not on the one hand claim to renounce the constitution whilst on the other retaining office under it.[32]

British officers were unimpressed by this argument. They claimed it was a new ground in law and that a declaration of independence did not necessarily mean the renunciation of the whole constitution. Whilst accepting that some doubt existed as to the power of the Governor to dismiss the government, they were clear that the Queen did have the authority to dismiss and so could validate the Governor's actions. For this to happen, however, the dismissal would have to be issued immediately after a UDI as it could not be retrospective.[33] British officials were also strongly of the view that new ministers would need to be appointed at once after the dismissal. This would ensure that a government was in position to countermand the orders of Smith and his colleagues, provide direction to the security forces and civil servants and advise the Governor. This would require the Leader of the Opposition to be notified shortly before the dismissal took place to secure his agreement to assume office.[34]

As a result of these deliberations, a plan was devised to cover the eventuality of a UDI taking place by October 1964. The Queen would approve the dismissal of Smith and his government, effective immediately following the Governor's decision to dismiss. The Governor would then appoint and swear in a new Prime Minister to avoid any power vacuum in the government or confusion by officials about who was in charge. The new Prime Minister would order the arrest of Smith, which would provide a crucial test of loyalty to the police and army.[35] In so doing, it would be made clear that the power to dismiss had come directly from the Queen and was being exercised on the ground by the Governor in her name.

At midday on 11 November 1965, this plan would be formally tested. Smith met with the Governor and informed him he would be declaring the UDI during his broadcast to the nation at 1.15 p.m. Gibbs responded by saying that this announcement 'would be an illegal and immoral act for which he had no mandate from the people'.[36] He asked Smith to reconsider his actions, but as the proclamation had already been signed by Smith and the Cabinet that morning, Smith refused the request, leaving Gibbs with no other choice but to dismiss him in the Queen's name. A copy of the message from the British High Commission confirming this was then handed to Smith. Undeterred by the Governor's actions, Smith continued to make his broadcast to the nation, announcing the UDI as planned. And this is when things started to go wrong from London's point of view, for Gibbs, for some unknown reason, had failed to appoint a new Prime Minister following his meeting with Smith, thus preventing the establishment of an alternative government that could countermand the actions of the recently dismissed Smith administration.

Unsurprisingly under the circumstances, the existing government did not recognise or accept its dismissal and argued that such a dismissal would have needed to be given directly by the Queen, not the British High Commissioner. As such, it continued to operate as the de facto government and was supported by the police, armed forces, civil service and judiciary as there was no effective alternative within the country.[37] Unbeknownst to the public at the time, it later emerged in 1990 that prior to Smith's dismissal and broadcast to the nation but after the government had signed the declaration of independence, four senior army officers arrived at Government House stating that they were ready to execute warrants for the arrest of Smith and his colleagues as rebels against the crown.

Taken aback by the offer, Gibbs refused to issue the warrants in contravention of the agreed plan of action and so no military action was taken against the Smith government. As an interesting aside into how a Prime Minister uses their memoirs to selectively tell the tale they wish to tell, Ian Smith categorically denies that Gibbs dismissed him from office but states that it was in fact Gibbs who said he would resign. He argues he was never a rebel at all but remained a lawful Prime Minister until he left office in 1979.[38]

This failure to appoint another government was a strategic mistake that greatly hampered Britain's ability to deal with the UDI at the time and was itself a constitutional breach that undermined the justification for the dismissal of the Smith government on the grounds of violation of the constitution. As Eugene Forsey states:

> The Crown cannot act without the advice of Ministers. If it refuses the advice of Ministers in office and they refuse to back down, it must find other Ministers who will take responsibility for the refusal; and the new Ministers must secure the support of either the existing Parliament or of the new Parliament.[39]

This story is tantalising, as things may have gone very differently in Rhodesia in 1965 if Gibbs had followed through with the agreed plan of action.[40] Had Gibbs dismissed Smith and appointed the Leader of the Opposition as a caretaker Prime Minister pledged to prevent a UDI and hold an election, the civil service would have found it difficult to follow the orders of a government that was known to have been dismissed by the Queen, the judiciary would have been freed to challenge any actions a Smith administration would have taken and the security forces would have been compelled to act to uphold the rule of law. What all of this shows is that whilst the monarch does have the power, in certain circumstances, to dismiss a Prime Minister for a breach of a constitutional principle, they can only do so in a way that is in line with the constitution they are looking to uphold.

LOSS OF AN ELECTORAL MANDATE

Our third ground for dismissal is the failure of the Prime Minister to resign if they have clearly lost the support of the people, following an election in which an opposition party or coalition of parties has emerged with a majority in the new House of Commons, thus showing that they no longer have a mandate from the people to govern. It is an accepted constitutional principle that the legitimacy of a government is based on the support of a majority of the people who have voted in an election. This is the democratic foundation on which our modern political system is based and any attempt to change that would be seen as unconstitutional. As a result, where an incumbent party has lost an election and an opposition party or coalition of parties has won a majority at that election, there is an obligation on the Prime Minister to resign. If they should fail to do so, the circumstances may warrant a dismissal. As Andrew Head observes in relation to the Canadian position, based on British constitutional practice, 'virtually all constitutional authorities appear to allow that a governor may dismiss a government with propriety ... if an opposition party has won a majority in an election and the existing government refuses to resign'.[41]

The principle is so deeply embedded in our political system that it is difficult to find any examples of its breach in a British, Australian, Canadian or New Zealand context. So fundamental is this assumption to our constitutional framework that the Canadian Supreme Court states:

> If after a general election where the opposition obtained the majority at the polls the government refused to resign and clung to office, it would thereby commit a fundamental breach of convention, one so serious that it could be regarded as tantamount to a *coup d'état*. The remedy in this case would lie with the Governor General or the Lieutenant Governor as the case might be who would be justified in dismissing the ministry and in calling the opposition to form the government.[42]

As this judgment clearly indicates, should such an event occur, the only solution could be found in the dismissal of the ministry by the monarch or their agent using the prerogative powers of the crown.[43]

This power would not, however, be used in the first instance, as constitutional precedent allows the government the opportunity to test its support in the Commons. We must remember that it is the House of Commons that makes and unmakes governments, not the people per se. It was the certain expectation of defeat in the Commons following the loss of an election that motivated Disraeli to resign in 1880 before the new House met, thus setting a precedent that is followed to this day.[44] As such, it is a matter for the House of Commons alone, rather than the head of state, to decide where confidence lies, but once that determination has been made, there is a duty on the monarch to observe the decision through the appointment of a Prime Minister who reflects that consensus.

The Golden Rule continues to define how the crown would act in this instance. The dual test will apply at all times and it will be for the Prime Minister of the day to demonstrate that they can continue to meet its requirements. An electorally defeated government can always seek to meet the new Commons and attempt to establish itself by passing a legislative programme and a Budget, just as Stanley Baldwin sought to do in 1923 when he lost his majority in the election of that year. It was only when he was subsequently defeated in the Chamber following the King's Speech that he resigned in MacDonald's favour, as it was clear he could no longer command the confidence of the Commons.[45]

If an election should prove to be inconclusive in the way that it did in February 1974, or indeed in 2010 and 2017, with no party winning an outright majority, an incumbent premier is entitled, and some may say obliged, to stay in office until Parliament has determined where confidence lies.[46] The existence of passive confidence does allow for a minority government to continue to govern despite having no majority. In such a case, the Prime Minister would continue in office as head of a caretaker government ensuring that no controversial actions are taken before Parliament has been re-called. For this reason, a Prime Minister who has lost an election has a right to meet the new House of Commons and try to pass a King's Speech before resigning if they feel that they are still able to govern. Should the sovereign refuse to let the incumbent Prime Minister face Parliament after an inconclusive election and instead dismisses them, replacing them with a new premier, they run the risk of criticism and allegations of political interference.[47] Should the government lose a confidence vote in the Commons but still refuse to resign, then a constitutional crisis might occur. It would initially be for the political parties themselves to try to resolve this situation, but should they fail to do so, the monarch may have to become involved and advise the Prime Minister to resign or face dismissal.

A historic example of this process occurred in British Columbia in 1898, following an election that produced a tie between the in-cumbent ministry and the opposition. The Lieutenant Governor, Thomas McInnes, took the view that the government had lost the election and informed the premier, John Turner, that he would no longer accept his advice with regards to appointments and expend-iture.[48] McInnes felt that the premier should have resigned as a consequence, but he simply carried on. Frustrated by this response, McInnes then dismissed Turner from office, without allowing him the opportunity to face the House and without a formal vote of the legislature to show its loss of confidence in the government. Turner countered by arguing he had a right to face Parliament before he was dismissed. McInnes rejected the validity of such arguments and, following considerable criticism of his actions, proceeded to appoint Leader of the Opposition Charles Semlin as premier. The end result was that the Lieutenant Governor was found to have lost the support of all political parties and when he clashed with the legislature again in 1900, he was removed from office, making him the only Lieutenant Governor to be dismissed in this way in the history of British Columbia.[49]

Notwithstanding this solitary example, the convention that a Prime Minister should resign following an election defeat is so well established a rule in the UK that it has not been ignored by any British government since Disraeli inaugurated the principle of immediate resignation in 1880 – save for inconclusive election results such as those in 1923, February 1974, 2010 and 2017. It is therefore highly unlikely that political parties would breach this convention and so compel a royal intervention.

LOSS OF POPULAR SUPPORT

The fourth ground for dismissal to consider is when the government is out of step with the people. The notion that the head of state could dismiss the government because it no longer holds the support of the electorate can be traced back to Albert Dicey at the turn of the twentieth century.[50] In his work on the constitution, Dicey said that the king would be justified in dismissing his Prime Minister if the government were found to be out of step with the wishes of the people, so long as the dismissal led to an election. The government was entitled to get its own way so long as it was the true representative of the people's will. In this way, the legal sovereign could force the government to appeal to the political sovereign in a controversial matter or else dismiss them and send for someone who would recommend an election.[51]

This view has been criticised by both H. V. Evatt and Sir Ivor Jennings, as it would place the monarch in an impossible position

THE KING AND CONSTITUTIONAL PRINCIPLES

of being able to determine the true public mood at any one time and deciding whether to dismiss their government or not.[52] Lord Hailsham, speaking as a former Lord Chancellor, also rejected this ground for dismissal, stating:

> Dicey's original view that the Crown is in some way an arbiter of the public opinion so as to put it in a position to force a dissolution after making a judgement concerning the popularity or unpopularity of a Government has long been rightly, and I think, universally, discredited. This would be a prescription for bringing the Crown directly into party politics … The Crown is the trustee of the constitution and not the arbiter of public opinion.[53]

Dismissal on these grounds is now considered by most authorities to no longer be justified by modern constitutional principles. Regular elections based on universal suffrage are seen as offering a more effective way of determining the will of the people, whilst ensuring the removal of the sovereign from the political realm.[54] In more recent times, this ground for dismissal has instead been used as a factor that should be considered when the head of state is contemplating the dismissal of a government on other grounds. In deciding on whether or not to intervene and dismiss a ministry, the monarch should only do so if they are confident that in any ensuing election, the government will be defeated. Should the government win the election, the monarch faces the prospect of being removed from office and the monarchy being significantly damaged.[55] This relies on dismissal being followed by an immediate election to determine the views of the people, who will show through their actions at the ballot box whether they support the monarch's decision. Given this, such an act could only be contemplated in the most extreme political crisis and could only be justified by reference to a defence of accepted constitutional norms.

The argument that the monarch has a duty to dismiss their Prime Minister if it was shown that the government was out of step with the people was used only once in the UK, during the passage of the Home Rule Bill in 1913. Invaluable sources exist that outline the arguments used and the points of view expressed between the King and Prime Minister during this crisis, which is extremely helpful to the student of constitutional practice. The debate between the two men began following the actions of the Unionist peers on 9 July 1913. During the second reading of the bill in the House of Lords, Lord Lansdowne put forward an amendment that stated 'this House declines to proceed with consideration of the Bill until it has been submitted to the judgement of the country' in an attempt to use the blockage of the bill in the Lords to trigger an election.[56] The Unionist opposition felt so strongly that the bill threatened the very fabric of the British state that any and all means of preventing it were justified. The Home Rule Bill had evoked strong opinions in the country at large and was threatening to lead to a civil war in Ireland that might well spill over into the rest of the kingdom. The possibility so worried the King that he met with Lansdowne at Balmoral to understand the Unionist position. George V outlined the advice that he had received from his ministers, which Lansdowne relayed: 'As a Constitutional Sovereign it would be impossible for him to disregard the advice of his Ministers, and that, whatever happened, His Majesty's position would be "unassailable" so long as he followed that advice.'[57]

Despite this assurance from his government, the King was concerned that passage of the bill could lead to bloodshed and would require the employment of troops to impose it on an unwilling populous. Sensing the King's concern that he wished to act constitutionally but was troubled by the government's policy, Lansdowne countered the government's advice by questioning its logic, as it all depended on the circumstances and whether or not the government had the support of the people. He argued, 'What are the circumstances of the case? It is doubtful whether any mandate for Home Rule has been given by the electors; they certainly had given no mandate for the Bill now before Parliament.'[58]

Lansdowne conceded that it was difficult for an election to focus on just one issue, as the Liberals had argued, but a referendum would solve this issue by placing one issue before the people and would remove all opposition if the government won the vote.[59]

Accepting the logic of this statement, the King wrote to the Prime Minister to set out his concerns and to seek further advice as to how he should proceed in light of them. Aware that the King was now wavering in his support for the government, Asquith sought to allay royal fears. His response, in September 1913, argued:

> We have now a well-established tradition of 200 years, that, in the last resort, the occupant of the Throne accepts and acts upon the advice of his ministers. The Sovereign may have lost something of his personal power and authority, but the Crown has been thereby removed from the storms and vicissitudes of party politics, and the Monarchy rests upon a solid foundation which is buttressed both by long tradition and by the general conviction that its personal status is an invaluable safeguard for the continuity of our national life.[60]

Asquith went on to point out that the monarch's rights and duties

ON HIS MAJESTY'S SERVICE

are now confined and circumscribed by convention to the ability to consult and be consulted, to advise and to warn, but in all other matters he must accept the advice of his ministers when it is presented. If he does not accept that advice, Asquith said:

> The Sovereign undoubtedly has the power of changing his advisers, but it is relevant to point out that there has been, during the last 130 years, one occasion only in which the King has dismissed the Ministry which still possessed the confidence of the House of Commons … Nothing can be more important, in the best interests of the Crown and of the country, than that a practice, so long established and so well justified by experience, should remain unimpaired. It frees the occupant of the Throne from all personal responsibility for the acts of the Executive and the Legislature. It gives force and meaning to the old maxim that 'the king can do no wrong.' So long as it prevails, however objectionable particular Acts may be to a large section of his subjects, they cannot hold him in anyway accountable. If, on the other hand, the King were to intervene on one side, or in one case – which he could only do by dismissing ministers in *de facto* possession of a Parliamentary majority – he would be expected to do the same on another occasion, and perhaps for the other side … He would, whether he wished it or not, be dragged into the areas of party politics … This is the constitutional catastrophe which it is the duty of every wise statesman to do the utmost in his power to avert.[61]

Although this cogent letter set out a rational and accurate view of the developments of the conventions that bound king and Prime Minister together, Asquith's letter did not fully convince the King that he had a duty to stand by and watch the kingdom be split apart, as he was also aware that he was the ultimate guardian of domestic tranquillity. This led the King to reply to Asquith and question the premise of his overall argument, saying:

> While you admit the Sovereign's undoubted power to change his advisers, I infer that you regard the exercise of that power as inexpedient and indeed dangerous. Should the Sovereign never exercise that right, not even, to quote Sir Erskine May, 'in the interests of the State and on grounds which could be justified to Parliament'?[62]

Taking advantage of his undoubted right to consult, the King sought to push his case further with Asquith in person, expressing his own views during an audience in February 1914. Asquith recounts the conversation:

> The King replied that, although constitutionally he might not be responsible, still he could not allow bloodshed among loyal subjects in any part of his Dominions without exerting every means in his power to avert it. Although at the present stage of proceedings he could not rightly intervene, he should feel it his duty to do what in his own judgement was best for his people generally.[63]

Asquith replied that such action on the part of the King would be politically dangerous for the monarchy.

What is most interesting to our contemporary eyes about this exchange is that neither correspondent doubted the existence of the monarch's power of dismissal in this case, unlike modern political commentators. Lord Esher, a close confidant of the King, put his finger on the heart of the matter when he highlighted that although the King had the power to dismiss his Prime Minister, he did not have the power to dictate government policy.[64] As it was more a change of policy than a change of government the King looked for, he in the end let the matter drop. Eventually, following the compromise that led to Home Rule being established in the south of Ireland but the counties of Ulster being excluded from the territory of the new Irish Parliament, he accepted the government's view and assented to the bill, ending the crisis.

The correspondence between monarch and premier offers a fascinating insight into the central working of the constitution. Although Asquith's advice is essentially correct, we must keep in mind that the King's right to dismiss was accepted. We should also note that the central tenet of the Unionist argument – that the King can and must dismiss his government, even if it has the support of a majority in the House, if it does not have the approval of the people – has never been answered. However, in truth, this argument was made by the Unionists to justify a dissolution and election rather than the dismissal of a government.

If the monarch believes that the government has lost the support of the majority of the people and the matter is of significant public interest and constitutional significance, it seems they can insist upon either a dissolution or referendum. If the government refuses this royal advice, they can either resign or face dismissal. Seen in this way, dismissal on this particular ground is very similar to the grounds of illegality and constitutional principle we have considered in this chapter. This would accord with the proper constitutional function of the monarch, which is to ensure the constitution is upheld. The monarch has the right and duty to refuse to assent to any policy that subverts the democratic basis of the constitution or engenders systemic and permanent change to the political system that could not be overturned at a later date. George V understood that Irish Home Rule was just such a change, as it would transform the constitutional framework of the kingdom, but acceded to the government's policy following the acceptance of a political compromise that led to partition.[65]

Brexit raised this as an issue once again, with the debate pitting the people against Parliament. Would the Queen have been justified in dismissing her Prime Minister to prevent Brexit, as some suggested?[66] The answer is no. Two acts of democratic accountability underpinned the Brexit process before Boris Johnson became Prime Minister – a referendum in 2016 and an election in 2017. In both cases, the majority of people supported Brexit and the government's actions. The 2019 general election returned the government with a large majority and showed that the policy of Brexit had the support of the people, even if that support was not uniform across the nations.

What would the situation have been, however, if the people, having voted to leave the European Union, were faced by a Parliament and government that refused to carry out the policy they had voted for? Should such a situation arise, would the monarch be justified in intervening by dismissing the Prime Minister? The answer is, in my opinion, no. So long as regular elections are held, there is no reason for the monarch to become involved, as the issue will resolve itself at the polls. Should a government seek to prevent itself being challenged at an election, the issue may become more relevant, but until it does there are no grounds for intervention. Should the monarch ever look to dismiss a government for this reason, they would need to be certain that the people would support them, else they may find themselves faced with a government who continues to have a majority in the House but no longer trusts the sovereign to be impartial. This could potentially lead to either the abdication of the incumbent at best or the abolition of the monarchy itself at worst.

INCAPACITY

The final ground for dismissal that we need to consider is incapacity, meaning a situation in which the Prime Minister is no longer able to perform their functions but lacks the ability to resign. This may happen due to an illness that incapacitates the Prime Minister to the degree that they are prevented from functioning. As we have seen, Churchill suffered a stroke in 1953, from which he fortuitously recovered. However, let us imagine that it had left him paralysed to the point that he could no longer communicate. In this state, he clearly could not continue as Prime Minister but nor could he offer his resignation and allow a new premier to be appointed. In such a situation, the monarch is the only one who can dismiss the Prime Minister and appoint a successor. For them to act, the monarch would need to be advised, most likely by the Cabinet, that the Prime Minister could no longer perform their duties and so should be dismissed. As we have seen, the sovereign must have a principal adviser, and if the current Prime Minister is no longer able to perform this function, the monarch, following medical and political advice, would be justified in dismissing them from office.

The potential for this power to be used arose in April 2020, when Boris Johnson was admitted to hospital suffering from Covid-19. Although Johnson recovered from his illness, it is clear from subsequent reports that he came remarkably close to death.[67] Let us suppose that Johnson had fallen into a coma as a result of his illness, which was also a highly likely outcome at the time. In this state, he would have been unable to perform his duties and his recovery would have been doubtful, which would create a dilemma for the government. He would clearly have lacked the physical ability to resign as either Prime Minister or leader of his party, but without a vacancy no new appointment could be made. It would have fallen to the Queen, acting on the advice of the Cabinet, to formally dismiss Johnson and appoint a new premier who could lead the government.

Far from being a theoretical question, this possibility came very close to being a reality. On 6 April 2020, the Cabinet was informed that Johnson had a 50-50 chance of surviving his bout of Covid-19 and plans would have to be made for any imminent succession to the premiership. Mark Sedwill, the Cabinet Secretary, was given the task of drafting these proposals, which give us an insight into just how important the prerogative power can be in a time of crisis. There were two scenarios that needed to be planned for. The first dealt with a situation in which Johnson was placed on a ventilator and thus rendered incapable of making decisions. In this scenario, the Cabinet would have been asked to recommend a stand-in Prime Minister for the duration of his absence. A draft letter to this effect was created and Dominic Raab was identified as the man who would be recommended. The Queen was briefed and the machinery was put in place to manage the transition.

The second scenario covered the eventuality of Johnson falling into a coma or dying. Either situation would instantly deprive the Queen of a Prime Minister, creating a vacancy that would need to be immediately filled. As it would take time for the Conservative Party to elect a new leader, an interim Prime Minister would need to be appointed. The palace was uncertain of how to proceed in this eventuality, as the spectre of 1963 coloured their perception. There could be no repeat of the controversy of the Home appointment and so politicians would have to resolve this situation without royal involvement. The Cabinet was informed they would be required to formally vote for a successor, who the Queen would duly appoint on the understanding they would resign once a new Conservative leader was in place.[68]

What is striking about this proposal was that in the hopes of avoiding the situation that occurred in 1963, the palace accepted a return to the process used to select Macmillan in 1957 – a process that was also viewed as flawed by some. Since these events, speculation has emerged that Raab would have been selected as interim Prime Minister had such a vote taken place, but this presupposes that Raab would have had no interest in seeking the leadership himself. It would be essential that the interim Prime Minister would not use their appointment to sway the internal party election. It is not beyond the bounds of probability, however, to imagine a situation where the various factions within a Cabinet might seek to manipulate the outcome of a forthcoming leadership contest by removing a candidate they were opposed to. We do not know if Raab would have accepted office under these conditions or whether any other acceptable candidate capable of securing the Cabinet's support would have emerged. What is clear, however, is that the Queen would have needed to formally dismiss Johnson to create a vacancy and then would have used her power of appointment to install a successor within hours. So, as we can see, this power is far from an irrelevance to our modern political environment, and with the increasing age of our political leaders, this may become an issue that future generations will need to deal with.

The power of dismissal undoubtedly exists, but by its very nature it highlights the binary and symbiotic relationship between the monarch and the Prime Minister. To put this into modern parlance, the King's role is not to govern – that is the Prime Minister's job, supported by the Cabinet – but it is his task to ensure that proper governance is carried out. Indeed, he took an oath to do just that at his coronation, when he swore to govern the people of his realms according to their respective laws and customs. This proper functioning of the crown can only be carried out if there is an atmosphere of total trust and respect between the head of state and the head of government. The two institutions work best when they support and trust each other, neither placing the other in a position of constitutional embarrassment.

For this reason, if the power to dismiss was ever seriously contemplated in the UK, it would be the responsibility of the monarch to warn the Prime Minister that such action may be taken. This would allow the Prime Minister the possibility of resolving the situation within the bounds of constitutional practice and without royal involvement – the lasting lesson of Sir John Kerr's actions in 1975. It is for this reason that the use of the power to dismiss can only ever be seen as a last resort, when all other options have been explored and action is required to preserve the constitutional framework of the country. The monarch is the guardian of the constitution and has a right and a duty to act in its defence and preservation but only when all other political and constitutional mechanisms have been exhausted.

PART IV

THE PREROGATIVES OF DISSOLUTION AND ASSENT

10

THE KING'S DISCRETION

We shall now turn our attention to the dissolution of Parliament, which remains another important royal prerogative. It has always been an ancient prerogative of the crown that our kings can summon, prorogue and dissolve Parliaments, but unlike the prerogatives discussed in the previous chapters, this is a power that has been steadily constrained by statutory limits over the centuries. To understand why that should be the case, we need to travel back in time to the turbulent reign of Charles I, when Crown and Parliament found themselves in conflict. You may recall that when confronted by the expansion of the state in the sixteenth century, the Tudor monarchs sought to use their prerogative powers to fill the gap. Working through their council of state, the monarch took on aspects of legislative and judicial functions to aid their administration. At first this was with the acceptance of Parliament, but under the Stuarts, things began to change.

Seeking to promote their divine right to rule, the early Stuart monarchs tried to govern, as far as possible, without the inconvenience of having to call and rely on Parliament, something that did not go unnoticed by their subjects. We can look to Charles I's reign to see this process in action. His first parliament was summoned in May and dissolved in August 1625; the second, called in February 1626, was dissolved in June without passing a single statute; and the third met from March to June 1628 and then again from January to March 1629. It is to this august assembly that we owe the Petition of Right, which directly challenged the King's ability to tax without parliamentary consent. Outraged by this interference in his affairs, Charles refused to summon another parliament for eleven years and was only compelled to do so because England and Scotland were at war. Confronted once again by a Parliament that would not grant him money without a limit on his power, Charles dismissed it a month later.[1]

This was an act that would prove to be his undoing. Charles showed himself incapable of preventing the Scottish invasion of England in the summer of 1640. Royal chickens were coming home to roost, as inadequate financial resources and an overdependence on unpaid administrators highlighted the weakness of the consular system. Looking to avert the inevitable defeat, Charles summoned a *magnum concilium*, or great council of peers, in York. This was a historic event, as the council had last been summoned at the end of the fifteenth century and would never be summoned again. This attempt to split the peers from the Commons proved fatal, as the peers merely recommended that the King summon Parliament.[2] Left with no alternative, Charles duly summoned Parliament in November 1640, an event which would prove seminal for the development of our constitutional settlement.

Know to history as the Long Parliament, this body would remain in some form until 1660, when it was at last declared dissolved by the Convention Parliament. It would be this Parliament that would ultimately challenge the King's authority and, in so doing, incite the English Civil War in 1642.

From the start, the King's opponents occupied a strong position. To end the Scottish occupation of the north of England, Charles had signed the Treaty of Ripon. The treaty bound him to two monthly payments of £25,000, which the Scots expected Parliament to guarantee.[3] Reform was thus in the air and Charles was compelled to accept changes. The most important of these, in light of our discussion, was his acceptance of the Triennial Act 1641, which required Parliament to meet for at least a fifty-day session once every three years. This measure aimed to prevent any kings from ruling without Parliament, as Charles had done between 1629 and 1640. Should the King fail in his duty to summon Parliament every three years, the Act required that the Lord Chancellor issue the writs instead or, failing that, the House of Lords could assemble and issue writs for the election of the House of Commons.[4] This Act proved to be a considerable limitation on the King's power to summon and dissolve parliaments and was a step on the road to Parliament becoming a permanent institution; yet MPs were still concerned that the King could not be trusted to honour his commitments. So they went further and passed another Act that made the dissolution of Parliament conditional upon their assent. In this way, Parliament had provided the means by which it could continue to exist for as long as it wished.[5]

This was a situation that proved to be counterproductive for good government, as the House of Commons steadily removed it rivals by abolishing the monarchy and then the House of Lords over the next few years. These were actions that proved to many that tyranny did not just flow from the actions of over-mighty kings but could originate in Parliament itself. This realisation ensured that when the Convention Parliament invited Charles II to assume the throne, it was with the widely held acceptance that the royal prerogative of dissolution should be restored to balance the constitution. To ensure this, Parliament passed a second Triennial Act in 1664 that made the summoning and duration of Parliament a matter of royal discretion alone, thus buttressing the prerogative with statutory authority.[6] As a result, Charles was able to rule for the last four years of his reign free from the encumbrance of Parliament.

The constitutional settlement that was laid down by the Glorious Revolution of 1688 was contained primarily in the Bill of Rights 1689, the Act of Settlement 1701 and a further Triennial Act 1694. This last Act once more sought to set limits on the royal power of dissolution by requiring the king to summon Parliament annually and to hold elections every three years. In so doing, it ensured that parliamentary business was transacted throughout the year and the institution gained a permanence that it had failed to enjoy until this point, something that was to prove invaluable to the development of parliamentary government in the years ahead.[7] Very quickly, Parliament's leading men were able to compel their appointment to office through their mastery of the Commons, thus creating the link between the executive and legislature that lies at the heart of our system today.

The need for elections every three years coupled with the right of the government to seek a dissolution at any time ensured that the country was gripped by perpetual electioneering, with ten elections being held in the next twenty years. This elevated level of political volatility not only made it far more difficult to establish a cohesive block of supporters for the government but also raised the cost of standing for election, which many now found to be ruinous. The political managers therefore decided to pass a Septennial Act in 1715, which stipulated elections should be held every seven years, rather than three, and correspondingly increased the value of seats in the Commons in the process. From now on, governments and MPs could rely on a degree of certainty as to their positions and plan accordingly, a blessed situation that would last for the next 200 years.[8]

The next great milestone came with the passage of the transformative Great Reform Act and the Scottish and Irish Reform Acts, its sister legislation, in 1832. Prior to the passage of these Acts, the monarch, nobles and large land holders had been able to exert tremendous influence over elections due to the system being designed to support property and mercantile interests.[9] The Acts amended this system by redistributing parliamentary seats (reducing the ability of the upper class to influence an election's outcome in the process), expanding the franchise from 4 to 20 per cent of the male population in England and stimulating the growth of electoral organisations that could canvass these new voters.[10] This facilitated the two rising forces of nineteenth-century politics: the expansion of the franchise and the development of organised parties. Between them, these had a profound effect on the direct use of power by the sovereign.[11]

In 1834, the first test of the new system came about. William IV dismissed Lord Melbourne, who still enjoyed the support of a majority in the Commons, and asked Robert Peel to form a minority government instead. From the start, Peel's government was dependent on the support of the Whigs to pass legislation and as a result it did not last long, falling to a vote of no confidence in April 1835.[12] This would mark a watershed moment in British constitutional development, being the last occasion when a monarch would seek to dismiss a government that had a majority in the House of

Commons and attempt to install in office one that was more conducive to their own opinions.[13] Peel's administration was, however, unable to secure the support of the people at the polls and thus a majority in the Commons due to the reforms of the franchise and he became the first Prime Minister who had the support of the king to lose an election. Faced with a hostile majority in the Commons, Peel had no choice but to resign and Melbourne was returned to office, a result which highlighted a profound change in British politics.

Prior to 1832, the king was very much the driving force of the government and personally exercised considerable power within it. From 1832 onwards, however, we see a significant change, with the government switching from one that was regally led to one that was increasingly headed by members of a political party.[14] Before the Reform Act, the monarch could, within certain limits, appoint whom they pleased to be Prime Minister, confident that they were sure to win a general election given the monarch's ability to influence the electoral outcome. We can see the importance of this influence when we note that from 1715 to 1835 no government ever lost a general election.[15] As a result of this ability to manipulate electoral outcomes, royal interference in the appointment and direction of government policy was a reality that no politician could ignore. The election of 1835 therefore marked a significant turning point in our political development, as it saw for the first time a Prime Minister who enjoyed the full confidence of the king lose at the polls, clearly demonstrating to the political class that the electorate was no longer to be swayed by deference to the monarch's wishes. From this point onwards, success at the polls and support within the House of Commons would become the deciding factors for the appointment of a Prime Minister, rather than the favour of the monarch.[16]

As the monarch was now no longer able to influence the outcome of the election, the use of the prerogative of dissolution became a risky undertaking. This was a fact known to Queen Victoria when she informed Lord John Russell that the sovereign's power of dissolution had become a weapon 'which ought not to be used except in extreme cases and with the certainty of success. To use this instrument and be defeated is a thing most lowering to the Crown and hurtful to the country.'[17] Despite this, she continued to hold the view, supported by the politicians of her age, that she had the right to decide whether to grant or hold a dissolution of Parliament when requested by her Prime Minister. This view rested on the constitutional principle that a dissolution was a personal appeal by the sovereign to the people, who could be relied on to break a political deadlock in Parliament.[18]

This brings us neatly to the early twentieth century, where the quiet stability that had been engendered by the Septennial Act was to be shattered on the rocks of Home Rule as the Commons and Lords found themselves at loggerheads over the Irish question, a conflict that would turn on the operation of something called the 'Salisbury Doctrine'. Created by the 3rd Marquess of Salisbury as part of his efforts to perpetuate the influence of the House in an age of widening suffrage, this doctrine states that the House of Lords should not reject at second or third reading government bills brought from the House of Commons for which the government has a mandate from the nation.[19] Salisbury asserted that where the will of the people and the views expressed by the House of Commons did not necessarily coincide, the House of Lords had an obligation to reject, and hence refer back to the electorate, particularly contentious bills, usually involving a revision of the constitutional settlement, that had been passed by the Commons.[20] This mechanism would trigger the prerogative of dissolution as a way to resolve a situation whereby the two Houses found themselves deadlocked on an issue.

When this power was used against the so called 'People's Budget' in 1909, it triggered a profound political conflict. Although robbed of their large majority in the ensuing election of 1910, the Liberal government remained in office with the support of the Irish Parliamentary Party, who demanded Irish Home Rule as the price of their support.[21] Looking to facilitate that goal and ensure the government could never be defeated on a Budget again, the government proposed the Parliament Bill, which would curtail the power of the Lords. The Lords duly rejected this proposal and a second election was held in December 1910, which saw the Liberals and Conservatives return an equal number of MPs. Regardless, the Liberal government retained office again due to the support of the Irish nationalists. Eventually, Lords resistance was overcome when the government induced the King to agree to create enough new peers to pass the bill. Determined to prevent this outcome occurring, the Lords passed the bill into law.[22]

This new Parliament Act stripped the Lords of its power to reject money bills and limited its powers of delay to three consecutive sessions, greatly increasing the power of the Commons in the process. To counterbalance this new authority, the Act shortened the duration of parliaments from seven to five years to ensure the Commons remained in step with the will of the people. In so doing, it ensured that the only remaining check on the government's authority would be the King's prerogative of dismissal and dissolution. This is a position which has remained to this day except for the brief interlude of the Fixed-Term Parliaments Act 2011, which sought to transfer the power of dissolution once more to the Commons.

With the repeal of that Act, we have reverted to the accepted practice that the monarch alone has the right to grant or not a dissolution of Parliament. Granted, under normal circumstances they have little choice but to consent, as to do otherwise would lead to the resignation of the government and its replacement with the opposition, a situation which would compel them to seek an election to secure the confidence of the Commons.[23] This has led some to argue that the power of dissolution no longer truly rests with the sovereign but with the Prime Minister. This is an argument that, in my opinion, simply does not hold water. It could just as easily be argued that the sovereign has not refused a dissolution in modern times precisely because no Prime Minister has improperly sought one – showing the 'good chap' theory once again working in practice. The possibility of the monarch refusing a request still exists should the Prime Minister seek a dissolution for an improper purpose, such as having lost the support of the Commons, their Cabinet or their party, looking to forestall their overthrow by a rapid dissolution.[24]

Consider for a moment what would happen if a Prime Minister, instead of resigning, were to ask for another dissolution, having just lost an election. Let us put a human face on this by supposing that Boris Johnson, having called and then lost the 2019 election, sought a second dissolution rather than resigning. Would the Queen have had to grant the request? Clearly not, as it would have been not only her right but her duty to refuse such a request. Likewise, let us suppose that Gordon Brown, after the general election of 2010, had failed to build a coalition of support and requested another dissolution after having been defeated in the Commons. In such a scenario, the Queen would have been able to refuse the request and would have instead invited David Cameron to form a government. It is for this very reason that we cannot regard the request for a dissolution as being merely a formality, nor can we take the view that it will automatically be granted, for there are still some circumstances in which the sovereign would be justified in refusing such a request.[25]

The issue before us is therefore not whether the king is able to refuse a dissolution request but rather under what circumstances would he choose to exercise his discretion. History tells us that the two primary grounds under which this discretion could apply are when there is an alternate government available or when the Prime Minister no longer enjoys the backing of their Cabinet and/or their party. Ivor Jennings observes:

> The Queen must not intervene in party politics. She must not, therefore, support a Prime Minister against his colleagues. Accordingly, it would be unconstitutional for the Queen to agree with the Prime Minister for the dissolution of the Government in order to allow the Prime Minister to override his colleagues.[26]

Situations of this type are more common in British politics than is often assumed, and the existence of the royal discretion has proved vital in ensuring not only that the monarchy stays politically neutral but also that Prime Ministers play the game according to the rules. Take, for example, Harold Wilson's actions in 1969. Faced with considerable opposition to his trade union reforms, outlined in the white paper 'In Place of Strife', he threatened his colleagues with an election unless they supported him. This was an approach also adopted by Margaret Thatcher when she contemplated calling an election to forestall her defeat in the party leadership election in 1990. John Major, when pursuing his European policy, ensured party discipline in the key votes around the Maastricht Treaty by making them confidence votes, ensuring that any defeat would lead to an immediate election. In each case, the Prime Minister contemplated an election, but the palace let them know that their request would be refused.[27]

Faced with such circumstances, the king has the right but not the obligation to refuse a request for a dissolution. The wisdom of refusing such a request will entirely depend on the circumstances of the time and the makeup of the House of Commons, for all will revolve on whether an alternative government exists or not.

Two key political events provide us with modern guidance on how this prerogative would be utilised should the need arise. The first was in March 1950, when Clement Attlee feared defeat on the King's Speech following his narrow election victory of the month before, and the second was Harold Wilson's similar predicament in October 1964.

When the dust cleared from the election of 1950, Clement Attlee surveyed the political landscape and found to his dismay that he had just squeaked in with a significantly reduced majority of five. Such a precarious majority did not bode well for the government's longevity in office and the Conservatives knew it. It was, therefore, unsurprising that the Conservatives would seek to test support for the government by challenging its flagship policy for the nationalisation of the steel industry.[28] A defeat would bring down the government and would raise questions as to how the King should act in such circumstances. To ensure that any transfer of power was handled appropriately and in a timely manner, the Cabinet

Secretary, Sir Norman Brook, undertook a contingency planning exercise with Buckingham Palace, which laid the groundwork for how a dissolution request should be managed.

If we look purely at the Cabinet minutes of this debate, we would be left with little understanding of the turmoil that engulfed the government at this time, for they are particularly unrevealing. They simply state:

> The Cabinet had some preliminary discussion about the situation which would arise if the Government were defeated in a division early in the lifetime of the Parliament. It was generally recognised that, from the point of view of the national interest, a very serious situation would result – especially as essential financial business had to be transacted by Parliament in March and April.[29]

Readers could be forgiven for failing to grasp the importance of this debate from the record above. Saharan winds are less dry than the official records of Cabinet discussions. Luckily for us, Sir Norman's record of events is far more enlightening of the issues that confronted the government in this situation. He recorded:

> The Prime Minister said that the two Conservative amendments to the Address, both that on the Iron and Steel Act and that on Housing, would be pressed to a division; and he had been considering what advice he should tender to His Majesty if the Government were defeated in either of these divisions. He did not think it would be right to ask for a Dissolution so soon after the General Election, and he was inclined to think that his proper course would be to advise the King to send for Mr Churchill. The resulting Parliamentary situation would be unsatisfactory, for

the Conservatives, being in a minority, would find it even more difficult to carry on the essential business of Government; but the situation would have been created by the Conservatives and he thought they should be forced to assume responsibility for handling it.[30]

Let us just stand back a moment and admire the various constitutional principles expressed so succinctly within this memo, as they can help inform our understanding of how our constitutional settlement operates under stress. First, note how Attlee raises the prospect of a dissolution but then dismisses it as inappropriate at this stage. Here is the 'good chap' theory in action, as Attlee is aware that such a request is unlikely to be granted given the fact the country has just held an election. Rather than be rebuffed, he simply dismisses the possibility. Second, Attlee accepts that a defeat on the King's Speech will be a confidence vote for the government and he will have to resign as a result. There is no question of him looking to stay in office. Third, he is aware that the King's government must continue with a new Prime Minister and so he says that Churchill must be sent for.

In so doing, he raises two interconnected points that help inform our understanding of the powers of appointment and dissolution. The first is that the Prime Minister must enjoy the confidence of the Commons and can remain in office only so long as they can demonstrate the House's support. The second is that if the opposition, through their actions in Parliament, compel the government to resign, they must be willing and able to assume the reins of office. In this case, Attlee understood this would be far from easy for the Conservatives and so they would suffer the political consequences of defeating a recently returned government.

As it was, the government would survive the vote and stagger on until compelled to call another election in 1951, but the crisis had raised expectations that Whitehall would know how to act the next time the government was confronted by such a situation. To ensure this was the case, Sir Norman commissioned his private secretary to research 'on the question that would arise if the Government were defeated in the House of Commons'. Opinions were sought far and wide from the great and the good in royal, political and academic circles to ensure a robust answer was produced for this crucial question in the Cabinet Office paper 'Government Defeats in the House of Commons'.[31]

The report argued that it was hard to imagine how the king could refuse a Prime Minister with a clear majority in the Commons when they sought a dissolution. Such an act would lead to the resignation of the government and the refusal of the Leader of the Opposition to accept office, as they could not guarantee the confidence of the House in the government so formed. Such an event would then lead to the king either reappointing his former Prime Minister and then granting the dissolution or else granting the new Prime Minister the dissolution he had denied the former premier, thus raising the spectre of partisan activity.[32] The Cabinet Office felt that a refusal was most likely when there was a hung Parliament and the Prime Minister faced defeat by a combination that could command a majority. Out of this appeared an answer:

> While there is some divergence of view among the authorities on the question whether the King can refuse a dissolution to a Prime Minister who asks for it, the better opinion is that the power still exists but that the prerogative could properly be exercised only in exceptional circumstances.[33]

Such was the accepted view in 1950, and this is still the position to this day.

So far so good, but this being Britain, it is never this easy to get at the heart of the constitution. This is because different parts of the government view any particular question from the vantage point of their own existence, which allows subtle but important distinctions to emerge. Just such an event occurred here, as the palace and Cabinet Office recorded the outcome in slightly different ways, which we can see when we examine the briefing Sir Alan Lascelles, the King's private secretary, provided for George VI on the options open to Attlee in such a situation. As this briefing was written to explain the King's role in this crisis, it is worth quoting in full for the insights it holds. Sir Alan informed the King:

If Mr Attlee is beaten, two courses are open to him:

1. He can ask The King to accept his resignation and (if asked) advise His Majesty to send for Mr Churchill. There could not be much doubt about what to do then, and The King's problem is simple. (I am told, however, on good authority that Mr Attlee would *not* adopt this course, though the temptation to try and put the other side in on a very sticky wicket would obviously be strong.)

2. He can ask The King to dissolve Parliament. The King would be perfectly entitled to refuse this request if he were convinced that the present Parliament has not exhausted its present usefulness and that the country's interests demand that the holding of another general election should be postponed as long as possible. It is doubtful whether the argument is valid in present circumstances; could anybody

else form a government capable of doing anything but exist precariously on a tiny majority – or even a minority? And would withholding a dissolution now do more than postpone the inevitable general election for more than a few weeks? So there does not seem to be sufficient reason here for the Sovereign to break the precedent followed by his predecessors for more than a century by refusing his Prime Minister a dissolution. In Canada, of course, Lord Byng did, on famous occasion, refuse dissolution; but, though he acted from the very best motives, it is questionable if this refusal did anybody any good in the long run, and it undoubtedly left certain quarters in Canada a considerable legacy of bitterness against the Crown. (I am aware that Mr Churchill might argue in a directly contrary sense, but I do not believe that more than a small minority of his party would do so.)

But even if The King decided to grant a dissolution, he should certainly not do so save on the condition that it should not become operative until Parliament has done its duty of making at least a minimum provision for the national finance; no Prime Minister should ever be allowed to close the national legislative premises – particularly at this time of year – unless he can leave them in good financial order. Consequently The King would be bound to insist that the dissolution asked for by Mr Attlee should not take effect until Parliament had dealt with a Minimal Finance Act, and an Appropriation Act, as explained in the attached copy of a Treasury paper given me this evening by Sir E. Bridges. As the Prime Minister himself called for this paper, it may fairly be presumed that, if he should ask The King for a dissolution, he would himself stipulate that Parliament should be made to sit until this minimal business were completed – a period, I understand, of at least ten days or even a fortnight. So, in the event of Mr Attlee asking his Majesty for a dissolution on Thursday, April 27th, it could not take place until May 10th.[34]

The reason such a divergence can appear is due to the different influences that have shaped each institution's thinking. Whereas the Cabinet Office sees constitutional issues primarily through the lens of domestic political developments, the palace has tended to be influenced as much by empire and Commonwealth issues as domestic ones – as we can see through Lascelles's deference to Canada. The palace's view is, as a result, often wider and more nuanced than that of either the Cabinet Office or Downing Street, as it has a far wider range of examples at its disposal. If we just look at the domestic scene then it seems obvious that, as no dissolution request has been rejected in modern times, it follows that no dissolution request can be refused. However, this is simply not the case if we survey the wider imperial and Commonwealth examples of the same time period.

To understand Lascelles's opinion better, we need to understand the influences that had shaped it, as they still define how the powers of dissolution should be utilised by the sovereign to this day.

Our first example is the embarrassing situation the Governor-General of Canada, Lord Byng, found himself in during 1926. Following the election of October 1925, the Liberals had emerged with fewer seats than the Conservatives, but William Lyon Mackenzie King had remained Prime Minister with the support of smaller parties. Faced with this precarious situation, Byng informed Mackenzie King that his options in these circumstances were that he could either seek another dissolution, which would not be granted, resign and allow the Conservatives to form a government or else choose to carry on.[35] Mackenzie King chose to carry on until confronted with a major corruption scandal in the summer of 1926. To prevent his government losing a confidence vote, Mackenzie King requested a dissolution three times, but Byng refused, as he felt that not only was the Parliament still viable but an alternate government existed.

He informed the Prime Minister of his decision by saying that Mackenzie King 'had had the opportunity to govern, and that it would be most unfair to call another election without giving Meighen and the Conservative Party, which had the most seats in the House, a chance to form a government'.[36] This prompted Mackenzie King to resign, allowing Byng to summon Arthur Meighen to form a government despite his party's preference for an election.[37] This was partly due to the fact that at the time, a convention required that any ministers of the crown appointed from the House of Commons were obliged upon their appointment to resign their seats in Parliament and seek re-election. This posed a significant problem for Meighen personally, as he and several other key ministers would have to be temporarily absent from the Commons during this period, making a defeat on a confidence motion highly likely.

Meighen sought to circumvent this requirement by advising the Governor-General that he should appointment several ministers without portfolio to Cabinet, as these appointments were not required to stand for re-election. The Progressives and Liberals reacted with outrage, seeing the use of this device of 'acting ministers' as against the spirit of the convention, and moved a no-confidence vote in Meighen's new administration.[38] Meighen subsequently lost the vote, and confronted by such a defeat, he had no choice but to request – and Byng had no choice but to grant – the dissolution long sought after. The Liberals won a majority in the ensuing election and decried the unconstitutional actions of Lord Byng, demanding changes to the role of the Governor-General in the process, a fact which ensures the King–Byng Affair remains a politically controversial issue in Canada to this day. Such was its effect that Lascelles could not ignore it in 1950.[39]

Most commentators then and now have taken the view that although Byng was correct on the constitutional principles involved, Mackenzie King was right politically.[40] Since an election ended up being inevitable, commentators feel Mackenzie King should have been allowed his way so the people could have decided. In doing so they tend to ignore the by-election rule that triggered Meighen's downfall, as it was this fact that made his government unviable, not the lack of confidence. In any event, the principle at stake has shaped the debate ever since.

This brings us to our next case. As the war clouds in Europe gathered in the 1930s, the uneasy alliance that lay at the heart of the South African government began to fracture under their pressure. This conflict was embodied by its two leading men, Prime Minister James Hertzog and Deputy Prime Minister Jan Smuts, who between them represented differing visions for their country. In short, whilst Hertzog wished South Africa to follow an independent and to some degree isolated policy centred on the Afrikaner community, Smuts wanted South Africa to remain an active member of the Commonwealth and an ally of Britain.[41] This divergence of opinion had not been too problematic in the early life of the government, but as war in Europe became more likely, it split the administration apart. Looking to keep the country neutral, Hertzog informed the British government that South Africa would not under any circumstances go to war with Germany in defence of Czechoslovakia, a position he reinforced by arguing that he regarded Eastern Europe as being rightfully in Germany's sphere of influence.[42] This outraged the pro-British elements in the government.

To ensure this policy was adopted, Hertzog presented his Cabinet with a compromise plan on 1 September 1938. South Africa would declare neutrality in the event of war but would be neutral in the most pro-British way possible, a policy known as 'qualified neutrality'. Far from creating the unity he hoped for, the Cabinet split apart as the philosophical disagreements that had long been simmering burst forth. Whilst some members supported his approach, others on the nationalist side of the government argued that, far from being neutral, South Africa should ally itself with Germany. This proposal so outraged Smuts and his supporters that they affirmed South Africa must declare war on Germany alongside Britain and the rest of the empire and Commonwealth.[43] Seven members backed Smuts and six supported the Prime Minister and so the meeting was adjourned to allow cooler heads to prevail. Hoping to prevent a rupture, Hertzog proposed the next day that the matter should be settled by Parliament instead, with a vote on the issue in the House of Assembly.[44]

Addressing the House on 4 September, Hertzog said that he could not support going to war with Germany as it was a country merely trying to restore is honour following the humiliation of the Treaty of Versailles. Given this, South Africa should look to remain neutral in any future conflict unless its interests were directly threatened. To take the side of Britain in such a conflict would merely revive the animosity between Afrikaans-speaking and English-speaking South Africans. Smuts immediately refuted this, telling the House that Hitler sought nothing less than world domination and had to be stopped. South Africa had no choice but to fight at Britain's side.[45] When the vote was at last held the government shattered, with the motion being defeated by eighty votes to sixty-seven. The Prime Minister had lost, and he immediately sought a dissolution from the Governor-General.

Faced with a collapsing government, Governor-General Sir Patrick Duncan looked over his options. It was clear to him that the Prime Minister no longer enjoyed the confidence of the House and he clearly no longer enjoyed the support of his Cabinet either. He was, therefore, unable to meet the requirements of the Golden Rule. In considering whether to agree to a dissolution, he was swayed by the fact that neutrality had been proposed by the opposition in the recent election in May and they had been defeated, an outcome that seemed to demonstrate the will of the electorate. He therefore refused Hertzog's request and summoned Smuts to form a government. He was confident that the newly elected Parliament could still function and that an alternative government was available, which seemed committed to a policy supported by the majority of the electorate.[46]

The precedent set by these events proved that a Prime Minister must enjoy the support of their Cabinet if they wish to be able to make a legitimate request for a dissolution. Failing such support, the king is free to refuse the request and summon the individual who can best lead a government that commands the confidence of Parliament – a fact that was very much on Lascelles's mind in 1950.

Armed with these examples and keen to protect the King's position in the event of any future conflict of this kind, Lascelles wrote to *The Times* to ensure the public appreciated the King's position. Writing under the pseudonym 'Senex' (the wise man), he sought to distil his advice to the King into a more concise and understandable format for the public. In so doing, he created the gold standard definition of how the royal prerogative of dissolution can be applied. He wrote:

> It is surely indisputable (and common sense) that a Prime Minister may ask – not demand – that his Sovereign will grant him a dissolution of Parliament; and that the Sovereign, if he so chooses, may refuse to grant this request. The problem of such a choice is entirely personal to the Sovereign, though he is, of course, free to ask informal advice from anybody who he thinks fit to consult. Insofar as this matter can be publicly discussed, it can be properly assumed that no wise Sovereign – that is, one who has at heart the true interests of the country, the constitution, and the Monarchy – would deny a dissolution to his Prime Minister unless he was satisfied that: 1) the existing Parliament was still vital, viable and capable of doing its job; 2) a General Election would be detrimental to the national economy; 3) he could rely on finding another Prime Minister who could carry on his Government, for a reasonable period, with a working majority in the House of Commons.[47]

This highly influential statement has been studied and debated ever since and will continue to be until it is replaced by a better statement of the way in which this particular prerogative operates. Looking closely at it, there are a few things that we should note as they reinforce the points made above. First, note how Lascelles is at pains to state that the power to grant a dissolution is a personal one to the king but that the default position is that the monarch should always grant such a request unless they can meet three important conditions. In so doing, he affirms that the king is the guardian of the constitution, whose job it is to ensure that the House of

Commons continues to reflect the will of the people. To this end, a request for an election should always be honoured, as it preserves the democratic nature of our political system.

Second, the third condition he outlines appears to be the most important. The monarch can only seek to act independently if they can be assured that there exists another individual who will assume the role of Prime Minister and carry on the government for a reasonable period with the confidence of the House. This is essential to the king's need that his ministers should be accountable to Parliament for all governmental acts. If he cannot find such an individual, it would be best to grant the request and let the people decide. The monarch must at all costs avoid the political embarrassment of refusing a dissolution to one politician only to grant it to another soon after, a fact that was highlighted by the King–Byng Affair in 1926.

That leaves us with the other two conditions, which are far from unproblematic and have often led to conflicts in the debate on the sovereign's independent role in the dissolution of Parliament. The state of the economy seems to many to be a complicated ground to assert royal independence on, as it will be hard for the monarch to determine the economy's state. Politicians will naturally argue about this point and so any attempt by the king to make his views known risks his entering the political sphere. Any attempt by the sovereign to be an arbiter of what is and is not 'detrimental to the national economy' without the prior consent of the main political parties risks them being charged with political bias and so endangering their position. That said, there are clearly moments when it is simply not possible to hold a general election without damaging the national interest – during a period of war, national emergency and economic crisis, for instance. This was a view taken by George

V in 1916 when he feared an election would be harmful to the war effort and in 1931 when he felt the country required a government to carry out the much-needed economic measures in the wake of the financial crash.[48] These two events clearly influence Lascelles's thinking.

The first condition is also problematic, as it requires the King to determine the viability of a Parliament, which is likewise a political judgement. What this essentially means, however, is that the state of the Commons is such that some combination of support other than that currently enjoyed by the government is possible. If a majority can be assumed by some other way, then the system allows for the king to explore that option. Likewise, the monarch can take note of whether an election will inevitably occur in the future or whether the Parliament is recently elected. The aim is to ensure a degree of political stability and place pressure on politicians not to create a crisis if one can be avoided.

Lascelles's views proved to be the standard for how situations of this kind were dealt with, as we can see from events that took place in 1974. In a surprising repeat of history, Harold Wilson would find himself confronted by the same issue that Attlee dealt with in 1950. The February election of 1974 had proved to be an indecisive one, creating a hung Parliament in the process. This compelled the resignation of Edward Heath following his failed attempts to form a coalition government with the Liberal Party. Wilson thus entered his second premiership as leader of a minority party, faced with the prospect that he could lose a confidence vote at any moment. Seeking to capitalise on this fact, Heath laid down an amendment on the Queen's Speech that Wilson was not sure he could defeat.

Faced with this prospect, discussions began in Whitehall about how and if Wilson could request another dissolution so soon after the conclusion of the last. In a fascinating account of not just the rules that surround the use of the prerogative but also the 'good chap' theory of government, it was concluded that Wilson could ask but the Queen may not grant, and it is worth quoting the advice Wilson received to understand how this worked in practice. In a seminal report, Lord Crowther-Hunt informed the Prime Minister that

> before deciding whether to grant your request for a dissolution we believe the Queen might consider it her duty to see if another election were avoidable. In that event she would presumably say formally to you that she thought it right to carry out consultations. She would probably invite you to offer advice on whom she might consult, though she would not be bound to restrict her consultations to the names you might suggest. She might consult elder statesmen ... And she might seek either through such consultations or through her Private Secretary or both to ascertain what were the possibilities of an administration being formed (not necessarily by one of the existing party leaders).
>
> If the Queen's consultations led her to the conclusion that no one else was in a position to form an administration which could command as much or greater support than your own, she would presumably send for you and grant your request for a dissolution. However, if her consultations led her to the conclusion that someone else could form an administration which could count on the support of at least as many and preferably more members than you could count on, she would presumably send for you. We doubt if she would then refuse the request for a dissolution outright. We believe that she would probably report the outcome of the consultations to you, and go on to say that she felt bound in the circumstances to ask you to consider your position.[49]

This was a classic exposition of the Lascelles formula. The monarch reserved the right to consult widely and determine if the current Parliament was still viable and another administration possible. Based on those findings, they would then decide to either grant or withhold the request for a dissolution. Knowing this, Wilson acted accordingly and said he would seek a vote of confidence if defeated on the Queen's Speech to show the need for an election and to place his request on a stronger footing, whilst simultaneously putting pressure on the minor parties in Parliament.[50] The trick worked and Wilson won the vote. The knowledge that the Queen could refuse the request for another election compelled the politicians to find a political resolution to the crisis, which ensured the monarch was not forced to act. This shows how the mere existence of the power ensures the effective operation of the system as a whole.

So, the king is entitled to refuse a dissolution in certain circumstances but is under no obligation to do so. Whether he does will very much depend on the circumstances of the moment and the attitudes of the political leaders of the time. The monarch would need to exercise a fine degree of political judgement as to whether commitments made by the opposition or government rebels were likely to be met. This did not prove to be the case in Canada in 1926 but was the case in South Africa in 1939. Likewise, Sir John Kerr could rely on Malcom Fraser to form a government in 1975 – though in that case, we must keep in mind that the Governor-General always wished to grant a dissolution and it was only following the repeated refusal of his Prime Minister to request one and the growing danger that the Budget would not be passed in time that finally compelled him to dismiss Whitlam and replace him with a Prime Minister who would make such a request. Similarly, when Thatcher threatened to request a dissolution in 1990 during the leadership election, it was made clear to her that the Queen was not bound to accept this advice and so no request was made.[51]

Therefore, as Vernon Bogdanor has so effectively argued, the king 'has a right to refuse a dissolution only where a grant of a dissolution would be an affront to, rather than an expression of, democratic rights'.[52] This discretion flows from the monarch's role as the guardian of the constitution and as such, can only effectively be exercised in defence of our parliamentary democracy.

Before we move on to look at the prerogative of assent, it is worth considering for a moment the related issue of the monarch's role in granting a prorogation of Parliament. In 2019, Boris Johnson sought a prorogation of Parliament for five weeks, from 9 September to 14 October, as a way of frustrating the opposition he was facing in the House of Commons and regaining control of the parliamentary timetable. This decision was challenged in the courts, which ultimately found the government's actions to be illegal.

During the debate surrounding the legality of the prorogation, the role of the Queen in approving the order was raised, though the Supreme Court found her to be blameless. This is because prorogation is not a power reserved for the sovereign in the way the power of dissolution is. The traditional view is that prorogation can only occur on the basis of ministerial advice, which the monarch has no ability to refuse. Royal discretion does not, therefore, arise in this situation. Peter Hennessy, however, has observed that as advice to prorogue Parliament 'touches on her [the Queen's] personal prerogatives it can only amount to informal advice, which cannot bind her actions'.[53] This is a view supported by Vernon Bogdanor, who, whilst giving evidence before the Lords Constitution Committee, stated that a 'wise constitutional monarchy' would not prorogue Parliament if the request came from a Prime Minister who no longer held the confidence of the Commons.[54]

So, what are we to make of this? Prorogation has not been subjected to the same level of scrutiny in the UK as it has been in Canada and Australia, a situation that has not been rectified by the outcome of the 2019 case. In Canada, the issue was brought to a head by the actions of Stephen Harper's government in seeking a long prorogation in 2008. Following the election in October 2008, the Conservatives had emerged with the largest number of seats but lacked an overall majority in the Commons. To this end, the Liberal and New Democratic parties sought to table a vote of no confidence when the government presented its fiscal update. To frustrate this, Harper sought to prorogue Parliament, delaying the vote of no confidence. This decision was approved by the Governor-General, much to the anger of Harper's opponents.

Academics are split on how to respond to the overt political use of this parliamentary mechanism, with some still steadfast in their opposition to prorogation being regarded as a power reserved to the monarchy alone, whilst a growing number argue that in some circumstances it should be treated as a reserved power. In Canada, both Peter Hogg and Andrew Head have argued for this new interpretation. Hogg argues that it would be wrong to grant a prorogation to a Prime Minister who has lost the confidence of the Commons. In this instance, the monarch or their representative should refuse the advice to prorogue.[55] Head takes a broader view, arguing that the Governor-General is obliged to reject advice to prorogue where it would interfere with the power of Parliament to determine confidence.[56] Both men argue that the monarch is only obliged to act upon what they call 'constitutionally valid' advice, a view which is very close to that expounded by the UK Supreme Court in 2019.

These arguments are built on the foundations laid by Eugene Forsey, who in 1984 discussed the possibility of an incumbent government that had failed to win a majority in an election seeking to continue to govern without facing Parliament by means of a long prorogation – an example which again has echoes of the events in the UK in 2019. He argued that the only way to prevent this from happening was for the crown 'to refuse such a prorogation or dissolution, and, if necessary to dismiss the Government which advised such a prorogation or dissolution'.[57] This view has support in Australia too. In *Odgers' Senate Practice*, the Australian parliamentary authority, it is noted that the advice to prorogue could be refused where a Prime Minister has lost their majority and seek to prorogue Parliament 'simply as a means of avoiding a no-confidence motion and of clinging to power'.[58]

As an alternative to refusing advice to prorogue, the king may well seek to persuade their Prime Minister to withdraw their advice or else shorten the length of time requested, allowing Parliament to meet again within a reasonable space of time. Such action would be the acceptable first step in any discussion of a controversial prorogation and one that would be preferable to an exercise of royal discretion. This would protect the principles of responsible government whilst not politicising the monarch or exacerbating a political crisis. We can see this process in action in Canada in 2008. The Governor-General, Michaëlle Jean, granted the prorogation that Harper had requested but revised the end date to 26 January, which was only ten days longer than the ordinary Christmas break. She also insisted that the Budget be presented when Parliament returned as a condition to the granting of the prorogation.[59]

Given the current conventions in place within the UK, it is far more likely, if a similar situation occurred, that the King would seek to use his rights to advise and warn as means of altering a governmental attempt to seek a long prorogation for political advantage, rather than seek to refuse the advice outright. This course of action is now bolstered by the judgment of the Supreme Court in 2019. Alternatively, the King would be within his rights to request advice from the government to confirm that any request for an extraordinary prorogation during a period of parliamentary conflict would be legal before granting his assent. This would compel the government to produce a legal opinion in support of their position, thus bolstering their claim for a prorogation. Should such legal advice not be forthcoming, the King would be within his rights to reject the request. This is indeed how the Queen approached the request for prorogation in 2019. When the idea was first raised with the palace, royal concerns were expressed. Downing Street reassured courtiers that the prorogation was lawful and constitutional, so the Queen granted the request. It then fell to the Supreme Court to determine that the advice was indeed illegal.[60]

So, although there is a wide-ranging academic debate on the monarch's ability to refuse advice to prorogue Parliament, their doing so is not accepted practice in the UK at the time of writing. A case could be made for future royal intervention should a situation arise whereby it was warranted, with numerous examples available from other Commonwealth realms to support the monarch's actions. But that would be for another day.

II

THE KING'S ASSENT

The final prerogative we shall turn our attention to is that of the royal assent to legislation. This prerogative is by far the most nebulous and contested of the bunch, because the third stage of the legislative process is held to be a mere formality, requiring no direct involvement by the sovereign. When the House of Commons and the House of Lords have both passed a bill, it is conveyed to the crown to give assent to the proposed legislation, transforming the bill into an Act of Parliament. This process is necessary because the sovereign body of the United Kingdom is not the House of Commons but the King-in-Parliament, which means that for an Act to be valid, both Houses of Parliament and the crown must have accepted it. This power is one that is invested in the monarch alone and is capable of being utilised by the sovereign without the advice of ministers, as there is no involvement by the Privy Council.[1]

To understand how this process came about, we need to travel back in time once more. At first, kings governed by their prerogative powers alone, but this proved to be a less than ideal situation, as opposition can and did emerge from amongst the leading nobles. To prevent this from happening, kings began to consult their more powerful lords in council before acting to gain their support for any proposed royal actions. Over time, this body would expand in number into a rudimentary parliament.[2] The King began to summon the leading commoners to attend the most important of these gatherings, as happened in the reigns of Henry II, John and Edward I. Petitions would be submitted, and if agreed to, these would become what we would now call statutes.[3]

By the reign of Edward II, the separation of Parliament into two Houses was well underway and their individual petitions and responses were submitted to the king jointly for decision. The assent of both the Lords and the Commons has been recited at the start of each statute to show their joint agreement since 1485.[4] In the following centuries, royal legislative power would ebb to the two Houses of Parliament, but royal assent would remain a crucial part of the legislative process, for only the King-in-Parliament can pass laws and make statutes.

Prior to 1541, it was an accepted constitutional fact that the monarch had to give their assent to proposed legislation in person in Parliament, with the result that bills remained in limbo until the end of the parliamentary session. To end the logjam this requirement created, the Royal Assent by Commission Act was passed, which provided for the exercise of this prerogative by the appointment of Lords Commissioners, who would let Parliament know of the king's approval at once rather than waiting for the end of the session, a process which has remained in place to this day.[5] The king was still able to issue their assent in person, but since the Hanoverian succession few have chosen to do so, with Victoria issuing the last in-person assent in 1854.[6] Though George VI did give an in-person assent to a bill in 1939, this was to the Canadian Parliament during a royal tour.[7] As a result, the monarch has been removed from the public operation of the prerogative for some considerable time, something that is further complicated by the fact that the last time royal assent was refused was in 1708 when Queen Anne rejected the Scottish Militia Bill on the advice of her ministers.[8]

In the present day, once a bill has been approved by both Houses, royal assent must be sought. To do this, the Clerk of the Parliaments provides the Lord Chancellor with a list of bills ready for assent, which they in turn give to the chief clerk in the King's private office, requesting a warrant be issued authorising the affixing of the Great Seal of the Realm to the letters patent to show the granting of royal assent. The warrant and the letters patent are the only documents that the monarch signs. The King writes 'Approved' on the warrant and signs the letters patent 'Charles R', but he does not sign any bill nor see the proposed text.

We then return to the Palace of Westminster for the conclusion of this procedure. At this stage, one of two processes may take place. In the first, the five Lords Commissioners appointed for the task sit on a bench in front of the throne and inform the House of Lords and representatives of the Commons in Norman French '*Le Roy [La Raine] le veult*' (The King/Queen desires it) as the title of each bill is read out to demonstrate that assent has been granted, a formula used since the fourteenth century to demonstrate the monarch's assent.[9] For finance bills, the term used is slightly different and points to the importance of Parliament in securing revenue through taxation. Here the words '*Le Roy remercie sens bon sujets, accepte leur benevolence, et ainsi le vault*' (The King thanks his loyal subjects, accepts their bounty and wills it so) are employed in a subtle reminder that tax revenue is a gift of the people, not a right in and of itself. The second process derives from the Royal Assent Act 1967, which invented a new means by which each House is informed by its Speaker that the bill has been approved, a process which takes a few minutes whilst preserving the relevant forms. This has become the primary means used to record the granting of assent, although the Lords Commissioners can be appointed when Parliament is dissolved.

If a situation were ever to arise when a royal veto was to be utilised, then the diplomatic term '*Le Roy se avisera*' (The King will consider it) will be issued instead by either the King, the Lords Commissioners or the Speakers.[10] This is a quaint term in use since the fourteenth century, which shows the King's lack of consent in a way that does not give undue offence. Notably, the use of this term does not kill a bill but simply places it in limbo, as theoretically the King could provide his assent at a later time. This makes this power unique in modern political usage, as no other head of state with a veto power has this discretion.

The accepted rule is that this prerogative is exercised by the monarch in support of the government of the day, a proposition based on the fact that the crown has accepted that only the House of Commons can approve taxation since 1688. To ensure no conflict can arise between the Commons and the crown, monarchs have felt it prudent to allow proposed legislation to be approved rather than risk a breach with the Commons and the loss of tax revenue. The acceptance of this principle led in turn to the fusing of the legislative and executive functions, with ministers serving in the House of Commons exercising the primary right to initiate legislation and propose taxation. Standing Orders 14 and 48 of the Commons enshrine this relationship, stating that government business must be given priority in the discussions of the House and only the government can introduce money bills. These rules reflect the fundamental constitutional principle that Parliament must have its say, but the government must get its way, because it is the government which runs the country, not Parliament. The government is, however, constrained by the fact that it must always retain the confidence of Parliament. This dynamic relationship forms the beating heart of our political process and reflects the balance between our legislature and executive.

The UK Parliament has, for a long time now, been primarily a policy-influencing body rather than a policy-making body, a fact which distinguishes it from the US Congress. For this reason, it has not been felt necessary to moderate the legislative process by use of an executive veto on legislation. However, this means an inherent tension now exists in our system between representative government and responsible government. The legitimacy of the House of Commons flows from its representative character, but the legitimacy of ministers is a function of their accountability to Parliament.[11] Normally these two concepts sit side by side in harmony, but conflict can arise when the government either loses control of Parliament or else is out of step with the people. In such circumstances, the question arises as to the use of the prerogative of assent.

An argument has been made by constitutional scholars that the power to refuse assent has fallen into desuetude through the lack of its use since 1708.[12] This is a view I take exception to, as the personal prerogatives are powers that are by definition only supposed to be used in extremely rare situations. If a power is only supposed to be exercised rarely, it seems perverse to say that it ceases to exist if not used regularly. This is a situation commented upon by Arthur Balfour when he observed, 'The contrary doctrine seems indeed absurd; since it would deprive the Sovereign of every power which he does not habitually exercise. It is surely obvious that if the prerogative *ought* rarely to be used, it cannot become obsolete, *merely because* it is rarely used.'[13]

It has long been accepted that the monarch's prerogative powers flow from the common law and, as such, are incapable of becoming extinct through lack of use. Common-law attributes can be amended or abrogated by the exercise of parliamentary sovereignty, but they cannot be extinguished, as was demonstrated when the Fixed-Term Parliaments Act was repealed in 2022.[14] As Lord Morris, the former Attorney General, stated in relation to the repeal of the Act, 'The Royal Prerogative would once again come into play, having been in abeyance for the life of this Act.'[15] We can also never be sure to what degree a prerogative power's existence is used to modify a proposed course of action by the government. As the discussions between the monarch and Prime Minister remain secret, we can never know the degree to which the monarch may have threatened to withhold assent unless legislation was altered in a particular way. It is only when reference is made in either archival material or diaries and biographies that we can perceive its use.[16] For these reasons, I feel the desuetude argument simply cannot apply here.

Yet if we accept that the power of assent is still capable of being utilised to reject legislation passed by Parliament, we are left with the question of under what circumstances could such a rejection take place and whether the monarch would have any autonomy in the act.

Anne Twomey, supported by Adam Tomkins, is clear in her assertion that the key issue here is that the sovereign must act on the advice of their responsible ministers.[17] If the government advises the king to refuse his assent to a proposed piece of legislation, he will have no choice but to act as he has been directed. To highlight this point further, Twomey uses the example of a newly installed government objecting to a bill passed by its predecessors and so recommending that the monarch refuse assent. Similarly, it could be argued that if a serious error is discovered in the bill before its ratification, it would be entirely proper for the government to advise its rejection.[18] This is a view that is supported by Rodney Brazier, who likewise believes that the 'only circumstances in which the withholding of the royal assent might be justifiable would be if the Government itself were to advise such a course'.[19] Therefore, if we accept the importance of the monarch being bound by ministerial advice, it seems certain that assent can be refused if exercised upon the advice of ministers, who will be held to account for the act by Parliament.

This is an argument which is supported by the last recorded refusal of royal assent. In 1708, Queen Anne refused assent to the Scottish Militia Bill, a fact long accepted but little understood. The bill had been introduced into the first post-Union Parliament to rectify an omission in the Treaty of Union, which failed to provide for the establishment of a militia in Scotland. Subsequently, on 11 March 1708, the Queen was presented with a series of bills for her assent. When the Militia Bill was read out, however, the words '*La Raine se avisera*' were uttered, to the surprise of those in the chamber. The Queen then informed Parliament she had received a report that morning. A French fleet was sailing from Dunkirk with James Edward Stuart, the pretender, on board one of the ships. The navy had been dispatched to intercept it and she concluded they would no doubt be victorious. Ministers felt that the continuation of an armed militia in Scotland with dubious loyalties was not something they wished to preserve and so they advised the Queen to refuse assent, an outcome that Parliament did not object to.[20]

Another way of looking at this might be to say that the general rule is that the crown cannot refuse assent except on advice, save in certain instances whereby the monarch may properly withhold assent. It would be right, for instance, for the monarch to refuse to accept any bill which altered the position of Northern Ireland within the UK without the consent of the people of Northern Ireland, an argument that has been extended to Scotland following devolution.[21] Likewise, there has been some speculation as to whether the monarch would consent to the abolition of the House of Lords without a clear replacement, if they would support a government prolonging the duration of a parliament indefinitely in peacetime or if they would accept the abolition of the monarchy without a referendum.[22] How the king may act when confronted by such circumstances remains uncertain, but what stands out is that all these examples deal with fundamental parts of our constitutional settlement. As such, it seems that alongside ministerial accountability and representative government, we must add the monarch's role as our constitutional guardian to the mix of things to consider.

With this in mind, let us look at the two historical events when this issue arose to see what they can tell us.

First is the passage of Home Rule for Ireland in 1912, which threatened to divide the nation irretrievably. No sooner had the crisis of reform of the House of Lords passed than the government entered into a graver constitutional crisis, which raised the spectre of civil war. The removal of the absolute veto of the House of Lords had reignited the prospect that Irish Home Rule could now be achieved, because the newly passed Parliament Act 1911 would allow the Liberal government to secure passage of the necessary legislation within the life of a single Parliament, without the need for a further appeal to the electorate. As the government was dependent on the support of the Irish Parliamentary Party, pressure was placed on Asquith to introduce a bill at once.

The Conservatives bitterly opposed the introduction and passage of such a measure and sought to frustrate its implementation. They appreciated that they may not have been able to prevent the application of Home Rule in the nationalist parts of Ireland, but they felt the forced inclusion of the Unionist communities in the north flouted the principle of self-determination.[23] To this democratic argument the Conservatives added a potent constitutional plank, declaring that the Parliament Act had created a significant gap in the constitution. The preamble to the Act had stated that 'it intended to substitute for the House of Lords … a Second Chamber constituted on a popular instead of hereditary basis'. This was a statement that had no legal effect, but the Conservatives felt it did have a moral one. They argued that until such a chamber was created and the power of the veto returned to the newly formed second chamber, the constitution was unbalanced, lacking as it did the normal checks and balances of parliamentary interchange. The resulting vacuum created by this imbalance could only be filled by the King, who would now be called on to either veto legislation or else dismiss his ministers if they refused to hold a general election to approve the implementation of Home Rule.[24]

Of crucial importance was the fact that the King seemed to agree with the Conservatives. He felt the Parliament Act had 'destroyed the very foundations of those precedents to which he would naturally look for guidance at the present time'.[25] As a result, the King feared the changed political relationship between the Commons and the Lords had placed him in an untenable position as only he 'alone can now compel a Government to refer to the Country any measure which hitherto would have been so referred by the action of the Lords'.[26] It was this predicament that had led him to oppose the passage of the Parliament Act in the first place.

Supported by this royal approval, the Conservatives felt secure in their belief that the Liberals were acting in a truly unconstitutional manner – a view that was similarly held by the Liberals with regards to the actions of the Conservatives. To resolve the impasse and to protect the King's position, Bonar Law looked to force an election. He hoped the Conservatives would win the contest, but if the Liberals were victorious then the Conservatives would accept the fact the government had the support of the people and so confine their opposition to orthodox political channels.[27] The question before him was one of how the party could compel the government to call such an election now the Lords' veto no longer existed. The answer seemed to be to play the King.[28] Bonar Law knew that the only way the government could be compelled to call an election would be if the King were to refuse royal assent to the bill, insist his ministers recommend a dissolution or threaten to dismiss his ministers unless they agreed to an election.

The government naturally rejected this argument, arguing instead that the Parliament Act had finally settled a major constitutional question by confirming that only the government of the day could compel an election. The Liberals had certainly never intended to remove this power from the Lords only for it to reappear in the hands of the King. George V therefore found himself faced with a terrible constitutional dilemma, a fact that Bonar Law and the Conservative leadership were keen to impress upon him. Speaking to the King in September 1913, Bonar Law made it clear that it

is my firm belief that he [the King] could not avoid personal responsibility, that whether the Bill were allowed to become law, or whether he exercised his right to secure a General Election, in either case his action would be condemned by half his subjects, and that it was an open question whether greater permanent harm would be done to the Monarchy by an attack from the extreme supporters of the Government, or by the bitter and lasting resentment of the people of Ulster and those who sympathised with them.[29]

To overcome this conflict, George V looked to act in a way that reflected his understanding of constitutional propriety. As the record of these events by Lord Stamfordham makes clear, the King was of the view that it was for the politicians to decide whether Home Rule should be adopted, but it was his duty to prevent a civil war.[30] He insisted that this issue be discussed at every meeting with the Prime Minister going forwards, as up to this moment, Asquith had never alluded to the matter nor sought the King's advice.[31] Making it clear that he reserved the right to either dismiss his ministers or else refuse his assent to the proposed legislation, he placed pressure on the government to compromise and recognise that the majority in Ulster were opposed to Home Rule.

Asquith bristled at the King's intervention, believing that not only was the Home Rule Bill merely an ordinary legislative measure but that Unionists were over-egging the opposition in Ulster to Home Rule for political advantage. As a result, the bill lacked the constitutional significance the King was granting it. Nevertheless, the pressure worked and Asquith proposed the temporary exclusion of Ulster from Home Rule two months later in March 1914.

If he felt this decision would mollify the King, he would be disappointed. George V was firmly focused on the issue of consent. If this could not be met through parliamentary channels, he felt certain that a general election would have to be held before Home Rule could come into effect. Alternatively, he felt that a referendum on this issue could also bridge the democratic divide that had bedevilled the government's policy. If neither approach were adopted, the King feared there would be civil war.[32]

In pursuing his aim of either an election or referendum, the King was able to pressure the government effectively due to the existence of the royal prerogative, which allowed him to either dismiss the government or withhold consent to the bill. In contemplating which power to use, it was accepted in royal circles that dismissal would be the best course of action as this would lead to the appointment of Bonar Law and the holding of a general election shortly afterwards. This course of action would not require the King to disregard ministerial advice but would lead to a democratic vote on the policy in question. Failing that, the refusal of assent at least had the benefit of limiting the action to the Home Rule Bill itself.[33]

Keen to uphold constitutional practices and to allow the government the possibility of pursuing a policy he could support, the King informed Asquith on 5 February 1914 that should this issue become one in which the peace of the kingdom was imperilled, he would '[exert] every means in his power to avert it'.[34] Asquith correctly interpreted this as informing him that the King reserved the right to use his personal powers. Although this action would lead to the dismissal of the ministry, the King would refuse assent should the situation arise. 'Assent might be given,' he felt, 'on the understanding that the will of the people should be consulted, and at once, as to whether the Act should be put into force or not.'[35] In making this statement we can see shades of Twomey's argument that assent can be withheld if a change of government takes place before the implementation of the legislative process is complete.

In the end, the government amended the Home Rule Bill to exclude the six counties of Ulster for six years and the King yielded, as the country had now entered the First World War. His decision not to refuse consent was based on his understanding that as the bill could only come into effect after the end of the war and the negotiations with Ulster had been concluded, the issue was still far from settled. The royal assent in such circumstances was thus merely a formal act, as there was still room for further legislation, debate in Parliament and an election before the issue was finally resolved. In other words, the constitutional mechanism would continue to run along accepted lines, thus ending a crisis that could compel royal intervention. He made clear, however, that he retained his right of veto, though this was a power he felt to be such an extreme course that it 'should not be adopted unless there is convincing evidence that it would avert a national disaster, or at least have a tranquil-lising effect on the distracting conditions of the time'.[36] However, this leaves us in no doubt that George V believed he could veto legislation should the need arise.

This brings us neatly to the second historical event when po-tential refusal of the royal assent became a matter of live political debate – Brexit. Friday 9 June 2017 will be forever remembered as one of the key pivotal moments in British politics, for this was the day it became clear that Theresa May had lost her gamble in calling a general election. As the constituency results trickled in, it became clear that although the Conservatives would remain the largest party in the House of Commons, they would lack an overall major-ity. Everyone in Westminster now understood that the fate of the Prime Minister's Brexit policy now lay in the hands of Parliament. This was the worst possible situation that May could find herself in, with the Brexit process still far from over. Rather than strength-ening her hand for the negotiations ahead as she had hoped, May found herself at the mercy of her colleagues.

Faced with strong headwinds, May doggedly looked to stitch together an agreement that would be acceptable to both the EU and her parliamentary colleagues over the next few months. It was far from easy going, but she at last was ready to seek approval for her agreement in November of the following year. With Cabinet approval gained, the Withdrawal Agreement made its way to Parliament, where it became clear to everyone involved that the battle for its passage would be far from easy. The electoral maths was against May from the start, and with a disunited party and a determined opposition, the government was always going to be in for a rough ride. However, what made matters worse was that Sir Keir Starmer, as shadow Brexit Secretary, picked his battleground well by focusing on the Attorney General's advice on the Withdrawal Agreement. He pushed for its release, but the government resisted and so he resorted to a historical parliamentary procedure called a humble address to force the government to release the advice. The issue was debated and the government lost the vote but still refused to issue the advice. The opposition responded by tabling a motion of contempt of Parliament, which, amazingly, the government lost by eighteen votes, making it the first government in history to be found in contempt.[37]

In the following months, the government would be defeated numerous times on its flagship policy of leaving the EU, but several votes of no confidence in the government did not pass. This emboldened the government's opponents to go further and seek to overturn Standing Order 14, allowing backbench MPs to seize control of the order paper and hold a series of indicative votes on Brexit alternatives. This rule had ensured that government business had to take priority in the Chamber, but following the passage of the Grieve amendment, it was now possible for the opposition and backbench MPs to promote legislation themselves, a fact which raised the spectre of the royal veto.[38] Should any of these backbench bills have passed, it was argued that May should recommend that the monarch refuse assent.[39]

This was a view taken by Sir Stephen Laws and Professor Richard Ekins, as they felt the move by the Commons to seize control of the order paper from the government created a profound constitutional crisis that could have brought the monarch into the realm of political controversy. In a paper for the think tank Policy Exchange, they outlined that the attempt by a cross-party coalition of MPs to move the initiative in policy-making from the government to the Commons ran contrary to the logic of our constitution because it undermined the political accountability of the government and, by extension, electoral democracy.[40] They pointed out that as the Commons itself was not equipped or able to govern, it should confine itself to the oversight of governmental actions. So long as the Commons was unwilling to withdraw its confidence, ministers alone exercised the right and responsibility to govern.

To preserve this balance, they argued that any legislation designed to usurp the government's functions should be blocked, in the first instance by relying on the House's own procedures. If the Speaker were to subvert the normal rules, however, the government could advise that Parliament should be prorogued, ending a session of Parliament prematurely to prevent a bill from being passed by both Houses. The government could also have treated its defeat as a matter of confidence by itself moving a motion under the Fixed-Term Parliaments Act to trigger a general election. If neither of these procedures managed to prevent the usurpation of government authority, then as a last resort the government might ask that the Queen refuse consent to any legislation passed by an abuse of constitutional process.

As the indicative Brexit votes engendered nothing but further confusion due to the House's rejection of all the proposed alternatives put before it, the issue did not become live. Instead, the government tried to hold a further meaningful vote on 29 March, which was predictably rejected once again by 344 to 286. With parliamentary government effectively derailed by these votes, the levels of hysteria within Westminster reached record levels. The government and Parliament found themselves deadlocked due to their inability to agree a way forward, as they both lacked the will to either undo the results of the referendum or else accept the compromises necessary to ensure Brexit. In the end, the issue would be resolved by the general election of 2019 that saw Boris Johnson retuned with a large enough majority to finally ensure the passage of the Withdrawal Agreement.

What these events and most of the academic opinion make clear is that royal assent can potentially be refused with ministerial consent, but there is no consensus on what should happen when these kinds of exceptional circumstances occur. Where the king's duty lies in these circumstances is also contested. As assent is given without formal advice being presented by the government, it appears that the monarch has the ability to refuse such a request in much the same way as they can refuse a dissolution. They can also proactively take action to preserve a greater constitutional principle. Therefore, in this situation, the government can only offer informal 'advice' not formal 'Advice'. This allows for a degree of royal autonomy to exist.

That said, most commentators accept that it is prudent for the sovereign to seek ministerial support in this event, as the king could not legitimately be criticised for following the advice of a government that must seek the confidence of Parliament. Criticism in such circumstances ought to be directed at the government, which is democratically accountable to Parliament and whose constitutional role is to absorb such criticism instead of the monarch.

The king could, however, be criticised for *not* seeking ministerial advice. In this situation, the monarch would lose their ministerial shield, opening them up to direct criticism from MPs. Bearing the brunt of criticism that would otherwise be directed at the monarch is the most ancient of ministerial functions. Removing that possibility would breach norms that have stood for centuries and would be a genuine failure of democracy and accountability.

None of this, however, helps us understand the monarch's role in a situation like Brexit, where the Commons rejected the government's policy, looked to take control of the business of the House but still resolutely refused to say that it had no confidence in the government. Could a government in such a position advise the monarch to reject legislation passed in direct opposition to its primary policy aim? Ministerial responsibility and democratic accountability will be at odds with each other in such a situation and so it seems wisest to accept a degree of autonomy for the king in these circumstances. As the internal discussions that took place between the palace and No. 10 during this period are yet to be released, we can but guess as to the Queen's reaction to this unprecedented situation.

What we can say with confidence, however, is that elected politicians have a duty to strive to avoid such scenarios occurring in the first place, and it is to be hoped that a negotiated solution can be found in the House of Commons to ensure that any constitutional crisis is avoided. In this way, the prerogative of assent operates to compel politicians to act in a way that preserves our constitutional system.

As part of a sovereign's right to be consulted, encourage and warn, any objections or misgivings about proposed legislation would undoubtedly be passed on from Buckingham Palace to Downing Street months before any question of royal assent could arise so ministerial answers could be given. These answers would either allay the monarch's concerns or lead to changes in the government's approach. It is through the operation of these rights and the direct engagement of the king with the Prime Minister that royal influence would be brought to bear, rather than by the direct use of the veto. As is the case with the other personal prerogatives of the monarch, its formal use would be a sign of the failure to achieve a political compromise to an existing crisis. The true value of the power lies in its ability to influence ministerial or parliamentary behaviour so that the formal exercise of the power becomes unnecessary. Whilst the legal power of veto remains, it is impossible to set out any rules which might govern its use, save to say that any discussion of its use will be confined to the private and vigorous exchanges between the sovereign and Prime Minister.

Before bringing our discussion to a close, it is worth briefly touching upon the related subject of the king's consent. Although this power is entirely different from the royal assent, it flows from the same prerogative root source, as both deal with the monarch's role in the legislative process. The king's consent is a process by which the consent of the crown is sought whenever a proposed bill will affect the crown's own prerogatives or interests, such as hereditary revenue, individual property or estates. A similar power is exercised by the Prince of Wales in relation to the activities of the Duchy of Cornwall.

Unlike royal assent, which is sought once a bill has passed both Houses of Parliament, the king's consent is looked for before a bill is even introduced. Its origins remain unclear, but there is evidence for its use in 1728, when George II gave Parliament permission to debate the suppression of piracy. This seems to show that the king's consent was an accepted part of the legislative process prior to that period.[41] Looking to investigate the use of this power, the House of Commons Political and Constitutional Reform Committee undertook an investigation into the practice in 2014 and concluded, after hearing expert legal and parliamentary evidence, that consent was a matter of parliamentary procedure rather than a prerogative power.[42] The committee noted that if Parliament wished to abolish consent, it could do so by resolution and without any need for legislation.

This is a view that was confirmed when a spokesperson for the Queen said, in 2021, 'Queen's consent is a parliamentary process, with the role of sovereign purely formal. Consent is always granted by the monarch where requested by government. Any assertion that the sovereign has blocked legislation is simply incorrect.'[43]

Accepted practice would seem to demonstrate this. Consent is usually signified in one or both Houses of Parliament, at either the second or third reading stage, by a privy counsellor and is recorded in Hansard as having been given. Where proposed legislation that might affect the royal prerogative or the private interests of the crown is proposed by the Cabinet, the department sponsoring the bill must write to the palace to notify them, giving as much time as possible but never less than fourteen days before the bill is introduced to Parliament.[44] Legislation is then only introduced if consent has been granted. If consent is required but not signified, a bill may make no further progress through Parliament, and if a bill is mistakenly allowed to progress without receiving the required consent and the error is discovered before royal assent has been given, the proceedings may later be declared void.[45]

Whilst it may be true to say that the monarch always consents to a government measure, the same cannot be said of a private members' bill. In those circumstances, the requirement for consent can be used by the government to kill off the bill without having to muster any votes or to waste parliamentary time, by simply saying that the king does not consent. Just such an event took place in 1999, when the Queen, on the advice of her ministers, refused to give consent for Parliament to debate the Military Action Against Iraq (Parliamentary Approval) Bill, a private members' bill that sought to transfer the crown's prerogative to authorise military strikes against Iraq to Parliament.[46]

Given all this, how does the king's consent tie into our discussion of royal assent, since one is a parliamentary procedure and the other a prerogative power? Superficially, that may seem to be the case, but the two are intimately linked, as becomes clear on closer examination. In the UK, Canada and Australia, where this process operates, the established practice is clear. Use of consent primarily relates to measures that affect the monarch's prerogatives or personal interests, a fact highlighted by Erskine May in the parliamentary handbook in 1851. May stated that the practice had a very practical advantage, as queen's consent (Queen Victoria being on the throne at the time of writing) enabled the crown to protect its rights without having to resort to blocking a bill after its passage by refusing royal assent.[47]

And there you have it. King's consent is the mechanism by which Parliament and the crown agreed to moderate the need for the monarch to refuse royal assent, as all measures that directly affect the king's prerogative and interests need to obtain royal consent before being debated in Parliament. As Erskine May pointed out, the practice of prior communication between Parliament and the crown was helpful to both parties. If Parliament were to seek to affect the prerogative of the crown against its wishes, the crown would be free to protect itself by refusing royal assent.[48] Interestingly, this statement has been removed from the more recent edition of the work, replaced instead by a simple statement describing the certain conditions under which consent must be sought – leaving unsaid the implication of it not being given.

CONCLUSION: THE KING'S PEACE

Throughout this work, I have sought to prove that the King is far from a mere ornament of the constitution but is instead a vital part of our democratic settlement. He is the guardian of our constitution and the independent authority that certifies the legality of governmental actions. To this end, he possesses certain unique powers that enable him to maintain the effective operation of our political system in times of crisis and ensure our political class honour the conventions that underpin our democracy.

During a state visit to Canada in 1964, Queen Elizabeth II set out this concept more fully in her speech to the Quebec legislature. She described her role as being 'to personify the democratic state, to sanction legitimate authority, to ensure the legality of means, and guarantee the execution of the popular will'.[1] In short, to maintain the ancient concept of the king's peace. In fulfilling this role, the monarch is aided by their ministers and advisers, who are charged with ensuring that nothing illegal or unconstitutional can be put before the sovereign. We can see this concept in action when we look at the Queen's actions during the end of empire. When faced with unconstitutional actions in colonial administrations, the palace took the view that it would be better to risk a formal break and the establishment of a republic than to see the Queen act in an unconstitutional manner, an approach adopted in Rhodesia in 1964.[2]

The king's peace is an ancient notion, originating in the time of the Anglo-Saxons and vaguely developed under the early English kings. Rooted in their role as the executive of God's will on earth, early kings were instilled with the primary task of ensuring the good order of the domestic realm in accordance with biblical teachings. Nominally tied to their own households and servants, this concept sought to prevent the use of violence in society. It was greatly expanded following the Norman Conquest to cover the whole realm and the wider public order, as outlined in the laws of Edward the Confessor.[3] As the concept of law developed in the Middle Ages, this idea was further refined with criminal and civic acts, separated into distinct categories. The king was still responsible for ensuring the enforcement of the law, but nuances as to what constituted crimes began to shape legal thinking.

The king's role in the enforcement of the law flowed from his responsibility to safeguard public order, as the monarch was seen to be the ultimate authority in the land. This concept underpinned the arguments between Charles I and Parliament, as his opponents felt he was failing in his duty to uphold the lawful government of the kingdom. As a result, they were freed of their allegiance to him, a realisation that led to civil war. This is why the revolutionary settlement expressly outlined the monarch's role as protector and enforcer of the law.

Constitutional monarchy is therefore a form of government that, above all else, ensures the legitimacy of both sovereign and subject through adherence to the rule of law. It does this by placing the head of state beyond political competition, an outcome that is only possible if it is accepted that a hereditary head of state will be responsible for the maintenance of the constitution itself. In so doing, a monarch can represent the whole nation, becoming in the process a national symbol of unity. That is the monarchy's central function and is the justification for its existence.

This is a process that is solidified by the act of coronation. Although not required by law, as the succession takes place automatically upon the death of the monarch, the coronation reflects the realisation that the succession must be based on consent and acceptance, rather than strictly hereditary right. For this reason, it is felt that the coronation helps 'maketh a perfect and true king'.[4] Borrowed from the ancient rights developed for the consecration of Byzantine emperors, this ceremony has evolved over the centuries into the one we know today and stands as an important civic event. The ceremony incorporates and perpetuates features which are designed to highlight and place specific limits and conditions on the king's use of power.[5]

The service traditionally focused on the idea that the king was a servant of God and the church and that loyalty to the king's person and office was an important Christian duty. This was modified slightly in the seventeenth century to include a sense of civic duty and the idea that the king was the servant of not just God but his subjects as well, something that was achieved by a public ceremony which demonstrated to the public that the king was in lawful possession of the crown, throne and kingdom. The coronation is thus an act of legitimisation, where brute power is converted into the more acceptable form of authority.

Central to this is the taking of the oath, where the king makes his solemn promise to serve the people of his kingdoms. Having sworn his oath publicly and in a solemn and sacred ceremony, the oath must be kept, for it is the basis of his reign's legitimacy. It is an oath enshrined in law under section 2 of the Act of Settlement 1701 and the Coronation Oath Act 1688 and so has the force of law behind it. This is also why ministers are considered incapable of presenting the monarch with an illegal act.

The archbishop administers the oath by asking, 'Will you solemnly promise and swear to govern the Peoples of the United Kingdom of Great Britain and Northern Ireland, your other Realms and the Territories to any of them belonging or pertaining, according to their respective laws and customs?'

To which the monarch responds, 'I solemnly promise so to do.'[6]

It is important to note at this point that the coronation ceremony belongs to the wider fraternity of the English-speaking peoples, as the King is head of state of fifteen separate realms, all of whom have their own laws and constitutional settlements. The oath recognises this fact and binds the king to act in a lawful and constitutional manner in each jurisdiction. In this way, the monarch's gaze is slightly wider than that of their domestic ministers, ensuring they enjoy a degree of autonomy in dealing with their separate governments.

In this way, our constitutional monarchy yields continuity in the form of the state, which ensures the effective operation of our political system by providing institutional legitimacy. It does this by offering fixed constitutional landmarks and institutional continuity within a constantly changing world. It allows for our political system to continually reinvent itself to meet the challenges of the times.

But the monarchy is far more than a mere piece of the wider constitutional mechanism, as the king is both head of state and head of the nation, the very living representation of this United Kingdom. To fulfil this function, the monarch must exist above the political fray, free from the ties of party and uncorrupted by the divisions of the moment. Political heads of state can too easily divide rather than unite their countries. The monarchy's neutral position in politics allows it to serve as a unifying and non-partisan force, providing stability and continuity in the midst of an ever-changing political landscape. Not only are the UK, Canada, Australia and New Zealand continually ranked at the top of global lists for stability and democracy, but so are their fellow European monarchies, with the Scandinavians and the Dutch leading the way on the continent. Unlike the situation in the US or France, where political Presidents have divided their societies, our King remains above mere politics. A constitutional monarchy settles beyond argument the crucial question of who is to be the head of state and in so doing, places the head of state beyond political competition. They alone can represent the nation as a whole, unifying rather than dividing, by interpreting our society and reflecting that image back to us in an emotional way. In our case, however, the king remains above mere politics. The idea of 'King and Country' has an ability to stir a civic nationalism, which transcends the political divide, uniting the nation in the process.

All of this ensures that the British monarchy is one of the most and least discussed institutions within our country. The dignified role that the monarchy performs in acting as the unifying force of national life obscures the efficient role it plays in ensuring the smooth running of our constitutional system. Throughout these pages, I have sought to draw back the curtain and reveal the true nature of the wizard, separating fact from fiction so that we may all have a better understating of how our political system operates.

Central to this has been the argument that the king is the guardian of the constitution and an independent authority that certifies the legality of governmental action, a function they perform by being the repository of certain unique powers that can be deployed in times of emergency to ensure the proper functioning of the state. The king is required by the principles of responsible government to act on the advice of his ministers, but in doing so, he must be satisfied that the actions requested are themselves lawful.

This is the concept that Queen Elizabeth II set out in 1964, when she described her role as a constitutional monarch to the Quebec legislature. The statement neatly outlined the role of a constitutional monarch in today's political system. However, this role is only possible if we accept that the monarch has the power to compel the maintenance of legitimate authority and legality, and the tools that ensure they are able to achieve this are the royal prerogatives. As the king alone possesses the power to appoint and dismiss our Prime Ministers, to dissolve Parliament and to assent to legislation, they have the means of ensuring that ministers abide by the constitutional covenants that underpin our political settlement. The king is protected from the overt use of these powers by an acceptance on the part of British officials that they will never place before him advice they regard as unconstitutional, regardless of whether or not the matter might be subject to judicial oversight.[7]

This is a degree of protection that is often missing for the King's vice-regal representatives within the other Commonwealth realms, who, to a far greater extent, are involved in requests that raise issues of illegality and unconstitutionality. It is for this reason that many of the examples we have as to the correct usage of the prerogative powers come from those jurisdictions, where there is not only a greater acceptance of the intervention of the crown but also a greater opportunity for the use of prerogative powers. Within these realms, we find that discussions of the powers inherent in the monarchy are more openly expressed as their use is more common. Politicians and academics in Canada, Australia and New Zealand are more willing to accept the premise that the king or their representative may refuse to act on ministerial advice that would require them to act in a manner that is illegal or unconstitutional than is the case in the UK, where officials go to great lengths to prevent such issues arising in the first place. In refusing such advice, it is argued, the king exercises a discretion made possible by their role as the guardian of the constitutional settlement, a role they swore to uphold during their coronation.

For those who accept the premise that the king has a degree of autonomy in the exercise of their constitutional functions, the arguments revolve around if and when the monarchy may act. These are issues which are often difficult to determine, as they so often rely on the variables at play in any given political crisis. Broadly, it comes down to the interplay of the three primary constitutional principles:

1. The principle of responsible government – that the King acts on the advice of their responsible ministers.
2. The principle of the rule of law – that the executive as a whole must adhere to the constitutional principles and the law.
3. The principle of the separation of powers – that the determination of legality is decided by the judiciary rather than the executive.

It is when these principles find themselves in conflict and the only way a situation can be resolved is by the exercise of royal agency that we find the true value of the monarch to our constitutional system.

When faced with a situation where ministers have presented advice that is either illegal or unconstitutional on a subject that excludes judicial oversight, there are some practical steps the king can take before they need worry about exercising their prerogative powers. This is where Bagehot's concept of the rights of the monarchy enters the frame, as the king has an unquestionable right to advise, consult and warn – actions which can compel ministers to either justify the legality of their actions or modify their conduct to conform to constitutional principles. In response, the government may either backtrack or insist on its advice being accepted. So long as the government acquiesces to the monarch's actions or lack thereof, it retains responsibility for its measures, as the king has not formally exercised their discretion.

The first action the king can take is to simply query the advice that has been presented. It may be that an error has been made, which can be simply corrected at this stage. In this way, the monarch acts as a vital sounding board for ministers, who can rely on the king's experience and greater knowledge of constitutional practice. If the government persists with its proposed course of action, the king may request formal legal advice from the government law officers. This request will compel the government to examine its actions and the strength of its legal argument. Officials will place considerable pressure on ministers not to present the king with advice that does not at least have the weight of a responsible legal argument. The request for a legal opinion will, in most cases, resolve the issues, because the production of a legal opinion will either remove any doubts that may have arisen as to the legality or constitutionality of a proposed course of action or will compel the government to withdraw its advice. Having requested legal advice, the monarch is then bound by it, thus insulating the institution from any legal or political fallout. It will then fall to either the courts or Parliament to determine the validity of the act, as was the case with prorogation in 2019.

The rejection of ministerial advice or acting contrary to that advice is the last resort open to the monarch. Whether the king should act in this manner will depend entirely upon the circumstances that confront them and the country, the gravity of the issue and the applicable constitutional principles involved. Such actions are the ultimate circuit breaker within the British constitutional settlement and should only ever be considered when all other avenues of action have been exhausted. Their use is a sign of political failure, for it will signal that ministers have pressed on the king actions which cannot be justified and so have exposed the monarch to controversy. To prevent this from happening, the King's private secretary, in coordination with the Cabinet Secretary and the Prime Minister, will seek to protect the King by ensuring that any proposals that are seen to be either illegal or unconstitutional are not placed before him, a process which extends to the submissions made directly to the monarch by the other Commonwealth realms.

All of this brings us back to where we began, with the actions of the Johnson administration in early 2019. It was during this period that the monarch's role became more apparent than it has been for some time. When requesting a long prorogation period during the crucial last weeks of the Brexit negotitations, the government sought to bypass parliamentary oversight. The palace expressed its concerns with the course of action, but the government insisted on pressing ahead with its request. To ensure the legality of what was proposed, legal advice was sought. Assurances as to its legality were duly given and the monarch's consent was obtained on these assurances. It was only during the subsequent court case that it was found no formal legal advice on whether the prorogation was lawful or justiciable was given, as Johnson had requested the Attorney General keep his advice limited in scope. That said, there were no strong voices within the wider government arguing that this was an illegal act.[8] For all these reasons, it was reasonable for the Queen to consent to the prorogation. This was a position accepted by the Supreme Court, which made clear it was the advice given by ministers that was illegal, not the Queen's actions. A case could be made that the palace should have scrutinised the proposals more formally and applied the lessons learnt in Canada and Australia, but this was new ground for the UK, which helps explain their actions.

The issues that had been experienced over prorogation meant officials were all the more diligent when they confronted the Prime Minister over his refusal to seek an extension to the Brexit deadline, as required by the Benn Act. First, when Johnson sought advice from Geoffrey Cox about his ability to advise the Queen to refuse assent to the bill, officials circled the wagons. There was enough concern about the political fallout that could result from the use of the royal prerogative in this manner that the issue was never formally placed before the Queen. Instead, palace officials let it be known that the Queen would refuse any such advice and the issue was dropped. Faced with a legal requirement to request an extension past 31 October, Johnson sought ways to frustrate the aims of the Act, going so far as to say he would refuse to comply with its terms. To counter this, legal officers informed him that he would have to send the letter as legally required, but Johnson persisted in expressing his intention to ignore the Act. This led to a heated discussion in Downing Street, in which Helen MacNamara had to point out the reality that the wider civil service and security forces would not support an illegal act by the Prime Minister. If he persisted in his actions, then they would have no option but to advise the Queen to dismiss him from office. This stark fact ensured the Prime Minister backed down and complied with the will of Parliament.

This underlines the principle that the King is anything but a mere ornament to our constitutional settlement. Rather, the monarch is a vital force, who ensures the integrity of our constitutional settlement in their role as the guardian of the constitution. By holding the key powers of appointment, dismissal, dissolution and assent, the monarch ensures that government actions can always be checked. No matter how mighty a Prime Minister becomes, they can still be held within the bounds of law and custom. For this reason, any power that the king holds can only be used in a manner that is constituent with and supports fundamental constitutional principles. The royal prerogatives are most effective when they are able to change government policy without being formally exercised. The use of influence and institutional heft allows the King to operate in way that is consistent with democratic values and constitutional principles.

The fact that these powers have not been overtly exercised in the UK in modern times is a testament to their effectiveness as they have ensured political participants have behaved in constitutionally acceptable ways. The king's ability to operate independently acts as a corrective, which ensures politicians either behave in accordance with established rules and conventions, especially around their responsibility to Parliament, or resign. In rare cases, the king needs to merely point to the existence of their powers to ensure correct behaviour – Bagehot's right to warn in action. The exercise of these powers, therefore, often takes place in private, preventing us from perceiving their use. It is only when a particular example emerges in the archives, histories and memoirs of a period that we catch glimpses of their existence. For whilst the king may perform a largely symbolic role, it's a symbolism that is given substance by the existence of the royal prerogatives, powers that may be used to uphold and maintain the fundamental constitutional principles of the UK and the other realms. The exercise of these powers may be rarely observed, but their effect is significant.

Our country is changing in a profound way as we confront the new digital revolution, a process which requires the monarchy to once more transform itself to meet the needs of the nation. It falls to the King to be the one to institute this transformation, which will be far from easy. For whereas the monarchy has managed to maintain its authority in the past through an aloof separation from the people, our new forms of digital communication will simply not allow this approach to be sustained in today's world. To survive, the monarchy will need to be more engaged in civic society than ever before and this will require the institution and its supporters to be more open about the role it plays in our society. Whilst the monarchy could sustain itself in the past by simply being seen, today's monarchy must be seen to do.

To that end, we should not be shy about discussing not only the King's role within our political process but also the powers he holds, which enable him to meet these obligations. The symbolic and the practical exist side by side within our constitutional monarchy, enabling the King to be an effective agent of the state. The King's ultimate role is to deny power to others, ensuring that no one politician can ever become so mighty as to threaten our parliamentary democracy. He does this by holding the powers of appointment, dismissal, dissolution and assent that he wields either singularly or collectively to ensure that the political system operates in the way that it is intended to. As the Duke of Edinburgh once said, 'I think it is a complete misconception to imagine that the monarchy exists in the interests of the monarch. It doesn't. It exists in the interests of the people.'⁹ So long as the King serves our interests, whether here or in the other Commonwealth realms, he will continue to reign over us. Should he or his successors fail in their duty, the monarchy simply will not survive.

NOTES

1. The King's Majesty

1   Robert Hardman, *Charles III: The Inside Story*, London, Macmillan, 2024, pp. 55, 68–9.
2   Ed Owens, *After Elizabeth: Can The Monarchy Save Itself?*, London, Bloomsbury, 2023, pp. 21–6.
3   Robert Rhodes James, *Churchill: A Study in Failure, 1900–1939*, London, Harmondsworth, 1973, pp. 34–5.
4   Robert Rhodes James (ed.), *Winston S. Churchill: His Complete Speeches, 1897–1963*, vol. VI, London, Chelsea House Publishers, 1974, pp. 5847–9.
5   Royal.uk, 'A speech by the Queen on her 21st Birthday, 1947', https://www.royal.uk/21st-birthday-speech-21-april-1947.
6   Owens, *After Elizabeth*, pp. 152–5.
7   Sir John Fortescue, 'On the Laws and Governance of England', in Shelley Lockwood (ed.), *Cambridge Texts in the History of Political Thought*, Cambridge, Cambridge University Press, 2002.
8   M. M. Knappen, *Constitutional and Legal History of England*, London, Harcourt, Brace & Company, 1942, pp. 448–51.
9   Walter Bagehot, *The English Constitution*, Oxford, Oxford University Press, 2009.
10 Kenneth Rose, *King George V*, London, Phoenix Press, 2000, p. 35.
11 'Notes on Bagehot's English Constitution', undated, Royal Archives, Z143.
12 K. C. Wheare, 'Walter Bagehot: Lecture on a Master Mind', *Proceedings of the British Academy*, vol. 60, Oxford, Oxford University Press, 1974, p. 26.
13 Sarah Bradford, *George VI: The Dutiful King*, London, Penguin, 2011, pp. 112–13.
14 John W. Wheeler-Bennett, *King George VI*, London, Macmillan, 1958, p. 797.
15 Kenneth Harris, *The Queen*, London, Weidenfeld & Nicolson, 1994, p. 14.
16 Letter to *The Times*, 27 July 1986.
17 Bagehot, *The English Constitution*, p. 7.
18 Buckingham Palace created this distinction between 'capital A advice' and 'small a advice.' See 'Sir Martin Charteris to Mr Armstrong', 9 October 1974, National Archives, FCO 24/1894.
19 Vernon Bogdanor, *The Monarchy and the Constitution*, Oxford, Clarendon Press, 1995, p. 66.
20 Anne Twomey, *The Veiled Sceptre: Reserve Powers of Heads of State in Westminster Systems*, Cambridge, Cambridge University Press, 2018, pp. 52–3.

21 Peter Hennessy, *Muddling Through: Power, Politics and the Quality of Government in Postwar Britain*, London, Victor Gollancz, 1996, p. 16.
22 Lord Blake, 'The Monarchy', lecture delivered from Gresham College at the Guildhall, City of London, 3 July 1984.
23 Peter Ridell, 'Reason is not Treason in Monarchy Debate', *The Times*, 7 September 1994.
24 Twomey, *The Veiled Sceptre*, p. 1.
25 Royal.uk, 'The Authorised Liturgy for the Coronation Rite of His Majesty King Charles III', https://www.royal.uk/sites/default/files/documents/2023-05/23-24132%20Coronation%20Liturgy_05%20May_0.pdf.
26 Sir Roy Strong, *Coronation: From the 8th to the 21st Century*, London, HarperCollins, 2005, p. 240.
27 Tim Harris, *Revolution: The Great Crisis of the British Monarchy 1685–1720*, London, Allen Lane, 2006, p. 349.
28 Thomas Erskine May, *A Practical Treatise on the Law, Privileges, Proceedings, and Usage of Parliament*, London, Butterworths, 1851, p. 3.
29 Graeme Watt, 'The Coronation Oath', *Ecclesiastical Law Journal*, vol. 19, issue 3, September 2017, pp. 325–41.
30 *R. (Miller) v. the Prime Minister*, UKSC 41, 2019, https://supremecourt.uk/uploads/uksc_2019_0192_judgment_6862a98b60.pdf.
31 William Pitt Cobbett, *The Government of Australia*, vol. IV, unpublished manuscript, University of Sydney, 1919, p. 431.
32 Bogdanor, *The Monarchy*, p. 65.
33 Anthony King, *The British Constitution*, Oxford, Oxford University Press, 2010, p. 249.
34 Peter Hennessy, *The Hidden Wiring: Unearthing the British Constitution*, London, Victor Gollancz, 1995, p. 48.
35 Jennings, *The British Constitution*, pp. 195–203.
36 Cabinet Office, 'Introduction', *The Cabinet Manual*, sec. 1–3, p. 2.
37 Bogdanor, *The Monarchy and the Constitution*, pp. 1–42.
38 Twomey, *The Veiled Sceptre*, p. 4–7.
39 F. W. Maitland, *The Constitutional History of England*, Cambridge University Press, Cambridge, 1913, p. 300.
40 A. V. Dicey, *Introduction to the Study of the Law of the Constitution*, Indianapolis, Liberty Fund, 1982, pp. 3–4.
41 'Vernon Bogdanor: Britain is in the process of developing a constitution', *The Independent*, 22 September 2004.
42 Aileen Kavanagh, 'The Constitutional Separation of Powers', in David Dyzenhaus and Malcolm Thorburn (eds), *Philosophical Foundations of Constitutional Law*, Oxford, Oxford University Press, 2016, pp. 234–237.
43 'Cabinet Office: Precedent Books "Prime Minister's Relationship with the Monarch,"' 1954, National Archives, CAB 181.
44 William Blackstone, *Commentaries on the Laws of England*, London, Forgotten Books, 2012, p. 10.
45 'His Majesty The King's Declaration', 10 September 2022, https://www.royal.uk/his-majesty-kings-declaration.

2. The King's Pleasure
1 Noel Cox, *The Royal Prerogative and Constitutional Law: A search for the quintessence of executive power*, Abingdon, Routledge, 2022, p. 20.
2 Alex Carroll, *Constitutional and Administrative Law*, 5th ed., Harlow, Pearson, 2009, p. 246.
3 *Glasbrook Bros Ltd v. Glamorgan County Council*, 1924, AC 20 HL.
4 Carroll, *Constitutional and Administrative Law*, p. 246.
5 *BBC v. Johns*, 1965, Ch 32 a 79, 1 All ER 923 at 941, CA.
6 Colin R. Munro, *Studies in Constitutional Law*, 2nd ed., London, Butterworths, 1999, p. 258.

7   Claudia Gold, *King of the North Wind: The Life of Henry II in Five Acts*, London, William Collins, 2018, pp. 103–5, 108–9, 127.
8   Cox, *The Royal Prerogative and Constitutional Law*, p. 31.
9   John Cannon and Ralph Griffiths, *The Oxford Illustrated History of the British Monarchy*, Oxford, Oxford University Press, 1988, pp. 148–9.
10 S. E. Thorne (ed.), *Bracton on the Laws and Customs of England*, vol. II, Cambridge, MA, Harvard University Press, 1968, p. 33.
11 J. Enoch Powell and Keith Wallis, *The House of Lords in the Middle Ages*, London, Weidenfeld & Nicolson, 1968, pp. 125–129.
12 C. H. McIlwain, 'Medieval Estates', in John Bagnell Bury (ed.), *The Cambridge Medieval History*, vol. VII, Cambridge, Cambridge University Press, 1932, p. 712.
13 Munro, *Studies in Constitutional Law*, pp. 261–2.
14 See Diarmaid MacCulloch, *Thomas Cromwell*, London, Penguin, 2019 for examples of all three; Powell & Wallis, *The House of Lords in the Middle Ages*, pp. 563–582; Sir David L. Keir, *The Constitutional History of Modern Britain, 1485–1937*, London, Adam and Charles Black, 1948, p. 151–2.
15 Sir William Holdsworth, *A History of English Law*, vol. VI, London, Methuen & Co, 1924, pp. 204–7.
16 Cannon, *The Oxford Illustrated History of the British Monarchy*, p. 299.
17 Fortescue, *The Governance of England*, p. 109.
18 Sir Thomas Smith, *De Republica Anglorum*, ed. M. Dewar, Cambridge, Cambridge University Press, 1982, pp. 78, 87.
19 Maitland, *The Constitutional History of England*, p. 197.
20 Ibid., pp. 268–71.
21 Keir, *The Constitutional History of Modern Britain*, pp. 198–9.
22 *Case of Proclamations*, 1611, 12 Co rep 74.
23 Munro, *Studies in Constitutional Law*, p. 265.
24 Harris, *Revolution*, pp. 312–14.
25 Maitland, *The Constitutional History of England*, pp. 283–85.
26 Thomas Pitt Taswell-Langmead, *English Constitutional History: From the Teutonic Conquest to the Present Time*, 8th ed., London, Sweet & Maxwell, 1919, pp. 618–22.
27 Colin Kidd, *Subverting Scotland's Past: Scottish Whig Historians and the Creation of an Anglo-British Identity 1689–1830*, Cambridge, Cambridge University Press, 2003, pp. 132–3.
28 Taswell-Langmead, *English Constitutional History*, pp. 622–3.
29 Harris, *Revolution*, pp. 392–4.
30 Munro, *Studies in Constitutional Law*, p. 265.
31 Knappen, *Constitutional and Legal History of England*, pp. 448–451.
32 Munro, *Studies in Constitutional Law*, p. 264.
33 Cox, *The Royal Prerogative and Constitutional Law*, p. 52.
34 Ibid., p. 54.
35 Holdsworth, *A History of English Law*, p. 207.
36 Cox, *The Royal Prerogative and Constitutional Law*, p. 267.
37 Ibid., p. 268.
38 Goldwin Smith, *A Constitutional and Legal History of England*, London, Dorset Press, 1990, pp. 382–3.
39 Bogdanor, *The Monarchy and the Constitution*, p. 66.
40 Ibid., p. 66.
41 Ibid., pp. 66–7.
42 Bagehot, *The English Constitution*, p. 70.
43 Bogdanor, *The Monarchy and the Constitution*, p. 69.
44 T. E. Kebbel (ed.), *Selected Speeches of Lord Beaconsfield*, vol. II, London, Longmans, Green & Co, 1881, p. 493.

45 Bagehot, *The English Constitution*, p. 64.
46 'Miners Petition the Queen', *The Courier*, 12 August 1984.
47 Dean Palmer, *The Queen and Mrs Thatcher: An Inconvenient Relationship*, Stroud, The History Press, 2016, pp. 167–8.
48 Andrew Neil, *Full Disclosure*, London, Pan, 1997.
49 Palmer, *The Queen and Mrs Thatcher*, pp. 168–9.
50 'Queen dismayed by "uncaring Thatcher"', *Sunday Times*, 20 July 1986.
51 *Today*, 18 July 1986.
52 'Queen dismayed by "uncaring Thatcher"', *Sunday Times*, 20 July 1986.
53 Charles Moore, *Margaret Thatcher: The Authorised Biography*, vol. II, London, Penguin, 2016, pp. 576–80.
54 'Michael Shea', *Daily Telegraph*, 19 October 2009.
55 Maurice V. Brett (ed.), *Journals and Letters of Reginald, Viscount Esher*, vol. III, London, Ivor Nicholson & Watson, 1938, pp. 126–8.
56 *The Times*, 28 July 1986.
57 Bogdanor, *The Monarchy and the Constitution*, p. 71.
58 Twomey, *The Veiled Sceptre*, p. 1.
59 Public Administration Select Committee, 'Taming the Prerogative: Strengthening Ministerial Accountability to Parliament', HC422, 16 March 2004, paras 5–8.
60 Office of the Parliamentary Counsel, 'Queen's or Prince's Consent', October 2013 para 2.7; Political and Constitutional Reform Committee, 'The Impact of Queen's and Prince's Consent on the Legislative Process', HC784, 26 March 2014, para 6.
61 Twomey, *The Veiled Sceptre*, p. 6.
62 Rodney Brazier, '"Monarchy and the Personal Prerogatives": A personal response to Professor Blackburn', *Public Law*, spring, 2005, pp. 45, 47; Geoffrey Marshall, *Constitutional Conventions*, Oxford, Clarendon Press, 1984, p. 36.
63 Twomey, *The Veiled Sceptre*, p. 6.
64 Anthony Seldon and Peter Snowdon, *Cameron at 10: The Verdict*, London, William Collins, 2016, p. 10; Suzanne Heywood, *What Does Jeremy Think?: Jeremy Heywood and the Making of Modern Britain*, London, William Collins, 2021, pp. 291–2, 305.
65 Bogdanor, *The Monarchy and the Constitution*, p. 75.
66 'Esher to Knollys', 9 January 1910, Royal Archives, K2552 (1).
67 Dermot Morrah, *The Work of the Queen*, London, William Kimber, 1958, p. 160.
68 Bogdanor, *The Monarchy and the Constitution*, p. 76.

3. The King's First Minister

1 Ben Pimlott, *The Queen: Elizabeth II and the Monarchy – Golden Jubilee Edition*, London, HarperCollins, 2001, p. 418.
2 Colin Turpin and Adam Tomkins (ed.), *The British Government and the Constitution: Text and Materials*, 7th ed., Cambridge, Cambridge University Press, 2011, p. 379.
3 'Cabinet Office: Precedent Books "Prime Minister's Relationship with the Monarch,"', p. 2; Philip Norton, *Governing Britain: Parliament, Ministers and our Ambiguous Constitution*, Manchester, Manchester University Press, 2020, p. 130.
4 Ronald Fraser to Sir Norman Brooks, 'Functions of the Prime Minister and his Staff', 1949, National Archives, CAB 21/1638.
5 Roy Jenkins, *Baldwin*, London, HarperCollins, 1987, p. 77.
6 Rose, *King George V*, pp. 371–77.
7 Anthony Howard, *RAB: A Life of R.A. Butler*, London, Papermac, 1988, pp. 195–9.
8 'Political Crisis', *Sydney Morning Herald*, 21 April 1939.
9 Ross McMullin, *The Light on the Hill: The Australian Labor Party 1891–1991*, OUP Australia, Sydney, 1991, pp. 234–5.
10 Alan Reid, *The Power Struggle*, Sydney, Shakespeare Head Press, 1971, pp. 122–3.

11 Turpin and Tomkins, *The British Government and the Constitution*, p. 382.

12 Rodney Brazier, *Choosing A Prime Minister: The Transfer of Power in Britain*, Oxford, Oxford University Press, 2020, p. 13.

13 Ibid., p. 14.

14 Robert Blake, *The Office of Prime Minister*, Oxford, Oxford University Press, 1975, p. 41–2.

15 Norton, *Governing Britain*, p. 128.

16 Cabinet Office, *The Cabinet Manual*, sec. 2.8.

17 Political and Constitutional Reform Committee, 'Lessons from the process of Government formation after the 2010 General Election', HC528, 2011, paras 16–22.

18 House of Lords Constitution Committee, '12th Report: The Cabinet Manual', HL107, 2011, para 61.

19 'Memorandum of Mr Geoffrey de Deney, Clerk of the Privy Council, para 7, 10 September 1987', in Rodney Brazier, *Constitutional Texts: Materials on Government and the Constitution*, Oxford, Oxford University Press, 1990, pp. 133–9.

20 Twomey, *The Veiled Sceptre*, p. 115.

21 Ibid., p. 18.

22 Bogdanor, *The Monarchy and the Constitution*, p. 84.

23 Rodney Brazier, *Constitutional Practice: The Foundations of British Government*, 3rd ed., Oxford, Oxford University Press, 1999, p. 11.

24 David Marquand, *Ramsay MacDonald*, London, Jonathan Cape, 1977, p. 628.

25 Ibid., p. 629.

26 Harold Nicolson, *George V: His Life and Reign*, London, Constable, 1952, p. 460–61.

27 Marquand, *Ramsay MacDonald*, p. 630.

28 Nicolson, *George V*, p. 464.

29 Marquand, *Ramsay MacDonald*, pp. 623–3.

30 Ibid., pp. 635–7.

31 Rose, *King George V*, pp. 371–77; Jenkins, *Baldwin*, pp. 126–133; Robert Self, *The Neville Chamberlain Diary Letters*, vol. III, London, Routledge, 2002, p. 276.

32 Rose, *King George V*, p. 377.

33 H. J. Laski, *Parliamentary Government of England*, London, George Allen and Unwin, 1938, p. 403.

34 John T. Saywell, *The Office of Lieutenant-Governor*, Toronto, University of Toronto Press, 1957, p. 88.

35 'Functions of the Prime Minister', National Archives, CAB 21/1638.

36 Peter Hennessy, *The Prime Ministers: The Office and Its Holders Since 1945*, London, Allan Lane, 2000, p. 34; David Pollard, Neil Parpworth and David Hughes, *Constitutional and Administrative Law*, 4th ed., Oxford, Oxford University Press, 2007, p. 138.

37 Eugene Forsey, 'Mr. King and Parliamentary Government', *Canadian Journal of Economics and Political Science*, vol. 17, issue 4, November 1951, p. 451.

38 Philip A. Joseph, *Constitutional and Administrative Law in New Zealand*, 4th ed., Wellington, Thompson Reuters, 2014, p. 734.

39 Twomey, *The Veiled Sceptre*, p. 128.

40 David Butler, *Governing Without a Majority: Dilemmas for Hung Parliaments in Britain*, London, HarperCollins, 1983, p. 80.

41 Twomey, *The Veiled Sceptre*, p. 125.

42 Norton, *Governing Britain*, p. 130.

43 Ibid., p. 131–2.

44 Rowena Mason, 'Labour leadership: Jeremy Corbyn elected with huge mandate', *The Guardian*, 12 September 2015.

45 Anushka Asthana, Rajeev Syal and Rowena Mason, 'Jeremy Corbyn to hold crisis talks as Labour MPs try to force him out', *The Guardian*, 26 June 2016.

46 Norton, *Governing Britain*, p. 136.

47 Pippa Crerar, 'Liz Truss wins Tory leadership race to become Britain's next PM', *The Guardian*, 5 September 2022.

48 Brazier, *Constitutional Practice*, p. 26–7.

49 Nigel Fisher, *The Tory Leaders: Their Struggle for Power*, London, Weidenfeld & Nicolson, 1977, p. 6.

50 Jenkins, *Baldwin*, p. 131.

51 Ibid., pp. 131–3.

52 Butler, *Coalitions in British Politics*, pp. 69–73.

53 Marquand, *Ramsay MacDonald*, p. 761–3.

54 Ibid., p. 768.

55 Jenkins, *Baldwin*, pp. 134–5; Marquand, *Ramsay MacDonald*, pp. 765–9; Jeremy Dobson, *Why Do the People Hate Me So: The Strange Interlude Between the Two Great Wars in the Britain of Stanley Baldwin*, Leicester, Matador, 2009, pp. 242–3.

56 Jenkins, *Baldwin*, p. 135.

57 Rose, *King George V*, pp. 395–6.

58 Marquand, *Ramsay MacDonald*, p. 776.

59 Walter Reid, *Neville Chamberlain: The Passionate Radical*, Edinburgh, Birlinn, 2021, p. 147.

60 Dobson, *Why Do the People Hate Me So*, p. 243.

61 Robert Crowcroft, *The End Is Nigh: British Politics, Power, and the Road to The Second World War*, Oxford, Oxford University Press, 2019, pp. 14–16.

62 Jenkins, *Baldwin*, p. 136.

63 Peter T. Marsh, *The Chamberlain Litany: Letters Within a Governing Family, From Empire to Appeasement*, London, Haus Publishing, 2010, p. 271; Reid, *Neville Chamberlain*, p. 147.

64 Reid, *Neville Chamberlain*, pp. 149–62.

65 Marsh, *The Chamberlain Litany*, pp. 271–80.

66 Iain Macleod, *Neville Chamberlain*, London, Frederick Muller Ltd, 1961, p. 194–5.

67 Alexander Larman, *The Crown in Crisis: Countdown to the Abdication*, London, Weidenfeld & Nicolson, 2020, pp. 241–50.

68 Jenkins, *Baldwin*, p. 161.

69 Marsh, *The Chamberlain Litany*, p. 283.

70 Marquand, *Ramsay MacDonald*, p. 788.

71 Jenkins, *Baldwin*, p. 161.

72 D. R. Thorpe, *Eden: The Life and Times of Anthony Eden, First Earl of Avon, 1897–1977*, London, Chatto & Windus, 2004, pp. 185–6.

73 Marsh, *The Chamberlain Litany*, p. 284.

74 Jenkins, *Baldwin*, pp. 161–2.

75 Bradford, *George VI*, p. 346.

76 Ibid., p. 347.

77 Andrew Roberts, *Churchill: Walking With Greatness*, London, Allen Lane, 2018, p. 417.

78 Macleod, *Neville Chamberlain*, p. 199.

4. The King's Knight Apparent

1 Paul D. Webb, *The Modern British Party System*, London, SAGE Publications, 2000, pp. 197–8.

2 R. J. Q. Adams, *Bonar Law*, London, John Murray, 1999, p. 329.

3 Pimlott, *The Queen*, p. 230; Roberts, *Churchill*, p. 949.

4 Martin Gilbert, *Churchill: A Life*, London, Heinemann, 1991, p. 939; Pimlott, *The Queen*, p. 232.

5 Fisher, *The Tory Leaders*, p. 69.

6 John Colville, *Fringes of Power: Downing Street Diaries 1939–1955*, London, Phoenix, 2005, p. 662.

7 J. A. Cross, *Lord Swinton*, Oxford, Oxford University Press, 1982, p. 284.

8 David Carlton, *Anthony Eden: A Biography*, London, Allen Lane, 1981, p. 297.

9 David Dutton, *Anthony Eden: A Life and Reputation*, London, Arnold, 1997, p. 217.

10 Bogdanor, *The Monarchy and the Constitution*, p. 99.

11 Pimlott, *The Queen*, p. 232.

12 Tim Bouverie, *Appeasing Hitler: Chamberlain, Churchill, and the Road to War*, London, Bodley Head, 2019, p. 212.

13 Roberts, *Churchill*, p. 735.

14 Thorpe, *Eden*, p. 272.

15 'Sir Winston Churchill to King George VI', 16 June 1942, Royal Archives, PS/PSO/GVI/C/069/17.

16 Wheeler-Bennet, *King George VI*, pp. 544–46.

17 Roberts, *Churchill*, p. 758.

18 Leo McKinstry, *Attlee and Churchill: Allies in War, Adversaries in Peace*, London, Atlantic Books, 2019, p. 374.

19 Twomey, *The Veiled Sceptre*, p. 49.

20 Robert Rhodes James, *Anthony Eden*, London, Weidenfeld & Nicolson, 1986, pp. 316–17.

21 Anthony Seldon, *Churchill's Indian Summer: The 1951–1955 Conservative Government*, London, Hodder & Stoughton, 1981, p. 39.

22 Seldon, *Churchill's Indian Summer*, p. 40; Brazier, *Choosing A Prime Minister*, p. 72; Bradford, *George VI*, p. 603.

23 McKinstry, *Attlee and Churchill*, p 289.

24 Ibid., p. 290.

25 Ibid., p. 291.

26 Ibid., p. 292.

27 Brazier, *Choosing A Prime Minister*, p. 71–2.

28 Thorpe, *Eden*, p. 364.

29 Bouverie, *Appeasing Hitler*, pp. 169–70, 212–13.

30 Rhodes James, *Anthony Eden*, p. 335.

31 Robert J. Wybrow, *Britain Speaks Out, 1937–87: A Social History as Seen Through the Gallup Data*, London, Palgrave Macmillan, 1989, p. 43.

32 Rhodes James, *Anthony Eden*, p. 158.

33 Ibid., p. 203.

34 Howard, *RAB*, p. 200.

35 Thorpe, *Eden*, pp. 456–7.

36 Peter Catterall (ed.), *The Macmillan Diaries: The Cabinet Years 1950–1957*, London, Macmillan, 2003, p. 208.

37 Thorpe, *Eden*, p. 419.

38 Michael Jago, *RAB Butler: The Best Prime Minister We Never Had*, London, Biteback Publishing, 2015, pp. 241–2.

39 Rhodes James, *Anthony Eden*, pp. 396–7; Howard, *RAB*, pp. 208–10, 213.

40 Elizabeth Longford, *Elizabeth R*, London, Weidenfeld & Nicolson, 1983, p. 174.

41 Twomey, *The Veiled Sceptre*, pp. 168–73.

42 Pimlott, *The Queen*, p. 232.

43 Author's conversation with Lord Butler of Brockwell.

44 Cate Haste (ed.), *Clarissa Eden: A Memoir, from Churchill to Eden*, Weidenfeld & Nicolson, London, 2007, p. 199.

45 Fisher, *The Tory Leaders*, p. 69.

46 Roger Mortimore and Andrew Blick, *Butler's British Political Facts*, London, Palgrave Macmillan, 2018, pp. 376–8.

5. The King's Dilemma

1 Rhodes James, *Anthony Eden*, p. 595.

2 Ibid., pp. 256–7.

3 Brazier, *Choosing A Prime Minister*, p. 117.

4 D. R. Thorpe, *Supermac: The Life of Harold Macmillan*, London, Chatto & Windus, 2010, p. 366.

5   Pimlott, *The Queen*, p. 257.
6   Thorpe, *Eden*, p. 546.
7   Victor Rothwell, *Anthony Eden: A Political Biography, 1931–1957*, Manchester, Manchester University Press, 1992, pp. 245–6.
8   Pimlott, *The Queen*, p. 257.
9   Jago, *Rab Butler*, pp. 322–327.
10 Pimlott, *The Queen*, p. 260.
11 Earl of Kilmuir, *Political Adventure: The Memoirs of the Earl of Kilmuir*, London, Weidenfeld & Nicolson, 1964, p. 285.
12 Thorpe, *Supermac*, pp. 360–62.
13 Kilmuir, *Political Adventure*, p, 285.
14 *The Times*, 9 May 1997.
15 Thorpe, *Supermac*, p. 361.
16 Howard, *RAB*, pp. 247–9.
17 Edward Heath, *The Course of My Life*, London, Hodder and Stoughton, 1998, p. 178.
18 Harold Macmillan, *Riding the Storm 1956–1959*, London, Macmillan, 1971, pp. 180–85; Thorpe, *Alec Douglas-Home*, p. 189; Thorpe, *Eden*, p. 547.
19 Alan Thompson, *The Day Before Yesterday*, London, Sidgwick & Jackson, 1971, p. 161.
20 Thorpe, *Alec Douglas-Home*, p. 189.
21 Pimlott, *The Queen*, p. 260.
22 Fisher, *The Tory Leaders*, p. 84.
23 Thorpe, *Supermac*, pp. 265–6.
24 Philip Goodhart, *The 1922: The Story of the Conservative Backbenchers' Parliamentary Committee*, London, Macmillan, 1973, p. 175.
25 *Daily Herald*, 15 September 1959.
26 Alistair Horne, *Harold Macmillan Volume I: 1894–1956*, London, Macmillan, 1988, pp. 455–8; Jago, *Rab Butler*, pp. 320–23.
27 Macmillan, *Riding the Storm*, pp. 181–4.
28 Interview with Iris Portal, *Reputations*, BBC Two, 1983.
29 'Eden Resigns', *Daily Express*, 10 January 1957.
30 Howard, *RAB*, pp. 246–7.
31 Pimlott, *The Queen*, p. 260.
32 Butler, *Governing Without a Majority*, p. 80.
33 'Note on resignation audience', Avon Papers, 20/33/12A, Cadbury Research Library.
34 'The Earl of Avon to Sir Michael Adeane', Avon Papers, 23/2/20A, Cadbury Research Library.
35 Rhodes James, *Anthony Eden*, p. 595.
36 Macmillan, *Riding the Storm*, p. 184.
37 Heath, *The Course of My Life*, p. 179.
38 Alistair Horne, *Harold Macmillan Volume II: 1957–1986*, London, Macmillan, 1989, pp. 3–4.
39 Macmillan, *Riding the Storm*, p. 199.
40 Horne, *Macmillan 1957–1986*, p. 185.
41 Ibid., p. 4.
42 Thorpe, *Supermac*, p. 378.
43 Heath, *The Course of My Life*, p. 181.
44 Ibid., p. 181.
45 Ibid., p. 181.
46 'Eden Resigns', *Daily Express*, 10 January 1957; Heath, *The Course of My Life*, p. 181.
47 Macmillan, *Riding the Storm*, pp. 200–203; Fisher, *The Tory Leaders*, pp. 89–90.
48 'Mr Macmillan becomes Prime Minister', *The Times*, 11 January 1957.
49 Pimlott, *The Queen*, p. 260.
50 Ibid., p. 324.
51 Blake, *Office of the Prime Minister*, pp. 56–7.

6. The King's Friend

1 Pimlott, *The Queen*, p. 324.
2 Thorpe, *Supermac*, p. 563.
3 'Conservative Party Conference', *Evening Standard*, 10 October 1963.
4 Michael White, '1963 and all that', *The Guardian*, 8 October 2003.
5 Thorpe, *Alec Douglas-Home*, p. 288.
6 Pimlott, *The Queen*, pp. 325–26.
7 Horne, *Macmillan 1957–1986*, p. 534.
8 Harold Macmillan, *At the End of the Day, 1961–63*, London, Macmillan, 1973, p. 490.
9 'The Tuesday Memorandum', 15 October 1963, National Archives, PREM 11/5008.
10 Pimlott, *The Queen*, p. 331.
11 Thorpe, *Supermac*, pp. 571–2.
12 Pimlott, *The Queen*, p. 392.
13 Ibid., p. 573.
14 Ibid., pp. 573–4.
15 Ibid., p. 570.
16 Geoffrey Lewis, *Lord Hailsham*, London, Jonathan Cape, 1997, p. 232; Simon Heffer, *Like the Roman: The Life of Enoch Powell*, London, Phoenix, 1999, pp. 326–7.
17 Heffer, *Like the Roman*, pp. 326–8; Jago, *Rab Butler*, p. 385.
18 Pimlott, *The Queen*, p. 329.
19 Ibid., p. 329.
20 See Thorpe, *Supermac*, pp. 621–6 for the full text of the Thursday Memorandum.
21 Horne, *Macmillan 1957–1986*, pp. 566–7.
22 Macmillan, *At the End of the Day*, p. 518.
23 Pimlott, *The Queen*, p. 331.
24 Ibid., pp. 331–2.
25 Ibid., p. 332.
26 Ibid., p. 332
27 Lord Home, *The Way the Wind Blows*, London, HarperCollins, 1976, p. 185.
28 Pimlott, *The Queen*, p. 333.
29 Howard, *RAB*, p. 320.
30 Lewis, *Lord Hailsham*, p. 234.
31 Thorpe, *Alec Douglas-Home*, p. 314.
32 Ibid., pp. 334–5.
33 Anthony Howard and Richard West, *The Making of the Prime Minister*, London, Richard Clay, 1965, pp. 102–3.
34 Thorpe, *Alec Douglas-Home*, pp. 378–80.

7. The King's Commission

1 Antonia Fraser, *Perilous Question: The Drama of the Great Reform Bill 1832*, London, Phoenix, 2014, pp. 224–5, 240–42.
2 David Cecil, *The Young Melbourne & Lord M*, London, Bello, 2017, p. 249.
3 Elizabeth Longford, *Wellington: The Years of the Sword*, London, Abacus, 2004, p. 450.
4 Ibid., pp. 451, 456.
5 Douglas Hurd, *Robert Peel: A Biography*, London, Weidenfeld & Nicolson, 2007, pp. 165–86.
6 William Hague, *William Pitt the Younger*, London, HarperCollins, 2004, pp. 141–6.
7 Turpin and Tomkins, *The British Government*, p. 383.
8 Basil Markesinis, 'The Royal Prerogative Revisited', *Cambridge Law Journal* vol. 32, issue 2, November 1973, pp. 287, 290–92.
9 Rodney Brazier, 'The Monarchy', in Vernon Bogdanor (ed.), *The British Constitution in the Twentieth Century*, Oxford, Oxford University Press, 2003, p. 83.
10 Markesinis, 'The Royal Prerogative Revisited', pp. 290–92.

11 'Note to the Prime Minister from Robert Armstrong', 15 March 1974, National Archives, PREM 16/231.

12 Cabinet Office, *The Cabinet Manual*, para 2.9, p. 14.

13 Author's conversation with Jeremy Heywood.

14 Hennessy, *The Hidden Wiring*, p. 57.

15 Ibid., p. 64.

16 W. E. Gladstone, *Gleanings of Past Years: Vol. I, The Throne and the Prince Consort, the Cabinet, and the Constitution*, London, John Murray, 1879, p. 245.

17 Brazier, *Constitutional Practice*, p. 11; Markesinis, 'The Royal Prerogative Revisited', pp. 290–92.

18 Frank MacKinnon, *The Crown in Canada*, Calgary, Glenbow-Alberta Institute, 1976, p. 122.

19 D. Michael Jackson, *The Crown and Canadian Federalism*, Toronto, Dundurn, 2013, p. 75.

20 For the two sides of the debate, see Sir David Smith, *Head of State: The Governor-General, the Monarchy, the Republic and the Dismissal*, Sydney, Macleay Press, 2005 and George Winterton, *Parliament, the Executive and the Governor-General*, Melbourne, Melbourne University Press, 1983.

21 Edward McWhinney, *The Governor General and the Prime Ministers: The Making and Unmaking of Governments*, Vancouver, Ronsdale Press, 2005, p. 70.

22 *R. (Miller) v. The Prime Minister, Cherry & Ors. v. Advocate General for Scotland*, 2019, UKSC 41.

23 'Can Queen Elizabeth sack Boris Johnson?', *Financial Times*, 1 October 2019.

24 See debate in Caroline Davies, 'Could the Queen sack Boris Johnson?', *The Guardian*, 7 August 2019.

25 *Daily Mail*, 6 October 2019.

26 Cox, *The Royal Prerogative and Constitutional Law*, p. 80.

27 Norman Ward, *Dawson's The Government of Canada*, Toronto, University of Toronto Press, 1987, p. 191.

28 Jackson, *The Crown and Canadian Federalism*, p. 75.

29 Dennis Baker, *Not Quite Supreme: The Courts and Coordinate Constitutional Interpretation*, Montreal & Kingston, McGill-Queen's University Press, 2010, pp. 72–3.

30 See Brazier, *Constitutional Practice: The Foundation of British Government*, p. 11 for an example of this.

31 Peter Russell and Loren Sossin (ed.), *Parliamentary Democracy in Crisis*, Toronto, University of Toronto, 2009, pp. 87–8.

32 Eugene Forsey, *The Royal Power of Dissolution of Parliament in the British Commonwealth*, Toronto, Oxford University Press, 1968, p. 259.

33 Butler, *Governing Without a Majority*, p. 80.

34 'The Right of the Governor-General to Refuse a Dissolution', 9 November 1939, Royal Archives, PS/PSO/GVI/C/131/14.

35 Twomey, *The Veiled Sceptre*, p. 240.

36 'Deadlock – The Queen's Government must be carried on', 16 October 1964, National Archives, PREM 11/4756.

37 Robert Blake, 'Constitutional Monarchy: The Prerogative Powers' in D. Butler, V. Bogdanor and R. Summers, *The Law, Politics, and the Constitution*, Oxford, Oxford University Press, 1999, pp. 19, 27.

38 Bogdanor, *The Monarchy and the Constitution*, p. 111.

39 Harold Wilson, *The Governance of Britain*, London, Weidenfeld & Nicolson, 1976, p. 25.

40 Heywood, *What Does Jeremy Think?*, p. 291.

41 Ibid., p. 292.

42 Gordon Brown, *My Life, Our Times*, London, Vintage, 2017, p. 381; Peter Mandelson, *The Third Man: Life at the Heart of New Labour*, London, HarperCollins, 2010, p. 551.

43 Brown, *My Life, Our Times*, pp. 381–2.

44 Heywood, *What Does Jeremy Think?*, p. 305.

45 Anthony Seldon, *Brown at 10*, London, Biteback, 2010, p. 460.

46 Author's conversation with Jeremy Heywood; *Five Days that Changed Britain*, BBC Two, 2010.

47 Brown, *My Life, Our Times*, p. 381; Mandelson, *The Third Man*, p. 545; David Laws, *22 Days in May*, London, Biteback, 2010, p. 40.

48 Andrew Adonis, *5 Days in May: The Coalition and Beyond*, London, Biteback, 2013, p. 108.

49 Seldon, *Cameron at 10*, pp. 115–25; Matthew D'Ancona, *In It Together: The Inside Story of the Coalition Government*, London, Penguin, 2014, pp. 73–85.

50 Patrick Monahan, 'The Constitutional Role of the Governor General', in Jennifer Smith and D. Michael Jackson (eds), *The Evolving Canadian Crown*, Montreal, McGill-Queen's University Press, 2012, pp. 73–4.

51 Joseph, *Constitutional and Administrative Law in New Zealand*, p. 735.

8. The King and Parliamentary Processes

1 Keir, *The Constitutional History of Modern Britain*, pp. 271–75.

2 Harris, *Revolution: The Great Crisis of the British Monarchy*, p. 353.

3 Keir, *The Constitutional History of Modern Britain*, p. 282.

4 Henry Roseveare, *Treasury, 1660–1870: The Foundations of Control*, London, Allen and Unwin, 1973, p. 80; Keir, *The Constitutional History of Modern Britain*, p. 282.

5 Keir, *The Constitutional History of Modern Britain*, p. 282.

6 Smith, *A Constitutional and Legal History of England*, pp. 372–3.

7 Twomey, *The Veiled Sceptre*, p. 267.

8 Andrew Woodcock, 'Is the government's message discipline slipping under Boris Johnson?', *The Independent*, 2 August 2019; *Daily Mail*, 15 August 2019; Tim Shipman, 'Speaker John Bercow "will lean on the Queen" to oust Boris Johnson as prime minister', *The Times*, 25 August 2019.

9 'Note to the Prime Minister from Robert Armstrong', National Archives, PREM 16/231; Bradley and Ewing, *Constitutional and Administrative Law*, p. 93.

10 Tim Shipman, 'Speaker John Bercow "will lean on the Queen" to oust Boris Johnson as prime minister', *The Times*, 25 August 2019.

11 'Note to the Prime Minister from Robert Armstrong', National Archives, PREM 16/231.

12 Twomey, *The Veiled Sceptre*, p. 326.

13 'MPs reject Senate amendment to budget bill leading to possible parliamentary showdown', CBC News, 21 June 2017; 'Senate passes budget bill with no amendment as parliament breaks for summer' CBC News, 22 June 2017.

14 Philip Magnus, *King Edward the Seventh*, London, John Murray, 1964, p. 540.

15 A. W. Bradley and K. D. Ewing, *Constitutional and Administrative Law*, 14th ed., Harlow, Longman, 2007, p. 203.

16 Roy Jenkins, *Gladstone*, London, Pan Books, 2018, p. 226.

17 Keir, *The Constitutional History of Modern Britain*, p. 477.

18 Roy Jenkins, *Mr Balfour's Poodle: An Account of the Struggle Between the House of Lords and the Government of Mr Asquith*, London, HarperCollins, 1989, p. 103.

19 Ibid., pp. 121–2.

20 Ibid., p. 243.

21 Paul Jackson and Patricia Leopold, *Constitutional and Administrative Law*, 8th ed., London, Sweet and Maxwell, 2001, p. 169.

22 Campbell Sharman, 'The Australian Senate as a States House', *Politics*, vol. 12, issue 2, 1977, pp. 64–75.

23 W. Harrison Morre, *The Constitution of the Commonwealth of Australia*, 2nd ed., Sydney, C. F. Maxwell, 1910, p. 144.

24 Gough Whitlam, *The Truth of the Matter*, London, Penguin, 1979, p. 121.

25 Malcolm Fraser and Margaret Simons, *Malcolm Fraser: The Political Memoirs*, Carlton, Victoria, Miegunyah Press, 2010, pp. 294–7.

26 John Waugh, 'Blocking Supply in Victoria', *Public Law Review*, vol. 13, issue 4, December 2002, pp. 241–5.

27 Paul Kelly and Troy Bramston, *The Dismissal: In the Queen's Name*, Australia, Penguin, 2015, pp. 99–100.

28 Sir John Kerr, *Matters for Judgment: An Autobiography*, Melbourne, Macmillan, 1978, pp. 301–5.

29 Michael Sexton, *The Great Crash: The Short Life and Sudden Death of the Whitlam Government*, Sydney, Scribe, 2005, pp. 224–7.

30 Fraser, *Malcom Fraser*, pp. 304–5.

31 Forsey, *The Royal Power of Dissolution of Parliament in the British Commonwealth*, pp. ix–xi.

32 Eugene Forsey, *Freedom and Order: Collected Essays*, Ottawa, Carleton University Press, 1974, pp. 48–9.

33 Kerr, *Matters for Judgment*, p. 358; Whitlam, *The Truth of the Matter*, p. 110; Fraser, *Malcom Fraser*, p. 307; Kelly & Bramston, *The Dismissal*, pp. 222–3, 251–6, 285.

34 Twomey, *The Veiled Sceptre*, p. 301.

35 Joseph, *Constitutional and Administrative Law in New Zealand*, p. 735.

36 Marquand, *Ramsay MacDonald*, pp. 636–7.

37 Twomey, *The Veiled Sceptre*, p. 301.

38 Colin Leys, *European Politics in Southern Rhodesia*, Oxford, Clarendon Press, 1959, p. 142.

39 Ibid., p. 143.

40 Claire Palley, *The Constitutional History and Law of Southern Rhodesia 1888–1965*, Oxford, Clarendon Press, 1966, pp. 277–8; Robert Blake, *A History of Rhodesia*, New York, NY, Alfred A. Knopf, 1977, pp. 307–11.

41 Jon Johansson, *Two Titans: Muldoon, Lange and Leadership*, Wellington, Dunmore Publishing, 2005, p. 72.

42 Barry Gustafson, *His Way: A Biography of Robert Muldoon*, Auckland, Auckland University Press, 2000, pp. 390–93.

43 Hugh Templeton, *All Honourable Men: Inside the Muldoon Cabinet 1975–1984*, Auckland, Auckland University Press, 1995, p. 221.

44 Gustafson, *His Way*, p. 393; Gavin McLean, *The Governors: New Zealand's Governors and Governors-General*, Dunedin, Otago University Press, 2006, p. 310.

45 Evan Whitton, *The Hillbilly Dictator: Australia's Police State*, Sydney, ABC Enterprises, 1989, pp. 116–136.

46 'Letter by Mike Ahern, Parliamentary Leader of the National Party, to Sir Walter Campbell', 26 November 1987, Queensland Government, 16 December 1988.

47 Kenneth Mackenzie QC, Solicitor-General, 'Memorandum', Queensland Government, 26 November 1987.

48 *Daily Sun*, 27 November 1987.

49 Geoffrey Barlow and James Corkery, 'Walter Campbell: A Distinguished Life', *Owen Dixon Society eJournal*, 1–32.

50 Thomas Penberthy Fry, *The Crown, Cabinets and Parliaments in Australia*, Brisbane, University of Queensland, 1946, pp. 85–6.

51 Kerr, *Matters for Judgment*, pp. 365–7.

52 Keith Middlemas and John Barnes, *Baldwin: A Biography*, London, Weidenfeld & Nicolson, 1969, p. 999.

53 Andrew Heard, *Canadian Constitutional Conventions: The Marriage of Law and Politics*, North York, Ontario, Oxford University Press, 2014, p. 59.

54 Peter Hogg, *Constitutional Law of Canada*, vol. I, 5th ed., Toronto, Thomson Carsewell, 2007, p. 292.

55 Heard, *Canadian Constitutional Conventions*, p. 59.

56 Fry, *The Crown, Cabinets and Parliaments in Australia*, p. 129.

9. The King and Constitutional Principles

1 Twomey, *The Veiled Sceptre*, p. 306.

2 Hogg, *Constitutional Law of Canada*, p. 294.

3   H. V. Evatt, *The King and His Dominion Governors*, Abingdon, Routledge, 2013, pp. 173–4.

4   Patrick Monahan and Byron Shaw, *Constitutional Law*, 4th ed., Toronto, Irwin Law, 2013, p. 80.

5   Eugene Forsey, 'Schreyer's position not as simple as it seems, Forsey says', *Globe and Mail*, 2 February 1982; R. MacGregor Dawson, *The Government of Canada*, 6th ed., Toronto, University of Toronto Press, 1987, p. 189.

6   Advisory Committee to the Constitutional Commission, 'Report on Executive Government', Sydney, 1987, p. 68.

7   Head, *Canadian Constitutional Conventions*, p. 56.

8   Twomey, *The Veiled Sceptre*, p. 310.

9   Saywell, *The Office of Lieutenant-Governor*, p. 142.

10 W. L. Morton, *Manitoba: A History*, 2nd ed., Toronto, University of Toronto Press, 1967, p. 342.

11 Ibid., p. 344.

12 Anne Twomey, 'The Dismissal of the Lang Government', in George Winterton (ed.), *State Constitutional Landmarks*, Annandale, The Federation Press, 2006, pp. 142–48.

13 'Governor may dismiss Lang ministry', *Sydney Morning Herald*, 16 April 1932; Bethia Foott, *Dismissal of a Premier: The Philip Game Papers*, Sydney, Morgan Publications, 1968, pp. 197–8.

14 'Minute by Mr Stephenson', Dominions Office, 23 April 1932, National Archives, DO 35/9374/15.

15 'Letter from H. Bushe, Legal Advisor to the Dominions Office, to Sir T. Inskip, Attorney-General', 10 May 1932, National Archives, DO 35/9374/15.

16 Winterton, *State Constitutional Landmarks*, pp. 152–154.

17 Foott, *Dismissal of a Premier*, pp. 208–10.

18 *Official Yearbook of New South Wales 1930–1*, Sydney, NSW Government Printers, 1931, p. 18.

19 Severin Carrell and Rowena Mason, 'Scottish judges rule PM's suspension of parliament is unlawful', *The Guardian*, 11 September 2019.

20 'Supreme Court: Suspending Parliament was unlawful, judges rule', BBC News, 24 September 2019.

21 Tim Shipman, *Out*, London, William Collins, 2024, p. 98.

22 Twomey, *The Veiled Sceptre*, p. 320.

23 Fry, *The Crown, Cabinet and Parliaments in Australia*, pp. 131–2.

24 Stanley de Smith and Rodney Brazier, *Constitutional and Administrative Law*, 8th ed., London, Penguin, 1998, p. 122; Marshall, *Constitutional Conventions*, pp. 26–7.

25 Evatt, *The King and his Dominion Governors*, pp. 299–300.

26 Thorpe, *Supermac*, pp. 457–9.

27 G. Heaton Nicholls, *South Africa in My Time*, London, Allen and Unwin, 1961, pp. 443–82.

28 Palmer, *The Queen and Mrs Thatcher*, pp. 169–172.

29 'Letter by Sir Alex Douglas-Home to Sir Humphrey Gibbs', 8 June 1964, National Archives, DO 183/497.

30 Draft 'Message from His Excellency the Governor', 23 June 1964, National Archives, DO 183/497.

31 'Memorandum by Mr W Dale to Sir Arthur Snelling', 26 June 1964, National Archives, DO 183/497.

32 Draft 'Message from His Excellency the Governor', 7 August 1964, National Archives, DO 183/497.

33 'Memorandum by Mr D Gordon-Smith to Mr Bass', 1 October 1964, National Archives, DO 183/497.

34 'Memorandum by Mr H Bass to Sir Arthur Snelling', 11 September 1964, National Archives, DO 183/497.

35 'Memorandum by Mr H Bass to Sir Arthur Snelling', 27 October 1964, National Archives, DO 183/497.

36 Alan Megahey, *Humphrey Gibbs, Beleaguered Governor: Southern Rhodesia, 1929–69*, Basingstoke, Macmillan, London, 1998, p. 109.

37 Megahey, *Humphrey Gibbs*, pp. 85–115; Peter Joyce, *Anatomy of a Rebel: Smith of Rhodesia, a Biography*, Salisbury, Graham Publishing, 1974, pp. 282–3.

38 Ian Smith, *The Great Betrayal: The Memoirs of Ian Smith*, London, Blake, 1997, pp. 103–4.

39 Forsey, *Freedom and Order*, p. 48–9.

40 'Obituary: Humphrey Gibbs', *The Guardian*, 8 November 1990.

41 Head, *Canadian Constitutional Conventions*, p. 54.

42 *Resolution to Amend the Constitution*, 1981, 1 SCR 753 882.

43 Ibid., p. 41.

44 Turpin and Tomkins, *British Government and the Constitution*, p. 568.

45 Jenkins, *Baldwin*, pp. 77–79.

46 Cabinet Office, *Cabinet Manual*, para 2.12.

47 Twomey, *The Veiled Sceptre*, pp. 266–7; Saywell, *The Office of Lieutenant-Governor*, pp. 48, 132.

48 Saywell, *The Office of Lieutenant-Governor*, p. 132.

49 R. E. Gosnell, *A History of British Columbia*, Toronto, Lewis Publishing Company, 1906, p. 267.

50 Twomey, *The Veiled Sceptre*, p. 343.

51 Dicey, *Introduction to the Study of the Law of the Constitution*, pp. 428–9.

52 Evatt, *The King and His Dominion Governors*, p. 105; Sir Ivor Jennings, *Cabinet Government*, 3rd ed., Cambridge, Cambridge University Press, 1961, p. 410.

53 Kerr, *Matters for Judgment*, p. xvi.

54 Twomey, *The Veiled Sceptre*, p. 344.

55 Fry, *The Crown, Cabinet and Parliaments in Australia*, p. 87.

56 Simon Kerry, *Lansdowne: The Last Great Whig*, London, Unicorn, 2017, p. 232.

57 Ibid., p. 232.

58 Ibid., p. 232.

59 Ibid., p. 233.

60 Ibid., p. 233.

61 Roy Jenkins, *Asquith*, London, Fontana Books, 1967, pp. 610–11.

62 Brazier, *Constitutional Texts*, p. 443.

63 Ibid., p. 443.

64 Rose, *King George V*, p. 121.

65 Ibid., p. 120.

66 'Can Queen Elizabeth sack Boris Johnson?', *The Financial Times*, 1 October 2019.

67 'Boris Johnson and coronavirus: the inside story of his illness', *The Guardian*, 17 April 2020.

68 Shipman, *Out*, pp. 308–9.

10. The King's Discretion

1 Maitland, *The Constitutional History of England*, pp. 292–3.

2 Ibid., p. 293.

3 Keir, *The Constitutional History of Modern Britain*, pp. 211–12.

4 'Charles I, 1640: An Act for the preventing of inconveniences happening by the long intermission of Parliaments', British History Online, http://www.british-history.ac.uk/statutes-realm/vol5/pp54-57.

5 Maitland, *The Constitutional History of England*, pp. 293–4.

6 'Charles II, 1664: An Act for the assembling and holding of Parliaments once in Three yeares at the least, And for the repeale of an Act entituled An Act for the preventing of Inconveniencies happening by the long Intermission of Parliaments', British History Online, http://www.british-history.ac.uk/statutes-realm/vol5/p513.

7 Keir, *The Constitutional History of Modern Britain*, p. 268.

8 Ibid., p. 325.

9 R. G. Thorne, *The House of Commons: 1790–1820*, vol. II, London, Secker and Warburg, 1986, pp. 50, 369, 380.

10 Matthew Cragoe, 'The Great Reform Act and the Modernization of British Politics: The Impact of Conservative Associations, 1835–1841', *Journal of British Studies*, vol. 47, issue 3, July 2008.

11 Bogdanor, *The Monarchy and the Constitution*, p. 16.

12 Norman Gash, *Sir Robert Peel: The Life of Sir Robert Peel after 1830*, London, Faber and Faber, 2011, p. 97.

13 Hurd, *Robert Peel*, pp. 170–89.

14 Hague, *William Pitt the Younger*, pp. 463–73.

15 Keir, *The Constitutional History of Great Britain*, p. 406.

16 Ibid., pp. 406–7.

17 A. C. Benson and Viscount Esher (ed.), *The Letters of Queen Victoria*, vol. III, London, John Murray, 1907, p. 449.

18 Keir, *The Constitutional History of Great Britain*, p. 486.

19 E. A. Smith, *The House of Lords in British Politics and Society 1815–1911*, London, Longman, 1992, p. 167.

20 Glenn Dymond and Hugo Deadman, 'The Salisbury Doctrine', House of Lords Library Note, 2006, p. 5.

21 Keir, *The Constitutional History of Great Britain*, p. 477.

22 Ibid., p. 478.

23 Bogdanor, *The Monarchy and the Constitution*, p. 79.

24 Ibid., p. 79.

25 Ibid., p. 80.

26 Jennings, *Cabinet Government*, p. 86.

27 Robert Rhodes James, 'The British Monarchy: Its Changing Constitutional Role', *Royal Society of Arts*, vol. 142, issue 5448, April 1994, p. 25.

28 John Bew, *Citizen Clem: A Biography of Attlee*, London, Riverrun, 2017, pp. 483–4.

29 'Parliamentary Procedure', March 1952, National Archives, PREM 8/1262.

30 Ibid.

31 'Parliament: Government Defeat in the House of Commons; the Constitutional Position', 1952, National Archives, CAB 21/3682.

32 Ibid.

33 Ibid.

34 Ibid.

35 Allan Levine, *King: William Lyon Mackenzie King – A Life Guided by the Hand of Destiny*, Vancouver/Toronto, Douglas & McIntrye, 2011, p. 147.

36 Ibid., p. 156.

37 Roger Graham, *Arthur Meighen, Volume Two: And Fortune Fled*, Toronto, Clarke, Irwin, & Company Limited, 1963, pp. 420–21.

38 Levin, *King*, pp. 159–60.

39 Jackson, *The Crown and Canadian Federalism*, p. 62.

40 See Forsey, *The Royal Power of Dissolution of Parliament in the British Commonwealth* for a wider discussion.

41 Richard Steyn, *Jan Smuts: Unafraid of Greatness*, Johannesburg/Cape Town, Jonathan Ball, 2015, p. 123.

42 Michael Graham Fry, 'Agents and structures: The dominions and the Czechoslovak crisis, September 1938', in Igor Lukes and Erik Goldstein (eds), *The Munich Crisis, 1938: Prelude to World War II, Diplomacy & Statecraft*, vol. X, London, Frank Cass, 1999, p. 305.

43 Ibid., p. 328.

44 Steyn, *Jan Smuts*, p. 129.

45 Ibid., p. 130.

46 Bogdanor, *The Monarchy and Constitution*, p. 81; Steyn, *Jan Smuts*, p. 130.

47 *The Times*, 2 May 1950.

48 Nicolson, *George V*, p. 288, Bogdanor, *The Monarchy and Constitution*, p. 160.
49 'Note for the Record: Events Leading to Mr Heath's Resignation on 4 March 1974', 16 March 1974, National Archives, PREM 16/231.
50 Ibid.
51 Rhodes James, 'The British Monarchy', p. 25.
52 Bogdanor, *The Monarchy and Constitution*, p. 162.
53 Peter Hennessy, *The Prime Minister: The Office and its Holders since 1945*, London, Palgrave, 2000, pp. 29–30.
54 Constitution Committee, 'Fixed-term Parliaments Bill – Eighth report', House of Lords, 1 December 2010.
55 Peter Hogg, 'Prorogation and the Power of the Governor-General', *National Journal of Constitutional Law*, vol. 27, 2009, pp. 197–8.
56 Andrew Head, 'The Governor General's Suspension of Parliament: Duty Done or a Perilous Precedent', in P. Russell and L. Sossin (eds), *Parliamentary Democracy in Crisis*, Toronto, University of Toronto Press, 2009, pp. 47, 51.
57 Eugene Forsey, 'Position of the Governor General if No Party gets a Clear Majority in the Election', 15 August 1984, https://www.documentcloud.org/documents/2462092-eugene-forsey-governor-generals-role-post/
58 Rosemary Laing (ed.) *Odger's Australian Senate Practice as Revised by Harry Evans*, 14th ed., Canberra, Department of the Senate, 2016, p. 605.
59 'Jean feared "dreadful crisis" when Harper sought prorogation: ex adviser', *Globe and Mail*, 25 June 2012.
60 Shipman, *Out*, pp. 49–50.

11. The King's Assent

1 Twomey, *The Veiled Sceptre*, p. 627.
2 Sir Ivor Jennings, *The Queen's Government*, London, Penguin, 1954, p. 66.
3 W. E. Hearn, *The Governance of England*, London, Longmans, 1867, pp. 51–8; K. Mackenzie, *The English Parliament*, London, Pelican Books, 1951, p. 26.
4 Keir, *The Constitutional History of Modern Britain*, p. 43.
5 Carroll, *Constitutional and Administrative Law*, p. 207.
6 Erskine May, *Parliamentary Practice*, 21st ed., London, Lexis Nexus, 1989, p. 529.
7 Wheeler-Bennett, *King George VI: His Life and Reign*, p. 379.
8 Munro, *Studies in Constitutional Law*, p. 55.
9 Jennings, *The Queen's Government*, p. 66.
10 Erskine May, *Parliamentary Practice*, 23rd ed., London, Lexis Nexus, 2024, p. 654.
11 Twomey, *The Veiled Sceptre*, p. 617.
12 Harold Laski, *Parliamentary Government in England*, London, Allen & Unwin, 1938, p. 409.
13 Balfour Papers, British Library, Add. MS 49869, fos. 123, 124.
14 Rodney Brazier, 'Monarchy', in Vernon Bogdanor, *The British Constitution in the Twentieth Century*, Oxford, Oxford University Press, 2004, pp. 69, 81.
15 Lord Morris of Aberavon, 'Parliament has trussed itself up like a chicken', *Daily Telegraph*, 26 January 2015.
16 MacKinnon, *The Crown in Canada*, p. 133.
17 Twomey, *The Veiled Sceptre*, pp. 624; Tomkins, *Public Law*, pp. 63–4.
18 Twomey, *The Veiled Sceptre*, p. 643.
19 de Smith and Brazier, *Constitutional and Administrative Law*, p. 127.
20 'Militia of Scotland Bill, refused the Royal Assent', *Journal of the House of Lords, vol. 18, 1705–1709*, British History Online, https://www.british-history.ac.uk/lords-jrnl/vol18, p. 506.
21 Harry Calvert, *Constitutional Law in Northern Ireland: A study in regional government*, London, Stevens & Sons, 1968, pp. 30–32.
22 Munro, *Studies in Constitutional Law*, p. 83.

23 Robert Blake, *The Unknown Prime Minister: The Life and Times of Andrew Bonar Law, 1858–1923*, London, Eyre & Spottiswoode, 1955, p. 163.
24 'The Constitutional Question, 1913', undated memo, Balfour Papers, BL Add. MS 49869, fo. 127, Pitt Rivers Museum.
25 Undated memo, Royal Archives, GV K2553 (5) 81.
26 Ibid., 98a.
27 Blake, *The Unknown Prime Minister*, p. 162.
28 Jeremy Smith, 'Bluff, Bluster and Brinksmanship: Andrew Bonar Law and the Third Home Rule Bill', *The Historical Journal*, vol. 36, issue 1, March 1993, p. 168.
29 'Memo to Lord Stamfordham from Bonar Law on his interview with the King', 16 September 1913, Royal Archives, GV K2553 (2) 16.
30 'Memo by Lord Stamfordham', 17 September 1914, Royal Archives, GV K2553 (6) 103.
31 Ibid.
32 'Memo by Lord Stamfordham', 19 March 1914, Royal Archives, GV K2553 (4) 33.
33 Brett, *Journals and Letters of Reginald, Viscount Esher*, p. 157.
34 Nicolson, *George V*, p. 233.
35 'Lord Stamfordham to Lord Salisbury', 5 June 1914, Royal Archives, GV K2553 (5) 44.
36 Nicolson, *George V*, p. 234.
37 Anthony Seldon and Raymond Newell, *May at 10: The Verdict*, London, Biteback, 2019, pp. 502–3.
38 'Queen could be asked to veto John Bercow's attempts to water down Brexit, Government confirms', *Daily Telegraph*, 21 January 2019.
39 Robert Craig, 'Could the Government Advise the Queen to refuse Royal Assent to a Backbench Bill?', UK Constitutional Law Association, 22 January 2019, https://ukconstitutionallaw.org/2019/01/22/robert-craig-could-the-government-advise-the-queen-to-refuse-royal-assent-to-a-backbench-bill/.
40 Sir Stephen Laws and Professor Richard Ekins, 'Endangering Constitutional Government: The Risk of the House of Commons taking Control', Policy Exchange, 31 March 2019, https://policyexchange.org.uk/wp-content/uploads/2019/03/Endangering-Constitutional-Government.pdf.
41 'The Impact of Queen's and Prince's Consent on the Legislative Process', House of Commons Political and Constitutional Committee, 26 March 2014.
42 Ibid.
43 'Queen shown legislation by convention, Buckingham Palace says', BBC News, 8 February 2021, https://www.bbc.co.uk/news/uk-55975199.
44 'The Impact of Queen's and Prince's Consent on the Legislative Process', House of Commons Political and Constitutional Committee.
45 HC Debs, 20 July 1949, col. 1385–6.
46 'Royal "consent" to laws revealed after FOI battle', BBC News, 15 January 2013.
47 Erskine May, *A Practical Treatise on the Law, Privileges, Proceedings and Usage of Parliament*, 2nd ed., London, Butterworths, 1851, pp. 336–7.
48 Ibid.

Conclusion: The King's Peace

1 Arthur Bousfield and Garry Toffoli (eds), *Royal Observations: Canadians and Royalty*, Toronto, Dundurn Press, 1991, p. 176.
2 Philip Murphy, *Monarchy and the End of Empire*, Oxford, Oxford University Press, 2013, pp. 156–7.
3 John Hudson, *The Oxford History of the Laws of England*, vol. II, Oxford, Oxford University Press, 2012, pp. 386–8.
4 R. Doleman, *Conference About the Next Succession, 1594*, London, Scolar Press, 1972, p. 136.
5 Cox, *The Royal Prerogative*, p. 194.

6 Ibid., p. 73.
7 Anne Twomey, *The Chameleon Crown: The Queen and Her Australian Governors*, Alexandria, Federation Press, 2006, pp. 179–80.
8 Shipman, *Out*, pp. 42–3.
9 Bogdanor, *The Monarchy and the Constitution*, p. 309.

BIBLIOGRAPHY

PRIMARY SOURCES

UK PRIMARY SOURCES

Bodleian Archives: Asquith Papers, Macmillan Papers

British Library: Balfour Papers

The Court of Appeal: Law Reports

The House of Commons: Hansard; Library Member Briefings; Office of Parliamentary Counsel, Political and Constitutional Reform Committee; Public Administration Select Committee; Standing Orders

The House of Lords: Constitution Committee, Law Reports, Library Member Briefings

The National Archives: Cabinet Office, Dominion Office, Foreign and Commonwealth Office, Premiership

Royal Archives, Windsor: George V, George VI

The Supreme Court: Law Reports

The University of Birmingham: The Avon Papers, The Chamberlain Papers

NON-UK PRIMARY SOURCES

Australian Bureau of Statistics: *Official Yearbook of New South Wales 1930–1*, Sydney, NSW Government Printers, 1931

National Library of Australia: Constitutional Committee, *Report on Executive Government*, Sydney, The Commission, 1987

University of Sydney: William Pitt Cobbett, *The Government of Australia*, vol. 4, unpublished manuscript, University of Sydney, 1919

ONLINE RESOURCES

Cabinet Office, *The Cabinet Manual*, https://www.gov.uk/government/publications/cabinet-manual

'Charles I, 1640: An Act for the preventing of inconveniences happening by the long intermission of Parliaments', British History Online, http://www.british-history.ac.uk/statutes-realm/vol5/pp54-57

'Charles II, 1664: An Act for the assembling and holding of Parliaments once in Three yeares at the least, And for the repeale of an Act entituled An Act for the preventing of Inconveniencies happening by the long Intermission of Parliaments', British History Online, http://www.british-history.ac.uk/statutes-realm/vol5/p513

'Militia of Scotland Bill, refused the Royal Assent', *Journal of the House of Lords, vol. 18, 1705–1709*, British History Online, https://www.british-history.ac.uk/lords-jrnl/vol18/pp504-506#h3-s15

R. (Miller) v. the Prime Minister, UKSC 41, 2019, https://www.supremecourt.uk/prorogation/index.html

Robert Craig, 'Could the Government Advise the Queen to refuse Royal Assent to a Backbench Bill?', UK Constitutional Law Association, 22 January 2019, https://ukconstitutionallaw.

org/2019/01/22/robert-craig-could-the-government-advise-the-queen-to-refuse-royal-assent-to-a-backbench-bill/

Royal.uk, 'His Majesty The King's Declaration', 10 September 2022, https://www.royal.uk/his-majesty-kings-declaration

SECONDARY SOURCES

JOURNAL ARTICLES

Barlow, Geoffrey and Corkery, James, 'Walter Campbell: A Distinguished Life', *Owen Dixon Society eJournal*, 1–32

Brazier, Rodney, '"Monarchy and the personal prerogatives": A personal response to Professor Blackburn', *Public Law*, spring 2005

Cragoe, Matthew, 'The Great Reform Act and the Modernization of British Politics: The Impact of Conservative Associations, 1835–1841', *Journal of British Studies*, vol. 47, issue 3, July 2008

Forsey, Eugene, 'Mr. King and Parliamentary Government', *Canadian Journal of Economics and Political Science*, vol. 17, issue 4, November 1951

Laws, Sir Stephen and Ekins, Professor Richard, 'Endangering Constitutional Government: The Risk of the House of Commons taking Control', Policy Exchange, 31 March 2019

Mackenzie QC, Kenneth, Solicitor-General, 'Memorandum', 26 November 1987

Markesinis, Basil, 'The Royal Prerogative Revisited', *Cambridge Law Journal*, vol. 32, issue 2, November 1973

Rhodes James, Robert, 'The British Monarchy: Its Changing Constitutional Role', *Royal Society of Arts*, vol. 142, issue 5448, April 1994

Sharman, Campbell, 'The Australian Senate as a States House', *Politics*, vol. 12, issue 2, 1977

Smith, Jeremy, 'Bluff, Bluster and Brinksmanship: Andrew Bonar Law and the Third Home Rule Bill', *The Historical Journal*, vol. 36, issue 1, March 1993

Watt, Graeme, 'The Coronation Oath', *Ecclesiastical Law Journal*, vol. 19, issue 3, September 2017

Waugh, John, 'Blocking Supply in Victoria', *Public Law Review*, vol. 13, issue 4, December 2002

Wheare, K. C., 'Walter Bagehot: Lecture on a Master Mind', *Proceedings of the British Academy*, vol. 60, Oxford, Oxford University Press, 1974

BOOKS

Adams, R. J. Q., *Bonar Law*, London, John Murray, 1999

Adonis, Andrew, *5 Days in May: The Coalition and Beyond*, London, Biteback, 2013

Bagehot, Walter, *The English Constitution*, Oxford, Oxford University Press, 2009

Baker, Dennis, *Not Quite Supreme: The Courts and Coordinate Constitutional Interpretation*, Montreal & Kingston, McGill-Queen's University Press, 2010

Benson, A. C. and Esher, Viscount (eds), *The Letters of Queen Victoria*, vol. III, London, John Murray, 1907

Bew, John, *Citizen Clem: A Biography of Attlee*, London, Riverrun, 2017

Blackstone, William, *Commentaries on the Laws of England*, London, Forgotten Books, 2012

Blake, Robert, *A History of Rhodesia*, New York, NY, Alfred A. Knopf, 1977

Blake, Robert, *The Office of the Prime Minister*, Oxford, Oxford University Press, 1975

Blake, Robert, *The Unknown Prime Minister: The Life and Times of Andrew Bonar Law, 1858–1923*, London, Eyre & Spottiswoode, 1955

Bogdanor, Vernon, *The British Constitution in the Twentieth Century*, Oxford, Oxford University Press, 2004

Bogdanor, Vernon, *The Monarchy and the Constitution*, Oxford, Clarendon Press, 1995

Bousfield, Arthur and Toffoli, Garry (eds), *Royal Observations: Canadians and Royalty*, Toronto, Dundurn Press, 1991

Bouverie, Tim, *Appeasing Hitler: Chamberlain, Churchill, and the Road to War*, London, Bodley Head, 2019

Bradford, Sarah, *George VI: The Dutiful King*, London, Penguin, 2011

Bradley, A. W. and Ewing, K. D., *Constitutional and Administrative Law*, 14th ed., Harlow, Longman, 2007

Brazier, Rodney, *Choosing A Prime Minister: The Transfer of Power in Britain*, Oxford, Oxford University Press, 2020

Brazier, Rodney, *Constitutional Practice: The Foundations of British Government*, 3rd ed., Oxford, Oxford University Press, 1999

Brazier, Rodney, *Constitutional Texts: Materials on Government and the Constitution*, Oxford, Oxford University Press, 1990

Brett, Maurice V. (ed.), *Journals and Letters of Reginald, Viscount Esher*, vol. III, London, Ivor Nicholson & Watson, 1938

Brown, Gordon, *My Life, Our Times*, London, Vintage, 2017

Butler, David, *Governing Without a Majority: Dilemmas for Hung Parliaments in Britain*, London, HarperCollins, 1983

Butler, D., Bogdanor, V. and Summers, R., *The Law, Politics, and the Constitution*, Oxford, Oxford University Press, 1999

Calvert, Henry, *Constitutional Law in Northern Ireland: A study in regional government*, London, Stevens & Sons, 1968

Cannon, John and Griffiths, Ralph, *The Oxford Illustrated History of the British Monarchy*, Oxford, Oxford University Press, 1988

Carlton, David, *Anthony Eden: A Biography*, London, Allen Lane, 1981

Carroll, Alex, *Constitutional and Administrative Law*, 5th ed., Harlow, Pearson, 2009

Catterall, Peter (ed.), *The Macmillan Diaries: The Cabinet Years 1950–1957*, London, Macmillan, 2003

Cecil, David, *The Young Melbourne & Lord M*, London, Bello, 2017

Colville, John, *Fringes of Power: Downing Street Diaries 1939–1955*, London, Phoenix, 2005

Cox, Noel, *The Royal Prerogative and Constitutional Law: A Search for the Quintessence of Executive Power*, Abingdon, Routledge, 2022

Cross, J. A., *Lord Swinton*, Oxford, Oxford University Press, 1982

Crowcroft, Robert, *The End Is Nigh: British Politics, Power, and the Road to the Second World War*, Oxford, Oxford University Press, 2019

D'Ancona, Matthew, *In It Together: The Inside Story of the Coalition Government*, London, Penguin, 2014

Dawson, R. MacGregor, *The Government of Canada*, 6th ed., Toronto, University of Toronto Press, 1987

Dicey, A. V., *Introduction to the Study of the Law of the Constitution*, Indianapolis, Liberty Fund, 1982

Dobson, Jeremy, *Why Do the People Hate Me So: The Strange Interlude Between the Two Great Wars In The Britain Of Stanley Baldwin*, Leicester, Matador, 2009

Doleman, R., *Conference About the Next Succession, 1594*, London, Scolar Press, 1972

Dutton, David, *Anthony Eden: A Life and Reputation*, London, Arnold, 1997

Erskine May, Thomas, *A Practical Treatise on the Law, Privileges, Proceedings, and Usage of Parliament*, London, Butterworths, 1851

Erskine May, *Parliamentary Practice*, 21st ed., London, Lexis Nexus, 1989

Erskine May, *Parliamentary Practice*, 23rd ed., London, Lexis Nexus, 2024

Evatt, H. V., *The King and His Dominion Governors*, Abingdon, Routledge, 2013

Fisher, Nigel, *The Tory Leaders: Their Struggle for Power*, London, Weidenfeld & Nicolson, 1977

Foott, Bethia, *Dismissal of a Premier: The Philip Game Papers*, Sydney, Morgan Publications, 1968

Forsey, Eugene, *Freedom and Order: Collected Essays*, Ottawa, Carleton University Press, 1974

Forsey, Eugene, *The Royal Power of Dissolution of Parliament in the British Commonwealth*, Toronto, Oxford University Press, 1968

Fortescue, Sir John, 'On the Laws and Governance of England', in Shelley Lockwood (ed.), *Cambridge Texts in the History of Political Thought*, Cambridge, Cambridge University Press, 2002

Fraser, Antonia, *Perilous Question: The Drama of the Great Reform Bill 1832*, London, Phoenix, 2014

Fraser, Malcolm and Simons, Margaret, *Malcolm Fraser: The Political Memoirs*, Carlton, Victoria, The Miegunyah Press, 2010

Fry, Thomas Penberthy, *The Crown, Cabinets and Parliaments in Australia*, Brisbane, University of Queensland, 1946

Gash, Norman, *Sir Robert Peel: The Life of Sir Robert Peel after 1830*, London, Faber and Faber, 2011

Gilbert, Martin, *Churchill: A Life*, London, Heinemann, 1991

Gladstone, W. E., *Gleanings of Past Years: Vol. I, The Throne and the Prince Consort, the Cabinet, and the Constitution*, London, John Murray, 1879

Gold, Claudia, *King of the North Wind: The Life of Henry II in Five Acts*, London, William Collins, 2018

Goodhart, Philip, *The 1922: The Story of the Conservative Backbenchers' Parliamentary Committee*, London, Macmillan, 1973

Gosnell, R. E., *A History of British Columbia*, Toronto, Lewis Publishing Company, 1906

Graham, Roger, *Arthur Meighen, Volume Two: And Fortune Fled*, Toronto, Clarke, Irwin, & Company Limited, 1963

Gustafson, Barry, *His Way: A Biography of Robert Muldoon*, Auckland, Auckland University Press, 2000

Hague, William, *William Pitt the Younger*, London, HarperCollins, 2004

Hardman, Robert, *Charles III: The Inside Story*, London, Macmillan, 2024

Harris, Kenneth, *The Queen*, London, Weidenfeld & Nicolson, 1994

Harris, Tim, *Revolution: The Great Crisis of the British Monarchy 1685–1720*, London, Allen Lane, 2006

Haste, Cate (ed.), *Clarissa Eden, A Memoir: From Churchill to Eden*, London, Weidenfeld & Nicolson, 2007

Heard, Andrew, *Canadian Constitutional Conventions: The Marriage of Law & Politics*, North York, Ontario, Oxford University Press, 2014

Hearn, W. E., *The Governance of England*, London, Longmans, 1867

Heath, Edward, *The Course of My Life*, London, Hodder and Stoughton, 1998

Heffer, Simon, *Like the Roman: The Life of Enoch Powell*, London, Phoenix, 1999

Hennessy, Peter, *The Hidden Wiring: Unearthing the British Constitution*, London, Victor Gollancz, 1995

Hennessy, Peter, *The Prime Ministers: The Officer and Its Holders Since 1945*, London, Allan Lane, 2000

Hennessy, Peter, *Muddling Through: Power, Politics and the Quality of Government in Postwar Britain*, London, Victor Gollancz, 1996

Heywood, Suzanne, *What Does Jeremy Think?: Jeremy Heywood and the Making of Modern Britain*, London, William Collins, 2021

Hogg, Peter, *Constitutional Law of Canada*, vol. I, 5th ed., Toronto, Thomson Carsewell, 2007

Holdsworth, Sir William, *A History of English Law*, vol. VI, London, Methuen & Co, 1924

Home, Lord, *The Way the Wind Blows*, London, HarperCollins, 1976

Horne, Alistair, *Harold Macmillan Volume I: 1894–1956*, London, Macmillan, 1988

Horne, Alistair, *Harold Macmillan Volume II: 1957–1986*, London, Macmillan, 1989

Howard, Anthony, *RAB: A Life of R.A. Butler*, London, Papermac, 1988

Howard, Anthony and West, Richard, *The Making of the Prime Minister*, London, Richard Clay, 1965

Hudson, John, *The Oxford History of the Laws of England*, vol. II, Oxford, Oxford University Press, 2012

Hurd, Douglas, *Robert Peel: A Biography*, London, Weidenfeld & Nicolson, 2007

Jago, Michael, *RAB Butler: The Best Prime Minister We Never Had*, London, Biteback Publishing, 2015

Jackson, D. Michael, *The Crown and Canadian Federalism*, Toronto, Dundurn, 2013

Jackson, Paul and Leopold, Patricia, *Constitutional and Administrative Law*, 8th ed., London, Sweet and Maxwell, 2001

Jenkins, Roy, *Asquith*, London, Fontana Books, 1967

Jenkins, Roy, *Baldwin*, London, HarperCollins, 1987

Jenkins, Roy, *Gladstone*, London, Pan Books, 2018

Jenkins, Roy, *Mr Balfour's Poodle: An Account of the Struggle Between the House of Lords and the Government of Mr Asquith*, London, HarperCollins, 1989

Jennings, Sir Ivor, *Cabinet Government*, 3rd ed., Cambridge, Cambridge University Press, 1961

Jennings, Sir Ivor, *The Queen's Government*, London, Penguin, 1954

Johansson, Jon, *Two Titans: Muldoon, Lange and Leadership*, Wellington, Dunmore Publishing, 2005

Joseph, Philip A., *Constitutional and Administrative Law in New Zealand*, 4th ed., Wellington, Thompson Reuters, 2014

Joyce, Peter, *Anatomy of a Rebel: Smith of Rhodesia, A Biography*, Salisbury, Graham Publishing, 1974

Kavanagh, Aileen, 'The Constitutional Separation of Powers', in David Dyzenhaus and Malcolm Thorburn (eds), *Philosophical Foundations of Constitutional Law*, Oxford, Oxford University Press, 2016

Kebbel, T. E. (ed.), *Selected Speeches of Lord Beaconsfield*, vol. II, Longmans, Green & Co, 1881

Keir, Sir David L., *The Constitutional History of Modern Britain, 1485–1937*, London, Adam and Charles Black, 1948

Kelly, Paul and Bramston, Troy, *The Dismissal: In the Queen's Name*, Australia, Penguin, 2015

Kerr, Sir John, *Matters for Judgment: An Autobiography*, Melbourne, Macmillan, 1978

Kerry, Simon, *Lansdowne: The Last Great Whig*, London, Simon Kerry, 2017

Kidd, Colin, *Subverting Scotland's Past: Scottish Whig Historians and the Creation of an Anglo-British Identity 1689–1830*, Cambridge, Cambridge University Press, 2003

Kilmuir, Earl of, *Political Adventure: The Memoirs of the Earl of Kilmuir*, London, Weidenfeld & Nicolson, 1964

King, Anthony, *The British Constitution*, Oxford, Oxford University Press, 2010

Knappen, M. M., *Constitutional and Legal History of England*, London, Harcourt, Brace & Company, 1942

Larman, Alexander, *The Crown in Crisis: Countdown to the Abdication*, London, Weidenfeld & Nicolson, 2020

Laski, Harold, *Parliamentary Government in England*, London, Allen & Unwin, 1938

Laws, David, *22 Days in May*, London, Biteback, 2010

Levine, Allan, *King: William Lyon Mackenzie King – A Life Guided by the Hand of Destiny*, Vancouver/Toronto, Douglas & McIntrye, 2011

Lewis, Geoffrey, *Lord Hailsham*, London, Jonathan Cape, 1997

Leys, Colin, *European Politics in Southern Rhodesia*, Oxford, Clarendon Press, 1959

Longford, Elizabeth, *Elizabeth R*, London, Weidenfeld & Nicolson, 1983

Longford, Elizabeth, *Wellington*, London, Abacus, 2004

Lukes, Igor and Goldstein, Erik (eds), *The Munich Crisis, 1938: Prelude to World War II, Diplomacy & Statecraft*, vol. X, London, Frank Cass, 1999

MacCulloch, Diarmaid, *Thomas Cromwell*, London, Penguin, 2019

McIlwain, C. H., 'Medieval Estates', in John Bagnell Bury (ed.), *The Cambridge Medieval History*, vol. VII, Cambridge, Cambridge University Press, 1932

Mackenzie, K., *The English Parliament*, London, Pelican Books, 1951

MacKinnon, Frank, *The Crown in Canada*, Calgary, Glenbow-Alberta Institute, 1976

McKinstry, Leo, *Attlee and Churchill: Allies in War, Adversaries in Peace*, London, Atlantic Books, 2019

McLean, Gavin, *The Governors: New Zealand's Governors and Governors-General*, Dunedin, Otago University Press, 2006

Macleod Iain, *Neville Chamberlain*, London, Frederick Muller Ltd, 1961

Macmillan, Harold, *Riding the Storm 1956–1959*, London, Macmillan, 1971

Macmillan, Harold, *At the End of the Day 1961–63*, London, Macmillan, 1973

McMullin, Ross, *The Light on the Hill: The Australian Labor Party 1891–1991*, Sydney, OUP Australia, 1991

McWhinney, Edward, *The Governor General and the Prime Ministers: The Making and Unmaking of Governments*, Vancouver, Ronsdale Press, 2005

Magnus, Philip, *King Edward the Seventh*, London, John Murray, 1964

Maitland, F. W., *The Constitutional History of England*, Cambridge, Cambridge University Press, 1913

Mandelson, Peter, *The Third Man: Life at the Heart of New Labour*, London, HarperCollins, 2010

Marquand, David, *Ramsay MacDonald*, London, Jonathan Cape, 1977

Marsh, Peter T., *The Chamberlain Litany: Letters Within a Governing Family, From Empire to Appeasement*, London, Haus Publishing, 2010

Marshall, Geoffrey, *Constitutional Conventions*, Oxford, Clarendon Press, 1984

Megahey, Alan, *Humphrey Gibbs, Beleaguered Governor: Southern Rhodesia, 1929–69*, Basingstoke, Macmillan, 1998

Middlemas, Keith and Barnes, John, *Baldwin: A Biography*, London, Weidenfeld & Nicolson, 1969

Monahan, Patrick and Shaw, Byron, *Constitutional Law*, 4th ed., Toronto, Irwin Law, 2013

Moore, Charles, *Margaret Thatcher: The Authorised Biography*, vol. II, London, Penguin, 2016

Morrah, Dermot, *The Work of the Queen*, London, William Kimber, 1958

Morre, W. Harrison, *The Constitution of the Commonwealth of Australia*, 2nd ed., Sydney, C. F. Maxwell, 1910

Mortimore, Roger and Blick, Andrew, *Butler's British Political Facts*, London, Palgrave Macmillan, 2018

Morton, W. L., *Manitoba: A History*, 2nd ed., Toronto, University of Toronto Press, 1967

Munro, Colin R., *Studies in Constitutional Law*, 2nd ed., London, Butterworths, 1999

Murphy, Philip, *Monarchy and the End of Empire*, Oxford, Oxford University Press, 2013

Neil, Andrew, *Full Disclosure*, London, Pan, 1997

Nicholls, G. Heaton, *South Africa in My Time*, London, Allen and Unwin, 1961

Nicolson, Harold, *George V: His Life and Reign*, London, Constable, 1952

Norton, Philip, *Governing Britain: Parliament, Ministers and our Ambiguous Constitution*, Manchester, Manchester University Press, 2020

O'Brien, Bruce R., *God's Peace and King's Peace: The Laws of Edward the Confessor*, Philadelphia, University of Pennsylvania, 1998

Owens, Ed, *After Elizabeth: Can The Monarchy Save Itself?*, London, Bloomsbury, 2023

Palley, Claire, *The Constitutional History and Law of Southern Rhodesia 1888–1965*, Oxford, Clarendon Press, 1966

Palmer, Dean, *The Queen and Mrs Thatcher: An Inconvenient Relationship*, Stroud, The History Press, 2016

Pimlott, Ben, *The Queen: Elizabeth II and the Monarchy – Golden Jubilee Edition*, London, HarperCollins, 2001

Pitt Taswell-Langmead, Thomas, *English Constitutional History: From the Teutonic Conquest to the Present Time*, 8th ed., London, Sweet & Maxwell, 1919

Pollard, David, Parpworth, Neil and Hughes, David, *Constitutional and Administrative Law*, 4th ed., Oxford, Oxford University Press, 2007

Powell, J. Enoch and Wallis, Keith, *The House of Lords in the Middle Ages*, London, Weidenfeld & Nicolson, 1968

Reid, Alan, *The Power Struggle*, Sydney, Shakespeare Head Press, 1971

Rhodes James, Robert, *Anthony Eden*, London, Weidenfeld & Nicolson, 1986

Rhodes James, Robert, *Churchill: A Study in Failure 1900–1939*, London, Harmondsworth, 1973

Rhodes James, Robert (ed.), *Winston S. Churchill: His Complete Speeches, 1897–1963*, vol. VI, London, Chelsea House Publishers, 1974

Roberts, Andrew, *Churchill: Walking With Greatness*, London, Allen Lane, 2018

Rose, Kenneth, *King George V*, London, Phoenix Press, 2000

Roseveare, Henry, *Treasury, 1660–1870: The Foundations of Control*, London, Allen and Unwin, 1973

Rothwell, Victor, *Anthony Eden: A Political Biography, 1931–1957*, Manchester, Manchester University Press, 1992

Russell, Peter and Sossin, Loren (ed.), *Parliamentary Democracy in Crisis*, Toronto, University of Toronto, 2009

Saywell, John, T., *The Office of Lieutenant-Governor*, Toronto, University of Toronto Press, 1957

Seldon, Anthony, *Churchill's Indian Summer: The 1951–1955 Conservative Government*, London, Hodder & Stoughton, 1981

Seldon, Anthony, *Brown at 10*, London, Biteback, 2010

Seldon, Anthony and Newell, Raymond, *May at 10: The Verdict*, London, Biteback, 2019

Seldon, Anthony and Snowdon, Peter, *Cameron at 10: The Verdict*, London, William Collins, 2016

Self, Robert, *The Neville Chamberlain Diary Letters*, vol. III, London, Routledge, 2002

Sexton, Michael, *The Great Crash: The Short Life and Sudden Death of the Whitlam Government*, Sydney, Scribe, 2005

Smith, Sir David, *Head of State: The Governor-General, the Monarchy, the Republic and the Dismissal*, Sydney, Macleay Press, 2005

Smith, E. A., *The House of Lords in British Politics and Society 1815–1911*, London, Longman, 1992

Smith, Goldwin, *A Constitutional and Legal History of England*, London, Dorset Press, 1990

Smith, Ian, *The Great Betrayal: The Memoirs of Ian Smith*, London, Blake, 1997

Smith, Jennifer and Jackson, D. Michael (eds), *The Evolving Canadian Crown*, Montreal, McGill-Queen's University Press, 2012

de Smith, S. A. and Brazier, Rodney, *Constitutional and Administrative Law*, 8th ed., London, Penguin, 1998

Smith, Sir Thomas, *De Republica Angolorum*, ed. M. Dewar, Cambridge, Cambridge University Press, 1982

Steyn, Richard, *Jan Smuts: Unafraid of Greatness*, Johannesburg/Cape Town, Jonathan Ball, 2015

Strong, Roy, *Coronation: From the 8th to the 21st Century*, London, HarperCollins, 2005

Templeton, Hugh, *All Honourable Men: Inside the Muldoon Cabinet 1975–1984*, Auckland University Press, Auckland, 1995

Thompson, Alan, *The Day Before Yesterday*, London, Sidgwick & Jackson, 1971

Thorne, R. G., *The House of Commons: 1790–1820*, vol. II, London, Secker and Warburg, 1986

Thorpe, D. R., *Alec Douglas-Home*, London, Sinclair-Stevenson, 1997

Thorpe, D. R., *Eden: The Life and Times of Anthony Eden, First Earl of Avon, 1897–1977*, London, Pimlico, 2004

Thorpe, D. R., *Supermac: The Life of Harold Macmillan*, London, Chatto & Windus, 2010

Throne, S. E. (ed.), *Bracton on the Laws and Customs of England*, vol. II, Cambridge, MA, Harvard University Press, 1968

Turpin, Colin and Tomkins, Adam (eds), *The British Government and the Constitution: Text and Materials*, 7th ed., Cambridge, Cambridge University Press, 2011

Twomey, Anne, *The Chameleon Crown: The Queen and Her Australian Governors*, Alexandria, Federation Press, 2006

Twomey, Anne, *The Veiled Sceptre: Reserve Powers of Heads of State in Westminster Systems*, Cambridge, Cambridge University Press, 2018

Ward, Norman, *Dawson's Government of Canada*, Toronto, University of Toronto Press, 1987

Watkins, Alan, *The Road to Number Ten*, London, Duckworth, 1998

Webb, Paul D., *The Modern British Party System*, London, SAGE Publications, 2000

Wheeler-Bennett, John W., *King George VI*, London, Macmillan, 1958

Whitlam, Gough, *The Truth of the Matter*, London, Penguin, 1979

Whitton, Evan, *The Hillbilly Dictator: Australia's Police State*, Sydney, ABC Enterprises, 1989

Wilson, Harold, *The Governance of Britain*, London, Weidenfeld & Nicolson, 1976

Winterton, George, *Parliament, the Executive and the Governor-General*, Melbourne, Melbourne University Press, 1983

Winterton, George (ed.), *State Constitutional Landmarks*, Annandale, The Federation Press, 2006

Wybrow, Robert J., *Britain Speaks Out, 1937–87: A Social History as Seen Through the Gallup Data*, London, Palgrave Macmillan, 1989

INDEX